How to Become a Better Writing Teacher

How to Become a BETTER WRITING TEACHER

Carl Anderson • Matt Glover

HEINEMANN
PORTSMOUTH, NH

Heinemann
145 Maplewood Avenue, Suite 300
Portsmouth, NH 03801
www.heinemann.com

The authors and publisher wish to thank those who have generously given permission to reprint borrowed material:

pp. 84–85: Excerpts from "Short and Curly, Long and Swirly" from *ASK* magazine, November/December 2022. Copyright © Cricket Media, Inc. Reproduced with permission. All Cricket Media material is copyrighted by Cricket Media, Inc. and/or various authors and illustrators. Any commercial use or distribution of material without permission is strictly prohibited. Please visit http://www.cricketmedia.com/info/licensing2 for licensing and http://www.cricketmedia.com for subscriptions.

p. 137, Figure 6-6: Adapted from *A Teacher's Guide to Mentor Texts* by Carl Anderson. Copyright © 2022 by Carl Anderson. Published by Heinemann, Portsmouth, NH. Reprinted by permission of the Publisher. All rights reserved.

p. 139, Figure 6-7: Adaptation of "Unit of Study Schematic" from *A Teacher's Guide to Mentor Texts* by Carl Anderson, p. 87, 2022.

Acknowledgments for borrowed material continue on page xvi.

Library of Congress Control Number: 2023943004
ISBN: 978-0-325-13641-7

Editor: Zoë Ryder White
Production: Vicki Kasabian
Cover and text designs: Suzanne Heiser
Typesetting: Kim Arney
Video: Sherry Day, Heather O'Bryan, Michael Grover, Dennis Doyle, and Alan Chow
Manufacturing: Jaime Spaulding

Printed in the United States of America on acid-free paper
1 2 3 4 5 VP 27 26 25 24 23 PO 4500879512

To all of the teachers we have worked
and learned with over the years who
have made this book possible.

CONTENTS

Video Contents

Online Resources Contents

This list of resources are accessed online. You will find references to them in the text; a few appear as figures.

Online Resources

How to Access the Online Actions, Online Resources, and Videos

To access the Online Resources for *How to Become a Better Writing Teacher:*

1. Go to http://hein.pub/anderglove-login.
2. Log in with your username and password. If you do not already have an account with Heinemann, you will need to create an account.
3. On the Welcome page, choose "Click here to register an Online Resource."
4. Register your product by entering the code BETTER (be sure to read and check the acknowledgment box under the keycode).
5. Once you have registered your product, it will appear alphabetically in your account list under "My Online Resources."

Note: When returning to Heinemann.com to access your previously registered products, simply log in to your Heinemann account and click on "View my registered Online Resources."

Acknowledgments

First, both of us, Carl and Matt, are thankful for one another and grateful we've had the opportunity to collaborate in the writing of this book. Early in the pandemic, we decided to create a webinar series about teaching writing. It didn't take long for us to realize that we loved working with each other and pushing each other's thinking. We came up with the idea for this book soon after. Working together closely on this project has been a great, great gift to us both.

We are grateful for Zoë Ryder White, our editor at Heinemann, who was excited about the idea for the book from the moment we discussed it with her. Her vision and expertise shaped this project from that moment onward. Every one of our many Zoom calls and email exchanges energized us and guided us as we wrote. Zoë, you're the best!

We're thankful for Katie Wood Ray, our mentor and friend. Although Katie wasn't directly involved with this book, her foundational thinking about teaching writing influenced much of what we've written about.

Of course, we appreciate the teachers, coaches, and administrators with whom we've worked in schools and districts around the world, from New York City to Jakarta, Indonesia. There are simply too many of you to list here, but it's been a joy to work in your classrooms and talk with you about teaching writing. We wrote this book with you in mind, and we hope it helps you grow as writing teachers.

We want to give special thanks to the folks who attended our webinar series. The pandemic was a difficult time for everyone, and the opportunity the webinars gave us to connect with teachers, coaches, and administrators around the world helped sustain us during those challenging times.

Ellin Keene, we thank you for your enthusiasm for this project and your expertise about teaching literacy—and for your wonderful sense of humor, something that helped us many times during the past several years.

We are grateful for Kathy Collins, Towanda Harris, Georgia Heard, Aeriale Johnson, Jessica Martin, Vicki Vinton, and Janet Zarchen for the weekly Zoom conversations we had during the pandemic about teaching and working toward a better world. Each of you influenced this book in important ways.

Several educators opened up their classrooms and schools to us as we worked on the book, and their students appear in its pages and videos. Thank you to Ryan Scala and Emily Callahan for sharing your students' work. And thank you to Casi Hodge for inviting us into your district so we could make classroom videos.

To the entire team at Heinemann, thank you for your hard work. We appreciate your dedication to helping teachers and to improving the lives of children.

Carl would also like to give thanks to these people:

Dan Feigelson, I'm thankful for our professional conversations and collaborations and also for the times we've spent together in art museums and jazz clubs.

Hannah Schneewind, thank you for picking up the phone whenever I wanted to talk about teaching writing, even early in the morning, and for the times spent with your wonderful family.

And finally, I thank my children, Anzia and Haskell, for growing up but not away. And my wife, Robin Epstein, for all the days we've spent together. I love you all *so* much.

Matt would like to give thanks to these people:

My wife, Bridget, is one of the best teachers I know, and many of the beliefs that form the foundation for this book grew out of long conversations with her about children and learning. She became an educator the same year I began consulting full-time. How lucky for me to have a partner to take long walks with and talk with about meaningful ideas.

My children, Harrison, Meredith, Natalie, and Molly, were fifteen years younger when I wrote my first acknowledgments for a book. During that time I've watched you grow into amazing adults who care about making the world a better place. Thank you for being such a source of joy.

Introduction

The goal of this book is to help you become a *better* writing teacher.

That's a different goal from many of the books published on teaching writing in elementary and middle school.

Many of these books are about how to get started with writing workshop. They discuss the structure of a writing workshop, explain the basics about how to do minilessons, small-group lessons, and writing conferences, give you tips on how to manage a workshop, and tell you other important things you need to know when you're starting out as a writing teacher.

Other books are about writing workshop curriculum. They describe units of study you can do across a year of writing workshop and detail the minilessons you can teach in these units. Some of these books are bundled in sets, and you have an entire year's curriculum at your fingertips when you purchase them; others are single books, which explain how to do one or more units of study.

But . . . once you've read these books, successfully launched a writing workshop in your classroom, and implemented a yearlong curriculum, what's next? What's the path, whether you've been teaching writing for a couple of years or for many years?

The answer is to become better at teaching writing. Really good, in fact. Why? Your students need you to be a great writing teacher. That's because writing is such a critical skill, and for students to learn to write well, they need you to teach writing well.

How do you become a better writing teacher?

That's where this book comes in.

The first thing you should know: as you read the book, you'll be in the company of two experienced writing teachers, Carl Anderson and Matt Glover (we will use *we* to refer to ourselves from now on). Between us, we bring a total of seventy-two years of varied and complementary experiences in education to the conversation about teaching writing. Carl taught in upper-elementary and middle school grades for eight years; Matt taught first grade for six years. Carl worked as a full-time staff developer at the Teachers College Reading and

Writing Project at Columbia University for eight years; Matt was a principal in the Lakota District in Ohio for fifteen. Both of us now work as consultants for schools and districts in the United States and in many countries around the world, Carl for the past twenty-one years and Matt for fourteen. And both of us are authors of professional books, most of which focus on teaching writing—this book is Carl's sixth and Matt's eighth.

And the second thing to know is that in this book, we'll share the kinds of work we did as educators to get better at teaching writing. And we'll share what we do today with teachers around the world—teachers who are relatively new to writing workshop and teachers who have been running writing workshops in their classrooms for many years—to help them become better writing teachers. Whether we're working directly with teachers in schools, doing on-site workshops and webinars, keynoting conferences, or writing books, everything we do is about helping teachers everywhere become really good at teaching writing.

In the book, we're going to replicate the work we do in schools. We'll describe the principles that guide what we do when we teach writing and show you how to align your practice with these principles by describing a wide variety of high-impact actions you can take on your own or with colleagues. We'll supplement these actions with classroom videos and videos of us discussing teaching writing. And we'll provide many Online Resources that you can use when you try the actions.

The work on this book began in mid-2020, when Matt called Carl and suggested they do a webinar for teachers. A few weeks later, nearly five hundred people attended the first of what would become an ongoing series of webinars on teaching writing.

We had a blast doing the webinars. Of course, that's because we love talking with teachers about how to teach writing to children, since that's what we've been doing for many years in our jobs as consultants. And we also had a blast working together, forging a new partnership as we did the webinars—and started writing this book.

Our partnership is built on several foundations.

Very quickly, we discovered we had lots in common. For example, we're both sailors. And we're also fathers to children who are of a similar age—for Carl, Anzia and Haskell; for Matt, Harrison, Meredith, Natalie, and Molly.

Most important, we discovered we have the same vision for our work. Whenever we spend time with teachers, everything we do is about helping them get better at teaching writing.

Several months after that first webinar, when we decided to write a book together, it wasn't hard to decide on the book's focus; we knew right away we wanted to write about how to become a better writing teacher. And now, several years later—after countless Zoom meetings, texts and emails, first drafts, conversations with our editor, Zoë Ryder White, more Zooms and texts and emails, and many, many revisions—that's the book you're finally holding in your hands. Enjoy!

You're embarking on a journey that will be deeply satisfying for you.

1

Start Your Journey

So you want to be a better writing teacher.

Perhaps this is your goal because writing will help your students be more successful in school and work.

Maybe it's because you want to help students use writing to communicate the things they have to say in powerful ways.

Perhaps you want to help students use writing to reflect on their lives, follow their own lines of thinking, analyze themselves, their communities, and the larger world around them, and imagine new possibilities.

Or maybe you're driven by the knowledge that people have used writing to change the world, and you want to be better equipped to help your students access this power.

Perhaps you teach students who face a lot of challenges in becoming good writers.

Or maybe your students don't have the socioeconomic advantages students elsewhere have, and if they don't learn to write well, that'll be one more strike against them.

Perhaps you had teachers who helped you love writing, and you want to be more like them so your students will love writing, too.

Or maybe you had negative experiences with writing when you were in school, and you want your students to have a different experience.

Perhaps your school has started an initiative to help every teacher get better at teaching writing.

Maybe you know how immensely gratifying—and fun—it is to be good at doing something important.

Video 1.1
Welcome

Or perhaps it's a combination of several of these reasons that's driving you to be better at teaching writing.

In any case, whatever the reasons, congratulations! You're embarking on a journey that will be deeply satisfying for you. And, most important, the better you get at teaching writing, the more likely it is your students will become good writers and develop this critical skill that will enhance their lives now and in the future.

While there are plenty of road maps you can follow to *get started* as a writing teacher, there are not many for what comes next: becoming a really good writing teacher. So, imagine such a road map, which today you would access via a navigational app. You open the app and type in this destination: "better writing teacher." When you finish, you tap Go. In an instant, these directions pop up on the screen:

1. Start by understanding the principles of teaching writing.
2. Align your practice with these principles.

Just *two* steps? Could it be so simple? Yes . . . and no. While these directions contain just two steps, taking them involves doing a lot of challenging—and exciting—work, on your own, with colleagues, and with students.

In this book, we'll help you navigate both steps:

1. In this first chapter, we'll ground you in the principles of writing instruction and give you an overview of how to use the book.
2. In Chapters 2–9, we'll help you align your practice to these principles by describing specific actions you can take.

All right. Let's go!

First Step: Understand the Guiding Principles of Writing Instruction

At the beginning of a journey, you often start at a welcome center to get an introduction to the place you're about to explore. In the center, you learn about key sites you can visit and things to do at each site. For example, if you go to a

Vermont welcome center, you'll learn about the state's maple sugarhouses and hiking trails; if you visit an Arizona welcome center, you'll get information about caves and state parks.

You're now in the metaphorical welcome center at the beginning of your journey to becoming a better writing teacher. In it, you'll learn about the guiding principles of writing instruction, principles that the field of teaching writing discovered starting in the mid-1980s, when educators began to run writing workshops in their elementary and middle school classrooms. Understanding these principles will give you the lay of the land, a preview of the landmarks you'll explore during the journey ahead.

If you learned how to teach writing in the 1980s, you learned about three foundational principles—*time*, *ownership*, and *response*—from educators such as Donald Graves (1983), Lucy Calkins (1986), and Nancie Atwell (1987). In their book *A Teacher's Guide to Writing Workshop Essentials: Time, Choice, Response* (2020), Katherine Bomer and Corinne Arens describe these principles as the "basic necessities we provide our students every day in the classroom, the over-and-over elements that allow for composition, thinking, creativity, and problem solving" (2).

Time

Students need time, and lots of it, to practice writing.

Just like athletes and musicians need time to practice their sport or instrument, students need time to write to develop the habits of writers and to learn to write well. By running a writing workshop most days of the week, you give students the time they need to get better at all aspects of writing.

Ownership

Students are more motivated to write when they have opportunities to make important choices about their writing.

These choices include what to write about as well as decisions about navigating each stage of the writing process and how to craft their writing. And having choice is important not only because it increases students' motivation but also because it gives students the opportunity to learn about and get better at making the many choices experienced writers constantly make.

Response

Students need frequent response to their writing.

Students need teaching that responds to their needs as writers. Students get responsive teaching when teachers have one-on-one writing conferences with them as they write. When they confer, teachers learn about each student's needs as a writer and teach them what they need to learn. Minilessons and small-group lessons are other kinds of responsive teaching, especially when teachers choose these lessons with students' needs as writers in mind.

Students also need response to the content of their writing. This can take place during the share session, the last part of the daily writing workshop, when students read their drafts in progress. And it comes when students are finished with their writing and share it with audiences that may include their classmates, adults in their school, family members, people in the community, and others. When students get responses from audiences who matter to them, they experience writing as a communicative act. They learn that writing can satisfy important purposes for them, and those responses motivate them to write again.

In the decades since Graves, Calkins, and Atwell taught teachers about time, ownership, and response, writing teachers have recognized that there are other important principles. We'll discuss eleven more here.

Relationships

Students learn about writing best when they feel known by their teachers and feel connected to them.

We learned from John Hattie's (2009) work on student achievement that "person-centered" teachers are the ones whose students are most likely to show growth. For writing teachers, being person-centered has two dimensions.

- The first, knowing students *as people*, helps teachers have genuine relationships with them and steer students toward meaningful writing projects. And when students feel the sense of connection that comes out of these relationships, they're more open to learning from teachers (Graves 1994; Mraz and Hertz 2015).
- The second, knowing students *as writers*, helps teachers figure out appropriate next steps for students as individual writers and make plans for where they would like to take each student across a year of writing (C. Anderson 2005; Serravallo 2014a, 2014b, 2017).

Engagement

Student engagement is crucial for learning to write well.

When students are engaged in the work they do in school, they're more likely to learn (Crouch and Cambourne 2020; Keene 2018). In writing, there are several conditions for student engagement:

- Since choice and engagement are intricately linked, it's important to give students the opportunity to make the same kinds of choices experienced writers make, such as choice of topic (almost always) and choice of genre (sometimes).
- Sharing mentor texts that reflect students' identities and interests (Cherry-Paul 2021; Ebarvia 2017) helps students feel invested in the work.
- Helping students find authentic audiences for their writing increases their motivation to write well.

Authenticity

Learning in writing workshop is meaningful and relevant when it reflects what writers do in the world.

Debra Crouch and Brian Cambourne (2020) explain that students are more likely to learn when they see themselves as "doers" of the "whole" behavior being taught, not the "broken down" or "subparts" of that behavior (64–65). In writing workshop, this means teachers should

- have students write in genres that exist in the real world, for purposes that are relevant to students of their age and experience,
- have students study examples of the genres they're composing,
- teach craft techniques that experienced writers use, and
- teach writing strategies that experienced writers use to navigate the stages of the writing process.

Knowledge Base

To be effective, writing teachers need to have extensive knowledge about what they're teaching.

We describe school subjects such as science, social studies, and math as content area classes. Writing is rarely, if ever, included in this list. Does this mean writing has no content? Far from it, as experienced writers' knowledge is vast.

- They know a great deal about the craft of writing and the craft techniques they can use when they compose drafts.
- They know a repertoire of strategies for navigating the writing process and draw from these strategies when they write.

- They know how to use writing conventions—punctuation, grammar, spelling, and so on.
- They know how to use oral language, illustrations, written text, or some combination of the three as part of their compositional thinking.

It follows, then, that for students to learn the content of writing, teachers must know this content well themselves. Acquiring this knowledge is a necessary first step in being able to teach it to students (Ray 2002, 2006; Glover and Berry 2012).

Curricular Decision-Making

Classroom teachers are best positioned to decide what their classes need to learn each day.

The young writers in classrooms around the world have different experiences, skills, and challenges. This is true across students within one classroom and across classes within one school.

Teachers in classrooms are the people who know *their* students as writers, as they are the ones who talk with them about their writing in conferences and read their writing. It follows, then, that teachers are in the best position to make the day-to-day curricular decisions (which minilessons to teach) that translate curriculum and standards into teaching that responds to students' individual needs as writers (Hertz and Mraz 2018; Glover and Berry 2012; Tomlinson 2014; Meehan and Sorum 2021; Roberts and Roberts 2016).

Mentor Authors

One way people learn to do something is by studying what more skilled people do. Thus, *one of the best ways for students to learn about writing is to study what more experienced writers do.*

In writing workshop, teachers help students do this in three ways: First, students need to have a *vision* for what they're going to compose. We make this possible for them by teaching with stacks of mentor, or model, texts.

Second, we introduce students to the concept of *reading like a writer*, the habit of mind of writers in which they notice what other writers do in mentor texts, such as use craft techniques and conventions (Smith 1983; Ray 1999), and then try them out themselves.

Third, we give students *experiences* with reading like a writer to teach them about craft and conventions and to help them learn how to read like writers themselves, enabling them to continue to learn about writing the rest of their lives (C. Anderson 2022b; Marchetti and O'Dell 2021; Ray 1999; Rief 2018). We give them these experiences in several ways during units of study:

- in the immersion phase of a unit—the first few days of the study when we introduce students to mentor texts and they begin to study them
- in whole-class text study, in which we help students study mentor texts for extended periods of time
- in minilessons, small-group lessons, and writing conferences

Differentiated Instruction

Student writers have varied needs that we must take into consideration during teaching.

For example, students have different levels of enthusiasm for writing, different experiences with English as their first or additional language, and different knowledge of craft and conventions.

While writing teachers can address needs shared by many of their students in minilessons, these lessons won't land in the same way for all students. And students have needs that won't be addressed in minilessons. To meet students' individual needs, we must differentiate instruction for them (Tomlinson 2014).

Over the past several decades, writing teachers have learned how to use writing conferences to differentiate instruction (C. Anderson 2000, 2005, 2018). And they've also learned to teach small-group lessons with students who have common needs as writers (Serravallo 2021).

Starting with Strengths

Teaching children how to write better begins with determining what they can already do as writers, that is, their strengths.

Students have *partial understandings* of every aspect of writing, from planning pieces to focusing a draft to using end marks. A student's strength in an aspect of writing is the part of it that they currently understand and can do (K. Bomer 2010; C. Anderson 2018).

To answer the question *What do I teach this child today?* we start by assessing their strengths. Once we know what a child can do, we can decide the next step for them.

To see a student's strengths as a writer, we need to be comfortable with them *approximating* writing in writing workshop each day, that is, writing as best they can, at the level that they're currently at, without propping them up by overscaffolding their work (that is, giving them too much support as they write). Over time, as students grow as writers, their approximations of writing will become more sophisticated as their partial understandings become fuller understandings.

Nudging

Student writers learn best when they're learning something that is just beyond what they can do on their own.

In his writing about what he called the zone of proximal development, psychologist Lev Vygotsky (1986) explained that the job of the teacher is to teach students what they can learn to do with just a bit of adult support. The term *proximal* refers to skills that a learner is close to becoming able to do.

When we teach, our job is to meet students *where they are* and nudge them to take an appropriate next step, regardless of benchmarks or what other children in the class can do.

The principle of teaching with nudges shapes every lesson in writing workshop (Glover 2009). For example, in a minilesson, the teacher's job is to show their class a next step that many students in the class will be able to take. And in a writing conference, their job is to figure out an appropriate next step for an individual student.

When we teach with nudges, we are cautious about overscaffolding, or providing so much adult support that children produce something that is well beyond what they can do on their own. While well intentioned, teachers sometimes overscaffold students when they're more focused on an end product than on students' learning and understanding.

In writing workshop, overscaffolding can take many forms, such as having every student include teacher-determined sections in informational books or feature articles in upper grades (intro, what your animal eats, where your animal lives, etc.). Another common example of overscaffolding is when in lieu of teaching students strategies for planning their writing (webs, outlines, flowcharts), a teacher gives every student in their class a graphic organizer to fill out.

Explicit Teaching

A writing teacher's responsibility is to teach, rather than tell, remind, or correct.

While knowing the content of writing is essential for writing teachers, knowing how to *teach* content to students is what will make writing accessible to them (C. Anderson 2018, 2022b; Angelillo 2008; Brunn 2010; Eickholdt and Vitale-Reilly 2022; Marchetti and O'Dell 2021). Telling and reminding students what to do and correcting them when they fail to follow instructions (usually with a red pen) has limited and often negative effects on student growth. Instead, by showing and modeling what mentor authors do to navigate the writing process and use craft techniques and conventions with clarity and precision, we help students envision what they can do themselves as writers and how to apply those things to their own work.

Independence

A writing teacher's job is to help students learn to write without them.

While student independence is important for the day-to-day running of a writing workshop, the term *independence* has grown to encompass the long-term goal of students being able to work effectively as writers when their schooling is finished. To help students meet this goal, teachers need to teach students the strategies experienced writers use to function independently as writers across their lives (Cruz 2004; Mermelstein 2013).

Second Step: Align Principles and Practice

Now that you've gotten the lay of the land in our metaphorical visitor center, you're ready to start planning your journey toward becoming a better writing teacher.

This involves aligning the principles of good writing instruction with your day-to-day and across-the-year practice. In this book, that's what we'll help you do. We'll describe a series of practical actions that will help you align your teaching to each principle. Each action has been field-tested numerous times by us when we were teachers as well as by teachers we have worked with in schools.

Over the course of our careers, we have found that aligning teaching to these principles is exciting and enjoyable work. Time and time again, we've seen how doing this work helps students learn to write well and with enthusiasm!

Following are some tips for using this book to align your practice to these principles.

TIP

You'll find most of the actions in the pages of the book. However, you'll find there are a few that are online. These actions are just as important as the ones in the physical book—they are online only because of space limitations! When selecting which actions to move online, we chose actions that could more easily stand alone than actions linked to another action.

Understand the Book's Structure

We've organized the rest of the book into eight chapters. Each chapter has as its primary focus one of the principles we've discussed (see Figure 1-1).

Some of the principles don't have their own chapter but influence several of them. See page 20 for information about how this works.

Principle	Chapter Number and Title
Relationships *Students learn about writing best when they feel known by their teachers and feel connected to them.*	**2** Get to Know Students as People and as Writers
Engagement *Student engagement is crucial for learning to write well.*	**3** Create Conditions for Student Engagement
Knowledge base *To be effective, writing teachers need to be knowledgeable about what they're teaching.*	**4** Develop a Repertoire of Teaching Points
Curricular decision-making *Classroom teachers are best positioned to decide what their classes need to learn each day.*	**5** Become a Curriculum Decision-Maker
Mentor authors *One of the best ways for students to learn about writing is to study what more experienced writers do.*	**6** Help Students Learn from Mentor Authors
Differentiated instruction *Student writers have varied needs that we must take into consideration during teaching.*	**7** Individualize Instruction
Explicit teaching *A writing teacher's responsibility is to teach, rather than tell, remind, or correct.*	**8** Teach Clearly and Precisely
Independence *The writing teacher's job is to help students learn to write without them.*	**9** Support Student Independence

Figure 1-1

Understand Each Chapter's Structure

Each chapter has two parts:

1. ***Why you should prioritize aligning your practice to this principle:*** These short introductory sections provide a rationale for taking action to align each principle with your teaching.
2. ***What you can do to align your practice with the principle:*** This section is the how-to part of each chapter. In it, we describe actions that will help you align practice and principle. To help you decide which actions to take, you can refer to a diagnostic chart like the one in Figure 1-2 (which is the chart from Chapter 2), which you'll find in every chapter.

Action	When to Take It
Action 2.1 Get to Know Students' Identities	• If you mainly learn about the visible aspects of students' identities, the ones they signal with the designs on shirts they wear or the backpacks they bring to school. • If you know students who readily engage with you but less so with others.
Action 2.2 Reflect on What You Assess	• If you usually pay attention to just one or two aspects of writing when you assess students.
Action 2.3 Learn About Students as Writers in Multiple Ways	• If you rely on one main source of information to learn about your students but could tap others.
Action 2.4 Work on Your Conference Tableside Manner	• If you would like to work on your listening skills in your writing conferences. • If you would like your students to be more enthusiastic about conferring with you and sharing information about themselves.
Action 2.5 Look for Student Strengths	• If you tend to focus on what students can't do as writers instead of on what they can do. • If you speak in general ways about student strengths ("He's really good at elaboration.") but could be much more precise in how you describe these strengths.
Action 2.6 Set Writing Goals for Students	• If you tend to think in the short term about your students (*What can I teach this student today?*) and could learn to think more about the long term for them (*What should I be working on with this student over the next few months?*).
Action 2.7 Use Record-Keeping Forms to Set and Track Goals	• If you aren't sure why you should keep notes about students. • If you have trouble being consistent with record keeping. • If you're looking for ideas about kinds of record-keeping forms.

Figure 1-2

The actions invite you to do many different kinds of things, including

- learning about students
- assessing students using multiple lenses
- analyzing student writing
- setting goals for students
- trying out new forms and tools
- teaching new types of lessons
- talking to students in new ways
- incorporating genre choice into your curriculum
- gathering stacks of mentor texts
- analyzing mentor texts
- writing your own texts to teach with
- developing your repertoire of teaching points
- revising and designing units of study
- engaging colleagues and supervisors in conversations about teaching writing
- analyzing your writing curriculum
- trying out new teaching strategies in your minilessons, small-group lessons, and writing conferences
- watching and analyzing teaching videos
- reflecting on your lessons
- writing and role-playing sample lessons
- trying out strategies to support student independence

Consider Taking Our Suggested Approach to the Book

Once you've been to a visitor center, you've got some decisions to make. For example, if you were visiting Washington, DC, you would quickly learn there are a huge number of things you could do, such as visit historical sites, museums, and government buildings. Unless you were planning on spending weeks in the city, there would be no way you could see or do everything!

What do you do in situations like this? You prioritize. Perhaps you decide to visit memorials—the Lincoln Memorial, the Martin Luther King Jr. Memorial, and the Vietnam Memorial. Or perhaps you decide to visit museums instead and spend time at the National Museum of African American History and Culture and the Smithsonian. Or perhaps you decide to do a mixture of a few of each of these different kinds of activities.

It's important you understand that just like you can't see everything in Washington, DC, in one visit, you won't be able to do all of the actions in this book in a few days or even weeks. Far from it. If you've skimmed over the table of contents, you've noticed there are more than fifty actions you can try! And you may already be curious about some and excited to try them out.

From our own experience as teachers and as staff developers, we've learned that the process of becoming a better writing teacher takes time. Years, in fact.

And we've also learned that this process happens step-by-step. That's what each of the actions in the book is designed to do—take you one step at a time.

- Some of the actions will challenge you to try something right away in your classroom, but to become good at them, you'll need to keep working on them over and over again.
- Other actions will invite you to try activities outside of writing workshop, either by yourself or with colleagues. These will take time to understand, work through, and ultimately make a seamless part of your practice.

We anticipate that at any given time, you might be working on one action. Or over a month or two, you might be working on two or three actions, with one as your primary focus and the others secondary.

Decide on Your Starting Point

How to start the journey depends on your current job as well as your level of experience:

- You're a *competent* writing teacher. You've probably been teaching writing for two to five years. You're comfortable with the day-to-day structure of writing workshop and with taking your students through the units of study in your yearlong writing curriculum—and you want to know what you can do to become really good at what you do. (Go to the next section.)
- You're a *very experienced* writing teacher. You've probably been teaching writing for five or more years. You're very good at what you do in some ways but would like to lift the level of your teaching in others. (Go to page 15.)

- You're *new* to teaching writing. You're probably in your first or second year. (Go to page 16.)
- You're a *literacy coach* or an *administrator* who is responsible for helping teachers become better at what they do. (Go to page 18.)

YOU'RE A COMPETENT WRITING TEACHER

We've visited many schools and districts where a teacher's professional journey as a writing teacher is considered finished when they're able to run a daily writing workshop and navigate the series of units of study in their writing curriculum.

Being competent, however, is not the same as being a great practitioner. In schools all over the world, we've worked with teachers who recognize this and want to examine their practice and push themselves to be much better at what they're doing.

If you see yourself in this way, we suggest one of these paths for you:

1. If your school is paying special attention to one of the principles of writing instruction—in conversations in grade-level meetings or study groups or with professional development—then go to the corresponding chapter and dig in or look for actions across the chapters that are connected to the principle.

2. If your journey is self-directed, or one that you're going on with several colleagues, start by assessing how well you've aligned your practice so far to each of the principles of good writing instruction. Use the Alignment Diagnostic (**Online Resource 1.1**; see also Figure 1–3) as a tool to help you with this process.
3. If you see from the Alignment Diagnostic that you frequently checked "I want to work on this" in response to most or all of the diagnostic questions for one principle, that principle would be a good starting point for you.
4. More likely, you've discovered you want to work on aligning your practice to several principles. We strongly suggest you focus on one of them at a time! How do you decide which one, when they're all important?
   - If you discovered you want to work on getting to know students better, or on student engagement, start there, because successfully aligning your teaching to these two principles will help you with every other aspect of teaching writing, and it will help your students be more enthusiastic and open to your teaching.
   - Ask someone who knows your teaching well—a teaching mentor, your literacy coach, or your supervisor—for feedback about which principle to prioritize.

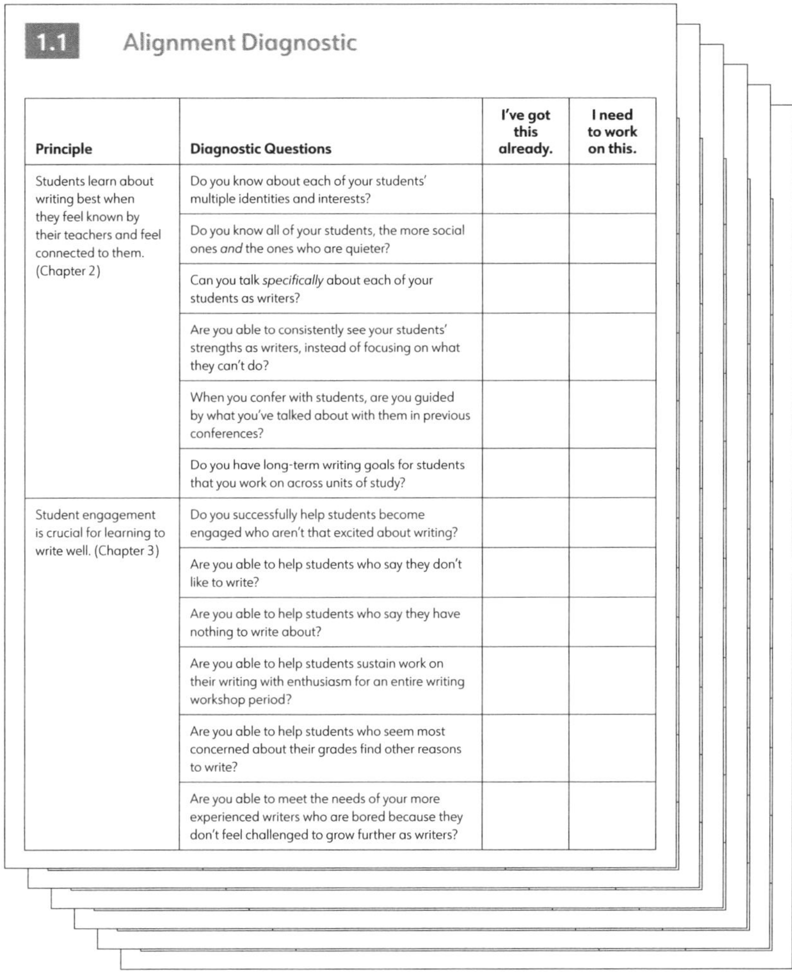

1.1 Alignment Diagnostic

Principle	Diagnostic Questions	I've got this already.	I need to work on this.
Students learn about writing best when they feel known by their teachers and feel connected to them. (Chapter 2)	Do you know about each of your students' multiple identities and interests?		
	Do you know all of your students, the more social ones *and* the ones who are quieter?		
	Can you talk *specifically* about each of your students as writers?		
	Are you able to consistently see your students' strengths as writers, instead of focusing on what they can't do?		
	When you confer with students, are you guided by what you've talked about with them in previous conferences?		
	Do you have long-term writing goals for students that you work on across units of study?		
Student engagement is crucial for learning to write well. (Chapter 3)	Do you successfully help students become engaged who aren't that excited about writing?		
	Are you able to help students who say they don't like to write?		
	Are you able to help students who say they have nothing to write about?		
	Are you able to help students sustain work on their writing with enthusiasm for an entire writing workshop period?		
	Are you able to help students who seem most concerned about their grades find other reasons to write?		
	Are you able to meet the needs of your more experienced writers who are bored because they don't feel challenged to grow further as writers?		

Figure 1–3

» If you're working with several colleagues, see which principles you all need and want to work on, and start there together, so you can give each other support.

If you're unsure about where to start, keep in mind that every one of the principles is important, and working on any one of them will help you improve your practice. Once you've worked on aligning your practice to one principle, then work on another.

YOU'RE A VERY EXPERIENCED WRITING TEACHER

If you're an experienced writing teacher, you've most likely been successful at aligning your practice in many ways to the principles of good writing instruction. However, there's probably still some work you can do to integrate the principles into your work, which will help you become a truly transformational writing teacher.

Do a self-assessment using the Alignment Diagnostic (**Online Resource 1.1**). We anticipate you'll check off "I need to work on this" in response to one or two of the diagnostic questions when you consider some or even many of the principles. You'll find that there is an action in one or two of the corresponding chapters that will address your needs.

Which principle should you address first?

- If you've checked off "I want to work on this" in response to one or more of the questions about getting to know students as writers, or student engagement, we suggest you start by aligning these principles even more closely to your practice.
- At this point in your career, you may be passionate about one of the principles and motivated to work on aligning it to your practice even further. Go to the corresponding chapter or see actions that are influenced by that principle in multiple chapters.
- Conversely, in your development as a writing teacher, you may not have worked on one of the principles as much as the others, perhaps because you didn't really know as much about it or because you didn't have the support you needed to get better at aligning it with your practice. If that's the case, perhaps now is the time!
- Ask for input from a similarly experienced colleague who knows your teaching or from your literacy coach or supervisor.
- If you're going on this journey with colleagues, share your self-assessments and find out which principle you all need to work on further.

YOU'RE A NEW WRITING TEACHER

If you're a new teacher, your primary goals are learning how to integrate the three foundational principles of time, ownership, and response into your practice by launching and learning how to run a daily workshop in your classroom:

- starting each workshop with a whole-class minilesson (ten to twelve minutes)
- managing independent writing time so that you can confer and do some small-group lessons (twenty-five to thirty minutes)
- ending each workshop with a share session in which some or all students share what they did that period (five minutes)

You're also working through each unit of study in your writing curriculum for the very first time. These two things are challenging, and you may feel you're drinking from the proverbial fire hose each day.

Nonetheless, we don't think becoming a great writing teacher is something you should wait to think about until you achieve a level of competency in running a writing workshop and navigating the curriculum. Instead, we think that becoming a really good writing teacher *should be your goal from the very beginning*. You should be aware of *all* the principles of good writing instruction, and you should be taking some of the actions in this book. Most likely, you won't be very good at these actions at the beginning. But at least you'll be making a start and can continue to work on and refine your skill with them as you get more experienced over the next couple of years. And then, as you become more competent and eventually very experienced, you can take on some of the other, more advanced actions in this book.

To give you a starting point, in Figure 1–4 we have listed the actions in each chapter that we think are important for you to begin to try when you're in your

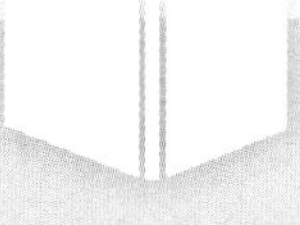

Further Reading

If you need help with launching a writing workshop in your classroom, see these valuable resources:

Kwame Alexander's *The Write Thing* (2019)

Nancie Atwell's *In the Middle* (2014)

Katherine Bomer and Corinne Arens' *A Teacher's Guide to Writing Workshop Essentials* (2020)

Randy Bomer's *Building Adolescent Literacy in Today's English Classrooms* (2011)

Ralph Fletcher and JoAnn Portalupi's *Writing Workshop: The Essential Guide* (2001b)

Katie Wood Ray and Lisa B. Cleaveland's *A Teacher's Guide to Getting Started with Beginning Writers* (2018)

Katie Wood Ray and Matt Glover's *Already Ready* (2008)

Laura Robb's *Teaching Middle School Writers* (2010)

Stacey Shubitz and Lynne R. Dorfman's *Welcome to Writing Workshop* (2019)

Chapter	Action(s)
2	2.1 Get to Know Students' Identities 2.4 Work on Your Conference Tableside Manner 2.5 Look for Student Strengths
3	3.1 Help Students Choose Engaging Topics 3.2 Create a Sense of Audience as Your Students' First Responder
4	4.1 Gather Stacks of Published Mentor Texts
5	5.1 Revise Existing Units 5.4 Improve Your Teaching When You Closely Follow a Unit
6	6.2 Do Whole-Class Immersion
7	7.2 Focus Conferences on What Students Are Doing as Writers
8	8.1 Keep Minilessons Truly Mini 8.2 Keep Conference Length in the Goldilocks Zone
9	9.1 Help *All* Students Write Independently

Figure 1-4

first year of teaching writing. As you try these actions, understand you probably won't be very good at them right away, and that's OK! With time and practice, you'll become skilled at doing them and they'll become a seamless part of your teaching.

YOU'RE A LITERACY COACH OR ADMINISTRATOR

As someone whose job it is to support the professional growth of all of the teachers in your school or department, how can you help them use this book?

1. If your school has already made it a priority to align its writing instruction with one of the principles, then your first step is easy: direct teachers to the corresponding chapter in the book or the actions across several chapters

that are influenced by that principle. Then there are several other steps you can take. For example:

- ***Help them decide which actions in the chapter to take first, and then discuss how this work is going.*** Will you do this as part of grade-level meetings? Study groups? Whole-faculty meetings? While working with a visiting staff developer?
- ***Support teachers as they try out actions in and outside of their classrooms.*** Are you able to provide in-classroom support and coaching? Can you be at meetings or PD sessions when teachers try outside-of-the-classroom actions?

2. If you're working on helping a group of teachers—in one grade or multiple grades—improve their practice, or you're helping individual teachers, you can do this in several ways:

   - ***Help them decide which principle to work on aligning first.*** First, suggest they use the Alignment Diagnostic (**Online Resource 1.1**) to help them identify which principle(s) to work on. At the same time, use the Alignment Diagnostic yourself to assess the group of teachers or the individual teacher you're working with, keeping in mind all you know about them from being in their classrooms and watching them teach and also from being in meetings with them where they've discussed teaching writing. With your assessment in mind, when you discuss with them which direction to go in first, you might be comfortable with where they want to go, or you might try to steer them in a different direction, which will involve an honest conversation about what you've been observing and hearing from them. Then you can refer teachers to the chapter that corresponds to a principle or actions across several chapters that are influenced by a principle.
   - ***Give them the support they need.*** Hopefully, you can visit teachers' classrooms to give them feedback and coaching and be in meetings when they try actions that are designed to be done outside of the classroom.

Why aren't there chapters on every principle you've discussed?

There are six principles that aren't the focus of individual chapters: time, ownership, response, authenticity, strengths, and nudging. Since we assume you've already launched a writing workshop in your classroom, you've already aligned your writing curriculum with the principle of time by doing so. Actions in multiple chapters will help you align the five other principles with your practice. To focus on these principles, see Figure 1-5, on the next page, for a road map to follow.

Principle	Actions
Ownership *Students are more motivated to write when they have opportunities to make important choices about their writing.*	**3.3** Help Students Identify Authentic Audiences **3.5** Make Time for Genre Choice **3.6** Help Students Choose Engaging Genres **5.5** Project a Yearlong Writing Curriculum **5.6** Assess Students' Curricular Experiences in Your School **9.2** Teach Students to Navigate the Writing Process Independently
Response *Students need frequent response to their writing.*	**2.4** Work on Your Conference Tableside Manner **3.2** Create a Sense of Audience as Your Students' First Responder **3.3** Help Students Identify Authentic Audiences **7.2** Focus Conferences on What Students Are Doing as Writers **7.7** Be Purposeful About Forming Small Groups **9.3** Envision How Students Can Help Each Other **9.4** Teach Students How to Work in Partnerships and Peer Conferences
Authenticity *Learning in writing workshop is meaningful and relevant when it reflects what writers do in the world.*	**3.4** Select Engaging Mentor Texts **3.7** Value and Teach into Illustration **4.1** Gather Stacks of Published Mentor Texts **4.4** Mine Process Texts for Teaching Points **6.8** Help Students See Mentor Authors as Real People **9.5** Help Students Find and Use Their Own Mentor Texts
Starting with Strengths *Teaching a child how to write better begins with determining what they can already do as writers, that is, their strengths.*	**2.5** Look for Student Strengths **2.6** Set Writing Goals for Students **2.7** Use Record-Keeping Forms to Set and Track Goals **7.3** Make Responsive Teaching Decisions **7.4** Give Individualized, Meaningful Feedback **7.7** Be Purposeful About Forming Small Groups
Nudging *Student writers learn best when they're learning something that is just beyond what they can do on their own.*	**2.5** Look for Student Strengths **2.6** Set Writing Goals for Students **2.7** Use Record-Keeping Forms to Set and Track Goals **6.7** Use Students as Writing Mentors **7.3** Make Responsive Teaching Decisions **7.7** Be Purposeful About Forming Small Groups

Figure 1–5

Getting to know students
as people and writers is one of the
most important things you can
do as a writing teacher.

2

Get to Know Students as People and as Writers

Why Is Knowing Students So Important?

Getting to know students as people and writers is one of the most important things you can do as a writing teacher (Graves 1994, 2006; Mraz and Hertz 2015).

- Students will feel seen and heard—and valued—and will be more willing to learn from you.
- You'll be more equipped to guide them toward finding and selecting high-engagement topics they'll be able to write well about.
- You'll be able to individualize instruction for them, especially in writing conferences and small-group lessons.
- You'll be able to meet them in the sweet spot of where they are as writers, which will help them learn.

Chapter 2

ACTIONS

What Can You Do to Get to Know Your Students?

Getting to know your students isn't just a happy by-product of spending time in a classroom with them. You'll get to know them because you take the deliberate stance that learning about them is important for teaching them well.

The actions in this chapter will help you be a writing teacher who gets to know students. Use the chart in Figure 2-1 to help you identify and prioritize which actions to take.

Action	When to Take It
Action 2.1 Get to Know Students' Identities	• If you mainly learn about visible aspects of students' identities, the ones they signal with the designs on shirts they wear or the backpacks they bring to school. • If you know students who readily engage with you but less so with others who don't.
Action 2.2 Reflect on What You Assess	• If you usually pay attention to just one or two aspects of writing when you assess students.
Action 2.3 Learn About Students as Writers in Multiple Ways	• If you rely on one main source of information to learn about students but could tap others.
Action 2.4 Work on Your Conference Tableside Manner	• If you want to work on your listening skills in your writing conferences. • If you want students to be more enthusiastic about conferring with you and sharing information about themselves.
Action 2.5 Look for Student Strengths	• If you tend to focus on what students can't do as writers instead of on what they can do. • If you speak in general ways about student strengths ("He's really good at elaboration.") but could be more precise in how you describe strengths.
Action 2.6 Set Writing Goals for Students	• If you tend to think in the short term about your students (*What can I teach this student today?*) and could learn to think more about the long term for them (*What should I be working on with this student over the next few months?*).
Action 2.7 Use Record-Keeping Forms to Set and Track Goals	• If you aren't sure why you should keep notes about students. • If you have trouble being consistent with record keeping. • If you're looking for ideas about kinds of record-keeping forms.

Figure 2-1

Action 2.1: Get to Know Students' Identities

Our eyes can see only the visible electromagnetic spectrum. Other kinds of light—infrared and ultraviolet, X-rays and gamma rays—are invisible to us. To see them, we need special instruments, such as the cameras that can view the universe in ultraviolet or infrared light on the Hubble and Webb telescopes.

Your students have multiple identities, some of which include

- who the child is—age, grade level, personality, gender, race, religion, ethnicity, languages they can speak
- family—parents or caregivers, siblings, pets, where they live as well as places they lived previously, cultural traditions, challenges their family may be facing
- school persona—attitude toward school, favorite subjects
- friendships—circles of friends, best friends
- activities and interests
- favorite aspects of pop culture
- opinions about their immediate world, as well as the world beyond them, and any ways they act on these opinions

Some of our students' identities are visible to us. For example, a child might wear a T-shirt featuring their favorite singer or bring a soccer ball to school. However, some identities are invisible to us—the child is the youngest in their family, or they recently moved from Guangzhou, China, to the United States.

What can you do to learn about and uncover children's visible *and* invisible identities? In his book *We Got This.: Equity, Access, and the Quest to Be Who Our Students Need Us to Be* (2019), Cornelius Minor reminds us that the goal of seeing students is to find an answer to the question "Where is the poetry in this young person?" (13). Following are seven strategies to help you see your students more fully.

1. ***Notice ways students signal their identities.*** Students tell you a great deal about themselves by the clothing they wear (sports jerseys and T-shirts with images on them), their jewelry (BFF necklaces), as well as what they bring to school (backpack clip-ons and collections of trading cards or

comic books). Students also signal some of their identities as they talk with each other about recent television shows or movies they've watched, or things they do outside of school, and eavesdropping on these conversations will help you learn more about them.

2. ***Ask them about themselves.*** When you sit down to have writing conferences with students, take a minute to ask how they're doing. Especially during the beginning of the school year, when you're prioritizing learning about your students, start writing conferences by asking them questions about aspects of their identities, such as their interests or their families.

3. ***Learn about them from reading their writing.*** Student writing is a rich source of information about student identities. It's important you read their writers' notebooks (in the upper grades) as well as their drafts with an eye toward learning about them as people, instead of solely to assess them as writers.

4. ***Notice what they choose to read.*** The books children are reading can teach you a lot about them. A child who is adopted may seek out books that feature characters who are adopted, or a child who is interested in Star Wars may read books set in that universe. The question "Why did you choose to read this book?" can sometimes lead to a conversation about one or more of a child's identities.

5. ***Ask their caregivers for information.*** You can learn a lot about students from asking their caregivers to tell you about them. (See **Online Resource 2.1**: Sample Letter.)

6. ***Have students write you a letter introducing themselves to you.*** To give students an image of how such a letter can go—and to help your students learn about you—write a letter to introduce yourself to them!

7. ***Ask students to write about their identities.*** There are multiple strategies you can teach to help students think about their identities and that will help you learn about them, too. These strategies include heart mapping (Heard 2016; see Figure 2-2) and identity maps (Ahmed 2018; Daniels 2017; Kleinrock 2021; see Figure 2-3). While the authors who have written about these strategies suggest teaching them to help students brainstorm topics (heart mapping) and to increase social comprehension and lay the foundation for anti-bias, anti-racist work (identity maps), these strategies have the added benefit of teaching you a great deal about your students as people.

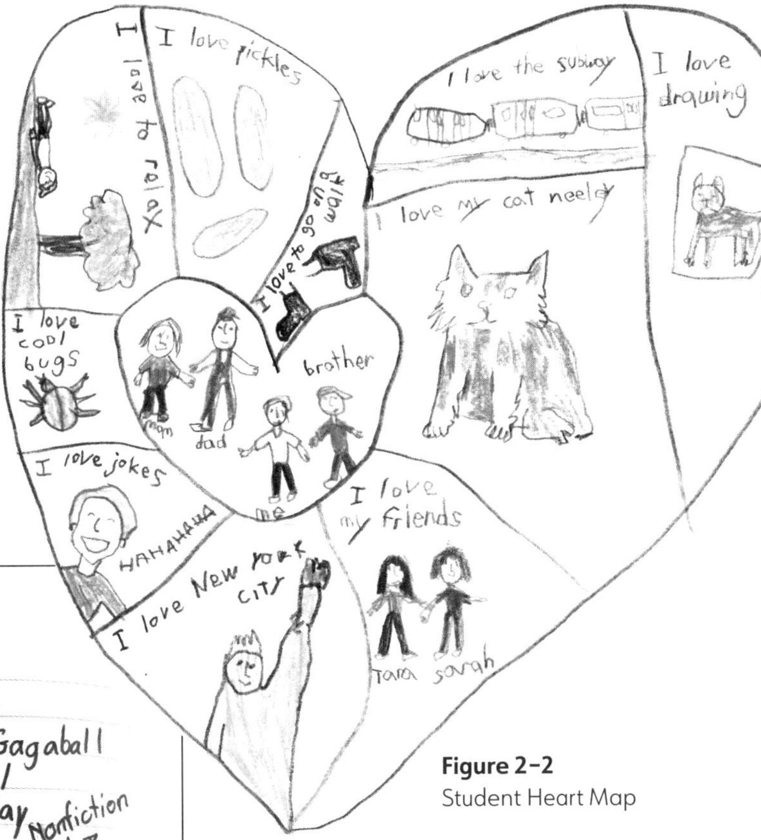

Figure 2–2
Student Heart Map

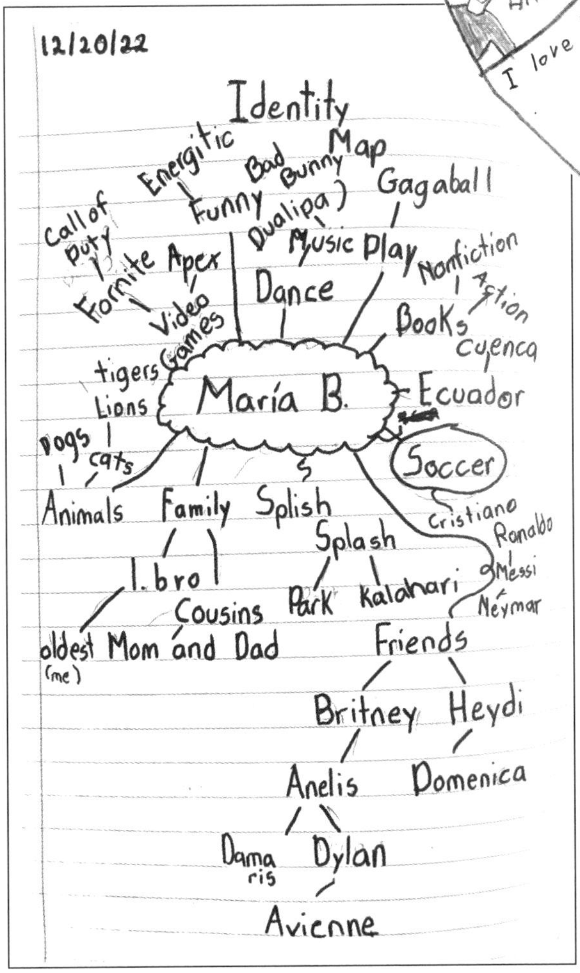

Figure 2–3 Student Identity Map

TIP

Use the Student Identities Form (**Online Resource 2.2**; see also Figure 2–4) to record things you learn about students. Keep this with your conference record-keeping forms, so you can jot down what you learn about students' identities during conferences.

2.2 Student Identities Form

Student	What Have I Learned About This Student's Identities?
Anna	– oldest child, younger brother Louis – lives w/ mom & dad – loves playing soccer! On team with Teresa – enjoys dancing – many relatives in Ecuador – best friends: Teresa & Daniella – LOVES Taylor Swift
Edmund	– youngest child, two older sisters – lives mostly with mom (divorce) – wants to be governor some day! – LOVES The Simpsons, has watched 500+ episodes – plays baseball, flag football – friends: Josh & Wyatt – enjoys writing about opinions, especially recycling
Alyssa	– lives w/ mom & dad, family emigrated from Shenzhen, China several years ago – older brother Albert in college – LOTS of pets: 1 dog, 1 cat, 5 hamsters, 1 bird – LOVES skateboarding + dancing – enjoys reading and writing fantasy – friends with Aurora & Syeda
Wyatt	– only child, lives with mom and dad – lives for BASEBALL, LOVES the Mets (wears a Mets hat + jersey to school every day) – big fan of Star Wars – friends: Josh & Gordon – family in Arizona, visits in summer – enjoys science and math especially
Syeda	– LOVES Olivia Rodrigo! – has a cat, Meny, that she adores – has a lot of responsibility for her younger brother, Syed – lives with mom and dad – enjoys singing and dancing – friends: Alyssa & Aurora

Figure 2–4

Assess What You've Learned About Students' Identities

After the first month of the school year, try one or both of these strategies to see how well you've gotten to know your students:

1. ***Write down three things you've learned about each student.*** This exercise may show you you've learned a lot about some students but not others. Also, see if there are any patterns in the kinds of things you've noted about students—for example, you might know a lot about your students' interests but little about their families.
2. ***Review the Student Identities Form.*** Which students have you learned a great deal about, and which ones have you not? And what aspects of your students' identities have you paid the most and least attention to?

Action 2.2: Reflect on What You Assess

Baseball is a game of statistics. You're probably familiar with some of the traditional ways statistics are used to assess baseball players. For example, BA (batting average) is the percentage of times a player comes to bat and gets a hit. You may be less familiar with some of the newer statistics that are used today. For example, WAR (wins above replacement) measures how many more wins an individual player adds to a team compared with the average player at their position. When we look at statistics, old and new, we come up with a more complete picture of a baseball player and their skill set.

Commonly, writing assessment is thought of as seeing how well students incorporate the qualities (or traits) of writing into their work. However, focusing exclusively on the qualities of writing gives you an incomplete picture. You can take a more expansive view of assessment by looking at multiple dimensions of your students as writers:

1. ***How engaged are students in their writing?*** Students who are engaged in writing are much more likely to learn what you want to teach them and to continue to write as they get older (Keene 2018). To help you think about how to help each student be engaged, it's important to assess each students' level of engagement (C. Anderson 2005), which you can do by paying attention to these things:

   » What is their affect as they write? How engrossed are they in their writing? Are they in a state of flow when they write?

   » How do students feel about the writing they're doing?

   » How well are students making the choices that lead to engagement—choosing topics and genres and finding meaningful audiences?

2. ***How do students move through the writing process?*** You should also assess how well your students navigate each stage of the writing process (rehearsal, drafting, revising, editing, publishing). What you learn will help you decide what to teach them so they can move through the process more effectively, which will help them write better, time and time again (C. Anderson 2005).

   Process is what you see happening all around you when you're with student writers. Here are some things to pay attention to at each stage:

   » ***Rehearsal (or prewriting):*** How do students pick topics? How do they gather material for their drafts? Plan their drafts?

   » ***Drafting:*** How do students get started with their drafts? Get restarted the next day? What strategies do they use when they get stuck? How do they use mentor texts to get ideas about how to craft their writing?

   » ***Revising:*** What kinds of revisions do students make? How do they decide which ones are needed?

   » ***Editing:*** What editing strategies do students use?

   » ***Publishing:*** How do students get their writing ready to publish (i.e., share their writing with an audience)?

3. ***How do students incorporate the qualities of good writing into their work?*** Of course, you'll be intensely interested in what students know about the qualities of writing—focus, structure, details, voice, and conventions (C. Anderson 2005; Culham 2003, 2005; Spandel 2012). These are some of the things to look for:

   » ***Focus:*** How do students focus their work—do they write all about a topic, write about part of a topic, or focus their writing on an idea about their topic? Does every part of their draft develop their focus?

   » ***Structure:*** How do students organize the parts of their pieces? How do they write beginnings? Endings? How do students transition readers from part to part?

   » ***Detail:*** What kinds of genre-specific details do students have in their repertoires? How precisely do they write details?

   » ***Voice:*** What voice techniques do students use to cue readers to read their writing with feeling and emphasis?

   » ***Conventions:*** How easy is their writing to read? What would make it easier for readers (and students themselves) to read their writing? What text conventions of written English do students use—spacing, writing left to right, and so on? What punctuation marks are in their repertoires? How do they use them to punctuate the kinds of sentences they write? What do students know about spelling? Do students spell words with grade-level-appropriate accuracy?

Assess What You've Been Assessing

To assesses students more comprehensively, the first step is to assess yourself and figure out what you typically look for and what you could start paying attention to more.

Use the What Do I Assess? Checklist (**Online Resource 2.3**; see also Figure 2-5) to make this self-assessment. You could work through the checklist yourself, or you could do so with colleagues.

Take Stock of What You Learned

Hopefully, the checklist helped you realize which aspects of writing you tend to prioritize and which ones you don't as much.

You may feel like you don't know that much about the aspects of writing you would like to start assessing, but no worries, you'll be able to get up to speed soon.

- Many of the actions in this book focus on engagement, process, and the qualities of writing, and as you work through them, you'll develop your knowledge base.
- Talk with a colleague who is more knowledgeable about an aspect of writing than you are.
- Read professional books to help you build your knowledge base. In many of the actions in this book, we'll steer you toward books we think you'll find helpful.

2.3 What Do I Assess? Checklist

Aspect of Writing	What to Look For	I *usually* assess this.	I *sometimes* assess this.	I *rarely* assess this.
Engagement	Students choose engaging *topics*.			
	Students choose engaging *genres* to write in.			
	Students choose to write for meaningful *audiences*.			
Process	Students have a repertoire of strategies for *rehearsing* their writing.			
	Students have a repertoire of strategies for *writing drafts*.			
	Students have a repertoire of strategies for *revising* their writing.			
	Students have a repertoire of strategies for *editing* their writing.			
	Students have a repertoire of strategies for getting a piece of writing ready to share (*publish*) with people in the world.			
Qualities of writing	Students *focus* their writing.			
	Students *structure* their writing.			
	Students write with *detail*.			
	Students use *voice* techniques.			
Conventions	Students use *conventions of print* (spacing, capitalization, etc.).			
	Students have a repertoire of *punctuation* marks they use to punctuate the kinds of sentences they write.			
	Students *spell* words with grade-appropriate accuracy.			

Figure 2–5

Action 2.3: Learn About Students as Writers in Multiple Ways

We're both sailors. When we go sailing, we start by learning about that day's conditions by tapping multiple sources of information. Before we leave home, we read websites to get information about wind direction and speed as well as the weather and online tide tables that tell us about the current. When we arrive at the water, we ask people who have already been out what the conditions were like. And we observe the sailing area, looking at wind indicators, like ripples on the water, and tide indicators, such as the way water is moving past the dock pilings. With all of the information we've gathered, we come up with a plan for the day's sail.

To get a multidimensional picture of each of your students as writers, you'll likewise need to tap multiple sources of information (C. Anderson 2005; Meehan and Sorum 2021; Meehan 2022):

- Observing them as they write.
- Talking with them as they write.
- Reading their writing.

By taking advantage of *all* of these sources, you'll get to know your students well. You'll be able to get information about their levels of engagement, learn how they move through the writing process, and find out how they incorporate the qualities of writing into their work.

Learn About Students by Observing Them at Work

You can learn about students' level of engagement and their writing processes by kidwatching, that is, watching them at work (Owocki and Goodman 2002).

Some of this observation will be incidental, done as you walk around your classroom to confer with students. For example, on some days, take a moment before each conference to watch the student for signs of engagement (looks of intense concentration, rapid writing, and so on) or for signs they might not be engaged (looks of boredom, avoidance behaviors such as getting out of their seats).

On other days, take a moment before conferences to notice which stage of the writing process a student is in, and watch to see what strategies they're using. For example, a student in the rehearsal stage might be brainstorming a list of topics to write about or planning their book by touching each page and thinking about what they're going to write on it. A student in the revision stage might be drawing arrows from where they want to add details to the margin and then writing those details there.

In this action, as you observe students at work, talk with them, and read their writing, jot down what you learn on your record-keeping forms for them. See Action 2.7 for ideas about useful forms.

You could even take a moment during a conference to observe a student at work. For example, to get information about a student's compositional strategies, ask them, "Let me watch you write a sentence," and then sit back and observe.

You can also take five to ten minutes to observe your entire class at work. On some days pay special attention to the variety of behaviors that indicate their level of engagement. On others, look for signs of where students are in the writing process and what strategies they're using.

Learn About Students by Talking with Them

Talking with students—especially during writing conferences—will teach you about them as writers (C. Anderson 2000, 2018; Johnston 1997).

Begin conferences with an open-ended question, such as "How's it going?" or "What are you doing as a writer today?" and then listen for which aspects of writing students talk about with you:

- What do you learn about their level of engagement from their tone of voice or what they say about their writing?
- What do you learn about the stage of the writing process they're in and what strategies they're using?
- When they're drafting, revising, and editing, what do you learn about a quality (or trait) of writing they're trying to incorporate into their drafts?

After you've started a conference, ask students some of these questions to get them talking about aspects of writing they don't bring up themselves:

- How are you feeling about writing today? How do you feel about writing this book (or piece)?
- Where are you in the writing process, and what strategies are you using?
- What are you doing to write this book (or piece) really well?
- How are you using punctuation in your writing? How is spelling going for you in this piece?

Learn About Students by Reading Their Writing

You can learn about every aspect of your students as writers by reading their writing. This includes finished drafts but also their writers' notebooks (in the upper grades) as well as their drafts in process, which contain revisions and edits. You'll read student writing in writing conferences and outside of writing workshop. (To help you with the assessments in this section, use **Online Resource 2.4**: Assessing Student Writing Guide.)

When you're reading student writing to assess their level of engagement, note the topics students choose to write about. For example, when a student who loves sports writes about their favorite NBA players, it's likely that student is engaged. And if students' writing is from a unit in which they can choose their own genres, note their genre choices. For example, a child who sees herself as an activist who is writing an opinion piece about a social justice topic is probably highly engaged.

When you're reading student writing to learn about how they navigate the writing process, look through their writing folders or notebooks to get information about how they navigate the rehearsal stage of the writing process. What strategies do they use to come up with topics? How do they gather information about topics before they draft? What planning strategies do they use? And by looking at the revisions and edits students make, you can learn what they do as they revise and edit.

Of course, when you read student writing, you'll learn a lot about their knowledge of the qualities of writing. When you're in a writing conference that focuses on the craft of writing, you'll focus the conference on one of the qualities of writing and learn about what the student knows about it. Or when you read student writing outside of writing workshop, you can learn about what students know about one or several traits.

Action 2.4: Work on Your Conference Tableside Manner

Patients who have a doctor with a good bedside manner—the ability to make them feel at ease and connect with them personally—have a much more positive attitude about seeing that doctor and are much more willing to talk with them about how things are going with their health.

You also have a manner when you confer with students—a deskside or tableside manner. When students are comfortable with *you*, they'll be more willing to share information about themselves. If your tableside manner is a good one, you'll put your students at ease as soon as you begin conferences with them (C. Anderson 2000, 2018; Kaufman 2000).

A good tableside manner is something you'll work on and develop over time. Following are several ways to work on how you talk with students.

Pay Attention to Your Body and Voice

How you position yourself physically and speak to children helps set a positive tone when you begin conferences:

- Sit next to the student, as close to eye level as possible, so you don't seem intimidating. If you work with younger students, try having them sit on a chair with a seat that's higher than yours, so they're more at your level.

- Turn toward the student and make eye contact.
- Smile *a lot*. Smiling lets students know you're glad to be with them!
- Speak in a friendly, inviting, conversational tone of voice.

Video 2.1
Observing conference tableside manner

Develop a Rapport with Students

At the beginning of conferences, take a few moments before getting down to business to chat with the student, to help build your rapport with them:

- Ask, "How are you doing today?"
- Ask a question about something you know about their life from the identity work you've done with them (see Action 2.1), such as "How's gymnastics going?"

Beginning a conference in one of these ways can help you break the ice with students. It demonstrates your interest in them as people. And you'll often learn things about students that will deepen your understanding of them and can become part of a back-and-forth with them that continues across the year ("How about the Lakers recently, huh?").

Another way to develop your rapport with students comes when they talk about their topics.

- When you know the student's topic comes out of one of their interests or identities, say so! Respond by saying, "Of course you're writing about basketball, given that you're on the basketball team!" Remarks like these are a quick and easy way to demonstrate your interest in them as people.
- When a student's topic surprises you because it doesn't seem to be connected to what you know about them, ask, "Why are you writing about this topic?" The student's answer may reveal an interest or identity you weren't aware of, deepening your understanding of the student. Or sometimes you'll realize they haven't made a good topic choice, in which case you'll teach them how to find a topic that's more aligned to their interests (see Action 3.1).

Sharpen Your Listening Skills

Listening well to students is essential. It communicates to students that you're interested in them and you find them fascinating as people and writers. This is a powerful message and will help students feel positive about conferences (Minor 2019; Feigelson 2022).

Video 2.2
Observing conference listening moves

One way to listen well to your students is to give them enough wait time—as much as five or ten seconds—after you ask a question, such as "How are you today?" or "How's it going with your writing today?" While it's tempting to jump in and speak for the student if they don't answer immediately, students will feel you aren't interested in discovering what they have to say when you don't give them time to come up with a response.

You should also get in the habit of responding to something interesting students say with "Say more about that . . ." (Feigelson 2014, 2022). Not only does this conversational move help you learn more about what students are telling you, but it's a clear statement of interest in what they're doing.

Show You Know Students as Writers

Conferences will also give you the opportunity to demonstrate how well you know your students as writers. When they feel known, students will be more open to talking about themselves as writers.

- ***Connect what students tell you about what they're doing as writers to what you already know about them.*** After you begin conferences with an open-ended question like "How's it going?" students will hopefully tell you about the work they're doing as writers. When students tell you about something they're doing that's connected to what you've talked about in previous conferences, say something like, "So you're working on adding more voice to your piece. Fantastic! We've talked about voice before when you were writing your book on spiders, and I know you're working hard on getting better at this."

- ***Ask students questions about what you know about them as writers.*** Bring up things you've learned about them as writers in previous conferences. For example, if a student is starting a draft, you might ask, "How is the planning going for this piece? That's something we've talked about before, and I'm curious about how you're planning this draft."

- ***Connect your teaching point to what you know about the student as a writer.*** When you name what you're going to teach the student, connect it to previous work you've done with them: "So today I'm going to teach you how to include character actions and thoughts in dialogue. We've talked about detail several times in the past couple of units, so in this conference, I'm going to show you another way you can elaborate."

- ***Use positive presuppositions when you talk with children.*** The way you ask questions says a lot about what you believe about someone and will affect how students respond in conferences. For example, instead of asking a child, "Have you tried something you learned from another author?" say, "What have you done in your writing that you learned from another author?" The second question communicates to the child you think they're the type of writer who tries things they've learned from other authors, while the first says you're not sure whether they are that type of person (Johnston 2004).

Action 2.5: Look for Student Strengths

In *Learning and Leading with Habits of Mind* (Costa and Kallick 2008), Arthur Costa discusses the habit of mind he calls "responding with wonderment and awe" (32–33), or the ability to be enthusiastic and passionate when you learn about a topic. When Katherine Bomer (2011) discusses this habit of mind in the context of writing instruction, she describes it as "reading with astonished eyes." Adopting this habit of mind is critical to the process of getting to know your student writers. It's important to be especially enthusiastic and passionate about students' *strengths* as writers and center those strengths in the decisions you make about how to teach them (K. Bomer 2010).

By *strengths*, we are referring to what a child *can* do, their present level of performance. The writing of most students shows a *partial understanding* of each aspect of writing, and their strengths are the part of each aspect of writing they understand and can do (C. Anderson 2018). When you can see a child's strengths, you're able to imagine appropriate next steps for them, ones that are based on what the child can already do.

Also, your ability to see children's strengths—and name them for students—helps them develop a positive image of themselves as writers. When you give students feedback about their strengths (usually in writing conferences), they are more open to your feedback and teaching, as students, like most people, respond better to people who see them positively.

Look at the writing of Joy, a kindergarten student, in Figure 2-6. Try responding to Joy's writing with a sense of wonderment and awe. What strengths do you see?

Flags by Joy Willis
Flags have different designs.
Flags are big and small.
Flags are metal. Flags are fabric.
Flags are around the world.
Flags are in parades.
Our American flag is on the moon.
Every country or state has a flag.

Figure 2–6

Did you notice that Joy has these strengths as a writer?

- She stays focused on the same topic across each page of her book.
- She zooms in and zooms out in her illustrations.
- She uses color in her illustrations to convey information about her topic.
- She introduces the topic of her book on the title page.
- She writes descriptive facts. ("Flags are big and small.")
- She uses topic-specific vocabulary (*metal, fabric, moon*).
- She puts spaces after many words.
- She knows how to spell some words correctly and uses her knowledge of sounds and letters to approximate the spellings of the other words.

Being able to see Joy's strengths helps us identify appropriate next steps for her. For example, a next step could be for Joy to learn to include action facts in her nonfiction writing. Other next steps could include learning how to write an introductory page and to use spacing even more consistently.

Learning to respond to student writing with a sense of wonderment and awe can be challenging. Seeing students' strengths can sometimes feel like looking for Waldo in the Where's Waldo? books! This action will help you develop this important way of seeing.

Develop Your Ability to See Strengths

Seeing student strengths begins with asking yourself this question: *What does this student understand* so far *about an aspect of writing?* You should be asking this question whenever you observe children at work, when you talk with them in conferences, and when you read their writing.

Start by doing a close study of one of your students, looking for this student's strengths in each aspect of writing. You can weave a study of this student into the day-to-day work you're already doing. Once you've studied one case-study student, you can focus on another.

Of course, you don't have time to do an in-depth study of each of your students! However, by studying even one student closely, you'll develop skills that will help you see strengths in each of your students as you interact with them day by day in writing workshop.

LOOK FOR STRENGTHS IN ENGAGEMENT

There are several ways to look for strengths in engagement:

- Observe the student at work in your writing workshop for five minutes.
- Read through their writing folder or writer's notebook, noticing what topics they choose to write about and (when given a choice) what genres they choose to write in.
- Have a writing conference with the student, and as the student talks about their writing, listen for evidence of engagement. You can also ask them directly about their level of engagement.

Use the Strengths in Student Engagement Tool (**Online Resource 2.5**) to help you with this part of the study.

LOOK FOR STRENGTHS IN THE WRITING PROCESS

Look for strengths in navigating the writing process in these ways:

- Observe the student for five minutes in whatever stage of the writing process they're in on a given day.
- Read their writing, looking for evidence of strategies they've tried at different stages of the writing process.
- Have a writing conference. Listen for what the student says about the stage of the writing process they're in and strategies they're using at that stage, asking about it directly if necessary.

Use the Strengths in the Writing Process Tool (**Online Resource 2.6**) to help you identify the student's strengths in moving through the stages of the writing process.

LOOK FOR QUALITIES OF WRITING STRENGTHS

Use these methods to look for the student's strengths in the qualities of writing:

- Read the student's writing. As you read through the first time, see what strengths stand out to you. Then reread several times, looking for strengths in one quality of writing at a time.
- Have a writing conference with the student and listen for what the student says about how they're incorporating qualities of writing into their work. If necessary, ask them about how they're doing this.

Use the Strengths in the Qualities of Writing Tool (**Online Resource 2.7**) to help you look for the student's strengths in each quality.

When you are studying a primary-grade student, you'll also find the Strengths in Print Fluency Tool (**Online Resource 2.8**) will help you name what they can do as they are learning to write words and sentences. Likewise, the Strengths in Illustration Tool (**Online Resource 2.9**) will help you identify strengths in their illustrations.

Action 2.6: Set Writing Goals for Students

The starting point for understanding how to support students' growth begins in your mind. Once you've identified their strengths, you'll be able to envision next steps, or goals, for them (C. Anderson 2005; Harris 2019; Serravallo 2014a, 2014b, 2017). These goals will transform your teaching, as helping students meet them will guide your work with them over several months of time, sometimes over an entire school year. And when many students have the same goals, they'll help you form small groups and also guide you in shaping your units of study to help students meet them.

How does this work exactly? Let's say you've identified an elaboration strength for one of your students—they write with a partial repertoire of details. A goal for this student could be to expand their repertoire. In practice, when you learn in a conference that most of a student's story consists of a series of character actions, you could teach them to include other kinds of details, such as character thoughts and dialogue. And in the next unit, when the student writes a nonfiction piece, and you notice the student's writing contains a lot of descriptive facts (which tell what something looks like), you could teach them about other kinds of details, such as action facts (which describe what something does) or number facts (which describe the size of something, the number of parts it has, etc.).

When you focus on goals when you work with them, students will be more likely to grow in response to your teaching.

Further Reading

For more guidance on how to see and respond to strengths in student writing, see Katherine Bomer's *Hidden Gems: Naming and Teaching from the Brilliance in Every Student's Writing* (2010) and *Starting with What Students Do Best* (2011).

Practice Setting Goals

Goals should be appropriate next steps for students. That is, a goal should be an incremental *step* for children, not the entire set of stairs! For example, when a child has a partial repertoire of one or two kinds of details, it would be reasonable to help that child increase their repertoire to two to three kinds of details, not the full repertoire. While ultimately we want children to learn to write with a full repertoire, there are many steps they can take along the way.

To practice setting goals, revisit the case-study student you worked with in Action 2.5. Or consider several students for whom you've identified some strengths. To set goals for them, ask yourself, *What reasonable next steps would help these students build on their strengths?*

If you're new to setting writing goals, learning to do this work will take some time. Once you get the feel for it, you'll be able to set goals for students more quickly. One reason for this is because you'll see that students have some similar strengths, and you can set similar goals for them.

Practice Prioritizing a Few Goals

To teach students effectively, prioritize two or three goals for each of them. Limiting the number of goals will make it more possible for you to keep working on them when you confer with students and when you put them in small-group lessons. This is important, as learning to write well is an over-and-over-again process—that is, students need continued teaching and support with goals to help them meet them.

Since young writers need to get better at every aspect of writing, how do you decide which ones to focus on first?

What do you mean by goals?

The kinds of goals we're discussing here are *writing goals*, ones that you can work on *across* units of study. For example, a student can work on the writing goal of *focusing on part of a topic* or the writing goal of *developing a repertoire of details* in any unit.

Writing goals are bigger than unit goals. In fact, you can translate a writing goal into a unit goal. For example, you can help a student with the writing goal of focusing on part of a topic by teaching them to write a small moment in a narrative unit of study, and you can help them with the goal of developing a repertoire of details by teaching them to cite research in an argument.

- ***Prioritize goals that students need the most support from you to meet.*** For example, students usually need one-on-one support to get better at elaboration. On the other hand, students who need to develop a repertoire of voice techniques, such as using bold words and punctuation marks like the exclamation mark and the ellipsis, will probably be able to get enough support from your minilessons to meet this goal.
- ***Prioritize engagement.*** If you learn a child isn't an engaged writer, this will be an important goal, especially early in the school year.

- ***Prioritize process goals that will help them move through the writing process independently.*** For example, in the beginning of the year, topic choice will be a goal for some of your students, since students who have trouble finding topics will have trouble getting started.
- ***Prioritize process goals that address stages of the writing process students may be skipping.*** For example, some students don't plan their writing and then have difficulty with writing a well-structured piece. Or some students skip the revision stage entirely and publish drafts that still need elaboration.
- ***Select goals that are higher on the food chain, such as focus or structure.*** For example, it usually makes more sense to help students who write bed-to-bed stories learn to focus their writing before you teach them about elaboration.
- ***Include a conventions goal.*** For example, you'll probably have one goal that addresses a convention, such as spacing (with younger children) or how to punctuate multiple-clause sentences (with older children).

See **Action 2.7** for a discussion about recording goals on record-keeping forms.

With these criteria in mind, review the goals you've envisioned for your case-study student, and narrow them down to two or three. If it's hard to decide, keep in mind that goals that you don't prioritize at first can become priorities later on in the school year.

Finally, remember that student growth takes place over many years. During their time with you, if you can help them grow significantly with several—but not all—aspects of writing, students will have had a good year. They'll learn about other aspects of writing in future years, with other writing teachers.

TIP

To help you envision appropriate goals, refer to the tools Strengths in Student Engagement **(Online Resource 2.5)**; Strengths in the Writing Process (**Online Resource 2.6**); Strengths in the Qualities of Writing **(Online Resource 2.7)**; Strengths in Print Fluency **(Online Resource 2.8)**; and Strengths in Illustration **(Online Resource 2.9)**.

Revisit—and Revise—Your Goals

Across the school year, review your goals to evaluate whether students have met them and, if so, set new goals for them. You can do this at any time, especially as you make sense of what you learn about them in writing conferences.

Since it usually takes several months (at least) for students to make progress with goals, we suggest you revisit your goals one or two times a year:

- when you are preparing for parent-teacher conferences, when you are already reviewing and synthesizing what you've learned about students so you can communicate this to parents
- when you are working on report cards

Action 2.7: Use Record-Keeping Forms to Set and Track Goals

When you visit your doctor, you expect they'll know about your health history and use what they know to make treatment decisions. Your doctor can do this because they've taken notes about what they've learned about you over the years and reviewed the notes before you came in for a visit.

Note-taking is equally valuable for teachers. You'll take notes about what you learn from students in conferences. You'll take notes about what you observe students doing and also about things you learn about them when you read their writing outside of writing workshop (C. Anderson 2005, 2018; Serravallo 2014a, Serravallo 2014b).

When you take notes, write down what they're doing as writers and their strengths in that work—and then use this information to formulate goals, and write them down, too. Having these notes is helpful in several ways:

- When you confer with students, you'll reread your notes beforehand and be reminded of your goals for them. Then, when you start your conferences, you'll be listening and looking for opportunities to address them.
- Your notes will help you identify trends of goals across your class. When you see that several students, or even most of the students in your class, have similar goals, address these shared goals in small-group lessons or in minilessons.

Select a Record-Keeping Form

If you're new to conference note-taking, your first step is to pick a note-taking form. If you've already been taking notes, you might want to try out another one to see if it works better for you.

There are two kinds of forms. The Class-at-a-Glance Record-Keeping Form (**Online Resource 2.10**; see also Figure 2–7) allows you to take notes about one conference each for all of your students. On the Individual Student Record-Keeping Form (**Online Resource 2.11**; see also Figure 2–8), you can record information about one student from several conferences. There are pluses and minuses for each kind of form (see Figure 2–9). Experiment with both to find the kind you're most comfortable with!

2.10 Class-at-a-Glance Record-Keeping Form

Class Conference Notes		Dates: 9/8	to		
Alyssa 9/8 PN "My Budgies" - writes "all about" her topic (TP) write small moment (G) Focus on part of topic	Erik 9/12 PN "Day I Got My Puppy" - added a few missing words (TP/G) revise by adding details	Tara 9/9 - lots of interests, not sure which one to pick as topic (TP) brainstorm list of topics (G) Topic choice strats	Atticus	Haskell 9/10 PN "Fishing Story" - adding details to story, but general (TP/G) write specific details	Arden 9/11 PN "Beach Story" - series of parts, time order - all parts equal length (TP/G) develop important parts
Kaelyn 9/11 PN "Skunk Story" - series of scenes, 1st scene unnecessary (TP) start close to problem (G) establish focus in intros	Henry 9/19 PN "Camp Story" - 1-2 actions per scene, general (TP) bit-by-bit actions (G) write precise details	Evie	Tunde 9/10 PN "Trip to DC" - all about focus (TP) write small moment (G) focus on part of topics	Kayla 9/12 PN "Cat Story" - introduces herself in lead (TP) dialogue lead (G) Repertoire of leads	Jonathan
Esteban 9/9 PN "Beach Story" - lots of dialogue (TP) add action to dialogue (G) use full repertoire of details	Ana	Edward 9/11 PN "Baseball" - has ending, very abrupt (TP) reflective ending (G) repertoire of endings	Tiffany 9/12 PN "Dad Story" - "I'm Done!" (TP/G) Revise by adding details	Josh 9/8 PN "Home Run Story" - has general sense of how story will go (TP) Plan w/ flow chart (G) planning strats	Wyatt 9/11 PN "The Best Dad" - trying to revise by adding on, no room on draft (TP) revise w/ post-its (G) revision tools
Terrence 9/12 PN "Beach Story" - well-developed parts, fizzles at end (TP/G) develop all important parts	Asha 9/8 Lots of interest unsure of what to write about (TP) heart maps (G) Topic choice strats	Madison 9/10 PN "Camp Story" - lots & lots of character details (TP) telling details (G) choosing just right details	Be[...] 9/9 - l[...] (TP) (G) u[...]		

Figure 2–7

2.11 Individual Student Record-Keeping Form

Name: Devon

Strength	Teaching Point	Goals, Next Steps, Postponed
Date: 10-2 One sentence to a page spelling	Background Details in Illustrations Info Book	Oral & written elaboration Periods
Date: 10-9 Background Details saying more 1 sent	How to say and write more using illust. details Info Book	Oral & written elaboration Periods
Date: 10-13 some periods	Consistent periods Fiction Story	Oral & written elaboration Periods
Date: 10-19 Consistent periods	Say and write more - emotions Fiction Story	Oral & written elaboration
Date: 10-27 Writing 2-3 sent per page	Say & write more - small actions Fiction Story	Planning ahead

Figure 2–8

Study How Experienced Teachers Take Notes

Studying the note-taking of experienced writing teachers will help you envision how you can do this well. Read the notes that Carl took on a Class-at-a-Glance Record-Keeping Form (see Figure 2–11) about a conference he had with Aurora, a sixth grader.

Carl made these note-taking moves:

- He wrote the date.
- He recorded what genre Aurora was writing in and the topic she was writing about.
- He noted an elaboration strength of Aurora's—that she has action facts in her repertoire of details.

Form	Pros	Cons
Class-at-a-glance record-keeping form	• You can quickly see which students need a conference. • Having less space forces you to be concise. • It's easy to see which students have similar goals, which can help you make decisions about minilessons and also about putting students together in small groups.	• To review your goals for students, you'll need to flip through previous forms in the binder or on the clipboard you carry with you when you confer.
Individual student record-keeping form	• Since you can take notes about several conferences on the form, it's easier to see all of your goals for a student before you have a conference. • You have more room for note-taking.	• You'll need another form to track when you see kids for conferences (**Online Resource 2.12**; see also Figure 2–10). • You'll need to flip through the forms to see which students have similar goals to help you make decisions about minilessons and forming small groups.

ONLINE RESOURCE

Figure 2–9

2.12 Tracking My Writing Conferences Form

Student	Dates								
Alyssa	10/10	10/19							
Ben L.	10/12	10/23	10/26						
Wyatt	10/16	10/19							
Bonnie	10/11	10/17	10/25						
Syeda	10/11	10/20							
Kayla	10/13	10/24	10/25						
Jonathan	10/12	10/18							
Kamara	10/10	10/24							
Chloe	10/12	10/19	10/27						
Dash	10/17	10/23	10/27						
Haskell	10/13	10/24							
Ben T.	10/11	10/25							
Ruby	10/16	10/17	10/26						
Tara	10/13	10/20							
Henry	10/17	10/20	10/25						
Tunde	10/10	10/23							
Danya	10/16	10/24	10/26						
Josh	10/13	10/18	10/27						
Anzia	10/11	10/23	10/26						
Cliff	10/16	10/18							
Sara	10/10	10/20	10/27						

Figure 2–10

- He wrote down what he taught Aurora (TP = teaching point): to include definitions in her writing.
- He came up with a goal for Aurora (G = goal): to develop her repertoire of details.

Now take a look at the notes Matt took on an Individual Student Record-Keeping Form (see Figure 2–12) about a conference he had with Albert, a first grader.

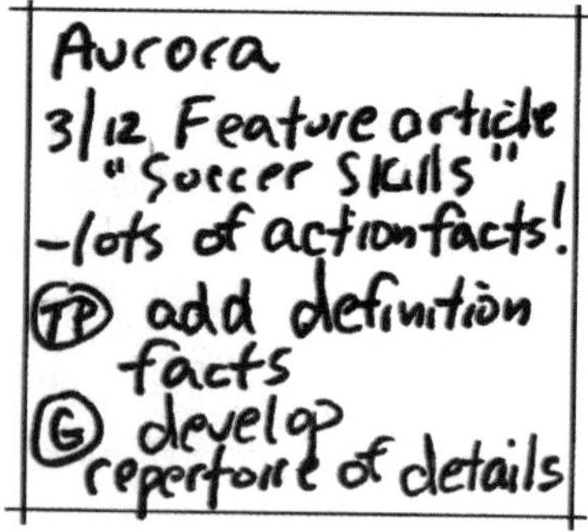
Aurora
3/12 Feature article "Soccer Skils"
–lots of action facts!
TP add definition facts
G develop repertoire of details

Figure 2–11

2.11 Individual Student Record-Keeping Form

Name: Albert

Strength	Teaching Point	Goals, Next Steps, Postponed
Date: Oct. 12 · Focused on a topic · Series of scenes · some periods	Genre · Per. Nar Topic: Park w/ sister TP - Focus on Part of a day	· Focus on part of a topic · more consistent periods

Figure 2–12

Matt made these note-taking moves:

- Matt wrote the date.
- He wrote down the genre Albert was writing in and the topic he was writing about.
- Matt wrote down several of Albert's strengths: Albert could stay focused on a topic ("writing about the whole day"), and he divided his topic up into "a series of scenes" that were in time order. Matt also noted he used periods to end some sentences.
- The second thing these notes reveal is Matt decided to teach Albert to focus his writing on part of a topic ("focus on part of the day"). (Since conferences focus on just one teaching point—and because Albert was in the middle of drafting his story—Matt didn't teach him about how to use periods more consistently on *this* day.)
- Finally, Matt wrote down two writing goals for Albert ("focus on part of a topic" and "more consistent use of periods") that were based on Albert's strengths. (If you're surprised that Matt set a focus goal after teaching Albert about this aspect of writing, remember that it often takes several conferences to help a child grow with any aspect of writing!)

Video 2.3
Conference with primary student

Video 2.4
Conference with upper-grade student

Practice Taking Notes Yourself

Now that you've studied how Carl and Matt take notes, you can practice taking notes about a conference by watching a video of either Matt conferring with a primary-age student (Video 2.3) or Carl conferring with an upper-grade student (Video 2.4).

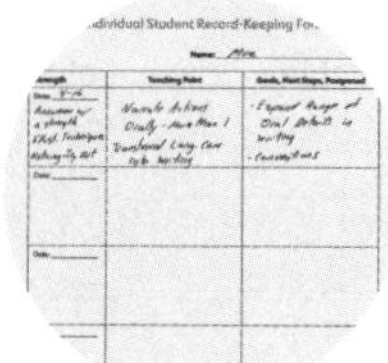

Video 2.5
Discussion of notes about primary conference

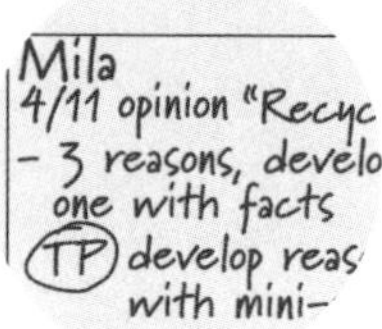

Video 2.6
Discussion of notes about upper-grade conference

You can take notes during or after the conference. (Both Carl and Matt take notes afterward because they prefer to give students their undivided attention. They usually take thirty seconds to write their notes.)

After you finish, you can literally compare notes with Matt or Carl by watching Video 2.5 or 2.6, where each shows and discusses their notes.

Practice Taking Notes About Your Students

Now it's time to apply what you've learned in your own writing conferences!

First, organize your note-taking forms:

- If you're using the class-at-a-glance form, put several copies on a clipboard or in a binder, whichever one you feel most comfortable with carrying from conference to conference. With several copies, you'll be set for a few rounds of conferences.
- If you're using the individual student form, put one for each of your students on a clipboard or in a binder. Since you can take notes about several conferences on each form, you'll be set for multiple conferences with each of your students.

Next, decide where to take notes:

- You could continue sitting by the student after a conference, which would allow you to provide follow-through reminders or extra coaching, as needed. Or you could write your notes as you walk from one conference to the next.
- You could also designate a spot in your classroom as your place to take notes. The routine of going to your note-taking spot after each conference can create a rhythm for you that will help you stick to the note-taking process.

Review Your Notes Before Conferences

Once you've had conferences with each of your students—and taken notes about them—it'll be time for the next round.

Before this next round, you'll have notes from the previous conferences. Review them before each conference, either before or just after you sit down with students. It's in these moments that notes will be a big help for you.

The most important notes to reread are the ones you wrote about students' writing goals. As you read them, ask yourself, *Based on these goals, what should I be listening for as this student tells me about their writing? What might I ask the student about? What should I be looking for as I read their writing?*

Then, as you confer, the answers to these questions will open up opportunities to continue helping students with their goals.

In **Action 7.3**, you'll learn more about how to use your notes to make good conference teaching decisions.

It's possible you may learn that a student needs help with an aspect of writing that isn't connected to one of your goals, which may in turn lead you to set another writing goal for that student. This is most likely to happen at the beginning of the school year, as you work to create a picture of a student as a writer over a series of conferences. However, once you've had a few conferences, you'll find that the goals you've set will start to inform your decision-making more and more, lifting the level of your teaching.

What about student-set writing goals?

We think it's a good idea to teach your students to have their own writing goals. However, we want to make clear the goals you set for them are different.

One of the points of having students set goals for themselves is to give them the experience of being successful goal setters. Therefore, we suggest you encourage students to set goals for themselves that they can accomplish mostly on their own, in a short amount of time, such as in a single unit of study. For example, students might set the goal of writing more neatly or writing more interesting leads.

The goals you set for your students, on the other hand, are ones that will require one-on-one support from you, and you'll give students support with them in a series of conferences over the course of several units of study.

TIP

When you see that students have met a goal you've set for them—which will probably happen after you've had several conferences with them about that goal, across several units of study—be sure to congratulate them! You can then start to focus on other goals you've set for them.

When students are engaged, they're more likely to learn what you teach them.

3

CREATE CONDITIONS FOR STUDENT ENGAGEMENT

Chapter 3

ACTIONS

Why Is Engagement So Important?

When students are engaged, they're more likely to learn what you teach them (Crouch and Cambourne 2020). Writes Ellin Keene, "We need to increase the amount of time kids spend deeply engaged because it proves intoxicating and has a real impact on whether children retain and reapply what they've learned" (2018, 17).

You can tell students are engaged when they

- are totally engrossed in their work
- lose track of time because they are so into their writing
- can't wait to write each day
- appear driven to write
- get into a flow where ideas come rapidly
- ask to sit where their flow can't be interrupted
- are so excited about their writing they want to talk about it as they write
    - want to talk about their writing at other times of the day besides writing workshop

- are disappointed when you tell them it's time to stop writing
- can't wait to publish (or share) what they've written

What Can You Do to Promote Engagement?

Student engagement happens by design, because teachers make decisions that lead to engagement (Crouch and Cambourne 2020). Cornelius Minor writes, "A kid can't be successful in my classroom if I have not created the opportunities for that child to be successful" (2019, 36).

In this chapter, we describe actions to help you create the conditions for engagement. Use the chart in Figure 3–1 to help you identify and prioritize which ones to take first.

Action	When to Take It
Action 3.1 Help Students Choose Engaging Topics	• If students say they don't know what to write about or have trouble initiating writing projects. • If students select general topics (my weekend, my vacation, animals, etc.). • If students usually choose the very first topic they come up with. • If students tend to write about very different topics from unit to unit, with varying degrees of engagement.
Action 3.2 Create a Sense of Audience as Your Students' First Responder	• If students don't seem eager to see you when you initiate conferences. • If students have less energy for writing by the end of conferences. • If students seldom take initiative to share their writing with you.
Action 3.3 Help Students Identify Authentic Audiences	• If students think of writing as an assignment to complete and turn in to you. • If students are puzzled when you ask them whom they plan to share their writing with. • If students name audiences for their writing, but these audiences don't make sense, given their topic and purpose for writing. • If students name the class as their audience, even when there are specific students who are a perfect audience for what they are writing about.
Action 3.4 Select Engaging Mentor Texts	• If students ask you, "Why do we have to write?" • If students are disinterested in your mentor texts. • If students have an engaging reading life but haven't yet found writing to be engaging.

Action	When to Take It
Action 3.5 Make Time for Genre Choice	• If students express interest in writing in a genre and ask you when they can write in it and you reply, "In the spring," or "You'll get to write in that genre next year." • If students write on their own at home, even though they seem disinterested in writing in school. • If students have varying degrees of engagement with the genre studies in your curriculum.
Action 3.6 Help Students Choose Engaging Genres	• If students are uncertain about how to choose genres. • If students are in a genre rut, that is, they usually choose genres they've written in recently or have written in frequently in school. • If students choose from a narrow range of genres.
Action 3.7 Value and Teach into Illustration	• If students enjoy drawing but are reluctant to write. • If students find it easier to draw than to write.
Action 3.8 Talk About Yourself as an Engaged Writer (in Online Resources)	• If students describe their own experiences with engagement with very basic language: "Writing went good today" or "I had fun writing today." • If students clearly are engaged with their writing but don't know why. • If students are sometimes engaged in writing, and sometimes not, but don't seem that aware of the differing qualities of their experiences.

Figure 3–1

Action 3.1: Help Students Choose Engaging Topics

When we give students the opportunity to make choices about their learning, they're often more engaged in that learning (M. Anderson 2016). Student engagement in writing begins with topic choice (Glover 2009).

When they choose their own topics, students can experience several kinds of engagement (Bomer and Bomer 2001; Ehrenworth, Wolfe, and Todd 2020; Keene 2018; Muhammad 2020):

- intellectual engagement
- emotional engagement

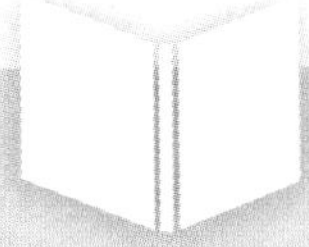

Further Reading

In Chapter 12 of *The Unstoppable Writing Teacher*, titled, "I want kids to write about what they care about, but so much of what they care about feels brainless and superficial to me," Colleen Cruz (2015) has an excellent discussion of how to help students with topic choice.

- perspective-bending engagement (when writing about a topic pushes you to reconsider your ideas or beliefs about it)
- aesthetic engagement
- political engagement

Since Donald Graves published his book *Writing: Teachers and Children at Work* (1983), topic choice has been at the center of writing instruction. However, as literacy educator Peter Johnston has pointed out, giving students the opportunity to make choices in writing workshop doesn't mean they'll know *how* to make good choices (Fletcher, Johnston, and Ray 2007). Educator Mike Anderson (2016) points out that it's the teacher's responsibility to teach students how to make good choices.

It follows that giving students the opportunity to choose topics doesn't *guarantee* students will have engaging writing experiences. Many students, then, will need guidance with generating engaging topics.

There are several tried-and-true strategies for identifying possible writing topics and choosing which ones will lead to engaging writing experiences. Once students have learned these strategies, they can use them again and again across the year, in any unit of study.

Teach Students How to Brainstorm a List of Topics

Brainstorming is one of the best strategies for choosing a topic. When students learn to brainstorm effectively, not only are they able to generate a list of topics but they also know how to decide which ones will be the most engaging to write about (Glover 2019).

Video 3.1
Minilesson: Brainstorming

The best way to teach this lesson is through demonstration. As you show students how you use the strategy, explain *how* you come up with a list of topics and *how* you select one to write about. For example, you can come up with topics by thinking of different aspects of your life, such as important people and places, interests, and opinions. You can then explain how to select a topic by rereading your list and seeing which ideas elicit an emotional response or a sense of excitement and wonder. As you do your demonstration, do a think-aloud throughout. This gives students insight into how to use the strategy themselves.

Teach Students About Writing Territories

Another strategy for finding topics is to use writing territories (Murray 1999; Atwell 2014). Writers often have a few favorite or important areas of interest in their lives, and they deliberately mine them for topics, whatever genres they're writing in. The topics that grow out of writing territories are likely to be more engaging.

Just as you would do when you teach students to brainstorm topics, teach students about writing territories through demonstration, by showing students how you come up with your own writing territories and then how you mine a writing territory for writing ideas. Once again, the key aspect of a demonstration lesson is thinking aloud as you teach.

Video 3.2
Minilesson: Writing territories

Teach Other Strategies

Of course, there are other strategies for discovering engaging topics. It's helpful to know about them, as the more strategies you have in your teaching repertoire, the more likely it is students will find one or two that will work for them.

You can learn about more strategies in professional books. For example, Georgia Heard discusses the strategy of heart mapping in *Heart Maps: Helping Students Create and Craft Authentic Writing* (2016).

Another source of strategies is your experience as a writer. Which ones do you use? They are just as legitimate as the ones described in this action.

Action 3.2: Create a Sense of Audience as Your Students' First Responder

The main purpose for writing is to communicate with other people. Engagement goes hand in hand with writers having real audiences in mind when they write.

While it's true students are more likely to be engaged in writing when they write for authentic audiences (the subject of Action 3.3), it's also important to think about your role in responding to student writing and how it's connected to student engagement (Crouch and Cambourne 2020). That's because you're usually the first responder to students' work *while it's in the process of being written*. Writes Cornelius Minor, "The role of the educator during the first part of any communicative act is to simply hear" (2019,16). The way you respond to students during this critical time can increase their engagement. By responding to students' topics with genuine interest and enthusiasm, even for just a few moments, you help students see that what they're writing about is worth being invested in.

Respond in Writing Conferences

When you confer with students, it's often the first time someone is interacting with them about their writing. Students often are insecure about their work and are thinking, *Is this a good topic?*

This is a perfect time to respond to students' topics with interest and, if a student is writing about a difficult experience, empathy. For students who are already engaged, this response affirms they're on the right track. For students who aren't that engaged, a positive response can be energizing.

One time you can respond to student topics is when students bring them up at the beginning of a conference. For example:

Teacher: *How's it going?*

Student [*Excited*]: Great. I'm writing about getting my new puppy.

Teacher: *You got a new puppy? Wow!*

Student [*Beams*]: I got to name her. I named her Snoopy!

Teacher: *I remember how exciting it was when my dog was a puppy. I can't wait to read your story about getting Snoopy. So what are you doing as a writer to tell the story?*

While it may seem like common sense to take a few moments to respond to what students are writing about, several things can get in the way, for example:

- *You might feel pressure to confer with as many students as possible in a period.* Since responding to what students are writing about can have a powerful energizing effect on students, it's worth the few extra moments you'll spend doing this in conferences.
- *There are times when you have trouble connecting with what students are writing about.* While you may not be interested in Star Wars or Fortnite,

working with student writers requires you to try to enter into their worlds and find value in what they're interested in! Colleen Cruz (2015) points out, "Our students need to know that we value their lives, all of what goes on in their lives, in order to feel that they can bring and share those lives with their writing in the classroom" (119). When students are engaged, they're writing to please themselves and their intended audience, not to please you!

Respond During Informal Topic Conversations

As you walk around your classroom in between writing conferences, you'll be glancing at students' work and noticing what they're writing about. Especially for students who you know aren't that engaged in writing—yet—dropping in for a short one-to-two-minute topic conversation and expressing interest in what they're writing about can help them feel more engaged.

Teacher: *I see that you're writing about Fortnite . . .*

Student [*Sighs*]: Yeah.

Teacher: *Fortnite is such a cool topic. What are some of the things you're writing about the game?*

Student: Well, there are a lot of different kinds of weapons, like sniper rifles and crossbows.

Teacher [Excited]: *You don't say!*

Student [*Sits up and smiles*]: And you can build forts with ramps and walls, but you need to use your axe to get materials first.

Teacher: *Wow, you're writing about such interesting facts about Fortnite. I bet your book will really help people who want to get good at this video game!*

Student [Beams]

Respond in Share Sessions

In the share session, students usually talk about things they tried as writers during that day's writing workshop. When students volunteer to share, tuck in your response to the topics they're writing about. For some students, a public response from you is even more affirming and energizing than a response given to them individually. Also, you'll be modeling for your class how to respond to the topics their classmates are writing about.

Teacher: *Who wants to share what they did today?*

Student: Me!

Teacher: *Luciana, what do you want to share?*

Luciana: In my short story, I'm writing about a kid who is being bullied.

Teacher: *Wow, bullying is such an important topic to be tackling, and writing a short story about it is a way to really help readers understand what it's like for a kid to go through such a tough experience.*

Luciana [Nods]

Teacher: *So what do you want to share about what you did as a writer today?*

Action 3.3: Help Students Identify Authentic Audiences

Students need authentic audiences for their writing. When they're able to write for audiences who matter to them—classmates, teachers, school officials, family members, members of their communities—about their experiences, interests, and ideas, they're more likely to be engaged (Boswell 2021).

One of the most powerful questions you can ask children is "Whom are you writing this for?" (Another way of asking this question is "Whom are you going to give this writing to when you're finished?") Too often, we find that students respond to this question in ways that reveal they're writing only because it's writing workshop, rather than writing *for* someone.

For example, Matt asked a child who was writing a book about soccer, "Whom are you going to give this to when your book is done?"

After a long, puzzled pause, the student finally said, "Uh . . . my mom?"

Matt then asked, "Does your mom like soccer?"

"No, she hates soccer!" the student exclaimed.

When Matt read the child's book, he saw he wasn't writing the book to help his mom understand or appreciate soccer. He said "my mom" only because that was the first name that popped into his head.

Contrast what that student said with how these other children responded:

- Zachary, a reluctant preschool writer and hermit crab expert, made his first book when he found out the class across the hall was getting a hermit crab but the teacher didn't know how to take care of it. Zachary made a book teaching her what he knew about hermit crabs. He gave it to the teacher when he finished.
- A seventh grader said, "I'm writing this story about the time I adopted my cat. When I'm finished with it, I'm going to give it to the people at the animal shelter so they can give it to people. Hopefully they will adopt cats also."
- A third grader said, "My friends and I are making a bunch of books, and then we're going to sell them out by the side of the road."

Given that these children each had an audience in mind for their writing, it wasn't surprising they were highly engaged in what they were doing. Children write with more energy when they believe there are people who will find their writing interesting and useful.

For students to have authentic audiences, they need to identify whom they could be writing for. Certain classmates? The principal? Their dad? The mayor of their town or city? And they need the opportunity to choose which audience they want to reach.

However, simply giving students the opportunity to identify and choose audiences for their writing doesn't mean they'll find audiences they want to write for. Just like you teach students how to find meaningful topics, you need to teach them how to find audiences for their writing.

Video 3.3
Minilesson: Identifying audiences

Conduct Minilessons About Audience

Give a minilesson early in each unit of study to help children identify possible audiences. Why? Children need to learn that their audience may change, depending on the topic they're writing about, the genre they're writing in, and the purpose for writing. For example, a child writing a story about a trip her family took to Myrtle Beach in a unit of study on personal narrative might decide she wants to share it with her family, so she can let them know how special it was to spend time with them. In a later unit of study on craft, the same student may choose to write a feature article on the Marines and decide to share it with classmates whose parents are also in the Marines.

A powerful time to teach students about audience is during units of study in which students can choose their own genres, as the range of possible audiences will be much wider than within a genre study. For example, a child who chooses to write a how-to book on making Star Wars spaceships out of blocks could make his book available in the block center. Another child, who wants to write about her opinion that there should be more vegetarian food on the school lunch menu, could share her writing with the principal or even send it to the school board.

Video 3.4
Writing conference: Identifying audiences

Teach About Audience During Writing Conferences

Conferences are another place to teach children about audience and, when necessary, give them support with identifying possible audiences.

Make it a habit to ask children, "Whom are you writing this for?" Simply by asking this question, you let students know this is an important thing to be thinking about as they write. And when children have some difficulty naming an audience, teaching them how to identify an audience can become the focus of the conference.

Talk About Audience in Share Sessions

In some share sessions, ask students whom they plan to give their writing to when they are finished with it. This kind of share nudges students to think about audience. And when they hear their classmates name different audiences, they get ideas about possible audiences for their writing and writing in general.

Do this kind of share session in every unit of study. Revisiting the idea is another way of communicating to your children the importance of having an audience for their writing and giving them ongoing support in identifying and choosing meaningful audiences for their work.

Plan Class Writing Celebrations

Teachers commonly organize writing celebrations at the end of units of study (Ayres 2013). Often, students read their finished writing aloud to their classmates as well as to parents and administrators who have been invited. In another kind of celebration, students walk around the classroom and sit down at their classmates' table spots or desks to read their writing and then write their responses on a piece of paper that's taped next to each student's writing.

When you have writing celebrations with your class, you can do a lot of teaching about audience:

- Ask your students if there are any people outside of the class—students from other classes, parents, school officials—whom they want to invite to the celebration to hear or read their writing.
- When you have students read their writing to the class, provide time after the celebration for students to meet with classmates or other attendees whom they wrote the piece for so they can hear their responses.
- When you have students sit at each other's desks to read their writing, suggest that students encourage specific classmates or other attendees who are their audience to read and respond to their pieces.
- Be sure to suggest that students share their writing with people who couldn't be at the celebration. This could involve bringing the piece home for their family to read or sending their writing to the president of the United States!

Action 3.4: Select Engaging Mentor Texts

A *mentor text* is a model text we use to teach students about the craft of writing and conventions (C. Anderson 2022b; Marchetti and O'Dell 2015, 2021; Meehan and Sorum 2021; Shubitz 2016). There are three kinds:

- a *published* mentor text—one written by an author outside of the classroom (e.g., a picture book or a poem in an anthology), in a newspaper or magazine (e.g., an opinion piece or a feature article), or on the internet (e.g., a TED talk)

- a *teacher-written* mentor text
- a *student-written* mentor text

Well-chosen mentor texts also help students become engaged writers because students have engaging experiences when reading them, which helps them realize they can write texts that will have the same effects on their own readers (C. Anderson 2022b; Meehan and Sorum 2021).

Another way mentor texts help students become engaged is to think of these texts as mirrors and doors, an idea that comes from the work of Rudine Sims Bishop (1990). Texts can be "mirrors," Bishop writes, because "literature transforms human experience and reflects it back to us, and in that reflection we can see our lives and experiences as part of the larger human experience. Reading, then, becomes a means of self-affirmation, and readers often seek their mirrors in books" (ix–xi).

When we select mentor texts that are mirrors, we help students become engaged. When texts reflect students' identities and experiences, they affirm these identities and experiences (Cherry-Paul 2021; Ebarvia 2017). This helps students see they have great material to write about. They also discover their interests are shared by other writers, which helps affirm that these interests are worth writing about.

Bishop explains texts can also be doors: "Books are sometimes windows, offering views of worlds that may be real or imagined, familiar or strange. These windows are also sliding glass doors, and readers only have to walk through in imagination to become part of whatever world has been created and recreated by the author" (ix–xi).

When we choose mentor texts that are doors, students can become engaged because they realize that writing can be a way for authors to explore experiences, interests, and ideas that are different from their own—or different from what people usually write about—and students can do the same. They also see that writing can be a way to get in someone else's shoes and try to see the world from their perspective.

By choosing just the right mentor texts, we help students answer the question *Why should I be engaged in writing?*

Provide a Variety of Reading Experiences

When you're selecting mentor texts, think about the kinds of engagement experiences students can have with them. The more ways that students are engaged as readers, the more ways they'll be able to envision engaging their own readers.

To do this, read widely in the genres your children will be writing in, and ask yourself, *What kinds of engagement experience can students have with this text?*

For example, consider the how-to genre. You might think of how-to books as texts that will primarily engage students on an intellectual level. But if you read many examples of this kind of writing, you'll see there are other engaging reading experiences that students can have:

- Amanda McCardie's *Our Very Own Dog: Taking Care of Your First Pet* (2019) can engage children on an emotional level as well as an intellectual level and also be a mirror for children who enjoy having animals and who may want to share their experiences with others.
- Mylisa Larsen's *How to Put Your Parents to Bed* (2016) can engage kids on a humorous and almost fantastical level (as it's usually parents who put children to sleep!)—and it will be a door for students that helps them see that how-to books can be funny and even ridiculous!
- Keilly Swift's *How to Make a Better World: For Every Kid Who Wants to Make a Difference* (2020) can engage kids on a political level—and it will be a door for students that will help them imagine new possibilities for this genre.

Select Texts That Center Students' Interests

Be open to choosing mentor texts about topics that you may not care much about but will validate your students' interests and help them see they can write about these interests. For example, you may not like video games, but some of your students probably do, and showing students nonfiction books or articles on this topic will help students realize they can write about what will be for them a highly engaging topic.

Use **Online Resource 3.1**: Choosing Engaging Mentor Texts Guide to help you select mentor texts.

Give Students Time to Read Mentor Texts as Readers

When students listen to or read mentor texts for the first time during immersion at the beginning of units of study (see Actions 6.1–6.3), give them time after reading each text to process their varied reading experiences. For example, when you read mentor texts aloud to the class, you could ask students to turn and talk to each other about their responses, have a class discussion, or (in the upper grades) ask students to jot their responses in their writers' notebooks before sharing them.

Action 4.1 includes a discussion of other criteria to consider when selecting mentor texts.

Resist the urge to discuss how mentor texts are crafted until *after* students have a chance to respond as readers! This helps them think about and deepen their responses, responses that are essential to helping them understand they can elicit the same reactions from readers when they write.

Name the Kinds of Reading Experiences Students Have

As students respond as readers the first time they listen to or read a mentor text, name the kinds of responses they're having. This kind of naming helps students understand the many different ways they are engaged with that text.

After reading Gaia Cornwall's *Jabari Jumps* (2017), for example, first graders shared these responses:

Aleema: I go swimming too! I know how to dive off the diving board. You can't look down, or you get scared!

Terrance: I was scared, too, when I dove off the diving board.

Syeda: I was scared when I climbed to the top of the monkey bars and jumped! It's really tall.

Tory: My dad helps me when I do scary things, too.

After facilitating the discussion, the teacher named the kinds of responses her students had:

Teacher: *Jabari Jumps* sure is a powerful story, because you had a lot of different kinds of responses to it. Some of you, like Aleema, were thinking about how you already know how to do what Jabari learns to do in the story. Some of you, like Terrance and Syeda, were thinking about how you felt when you did the same thing Jabari did or something similar. And some of you, like Tory, were thinking about important people in your life and how they help you when you do scary things.

Connect Students' Reading Experiences with Those They Want to Create

After students respond to mentor texts as readers, explain that they can elicit the same kinds of responses in their readers. By doing this, you help students envision the authentic purposes they can have for their writing, a key to being engaged writers.

For example, a first-grade teacher could say this after her students have read and responded to several all-about informational books:

Teacher: Now that we've read several all-about books, it's time to start thinking about the books you're going to write in this unit. As we do that thinking together, I want you to remember all of the different ways you responded to the books I've read you. That's because the books you'll write can have the same effects on the people who read them! Just like many of you had lots of questions—and got answers to them—when we read Gail Gibbons' *Frogs* (1993), your books will get readers asking and answering questions, too. Just like some of you got ideas for how to make the world a better place when we read Todd Parr's *The Earth Book* (2010), you might write books that have ideas about how to make the world better. And just like how some of the books we read, like Nicola Davies' *Surprising Sharks* (2003), helped you understand that there's a lot more to know about some subjects than you first thought, you might write books that help other people see how there are a lot of surprising things to learn about some topics. These are some really good reasons why you can write your own books!

Action 3.5: Make Time for Genre Choice

Like topic choice, genre choice is linked to student engagement (Fletcher 2006, 2017). In fact, for some children, the genre they write in is more motivating than the topic they write about! Observes Matt in his book *Craft and Process Studies* (2019), "A type of writing is more enticing [for them] than a particular topic" (3).

Why is genre choice linked to engagement?

- There are genres many children love to write in, such as fantasy and poetry.
- Some of children's purposes for writing are better realized in some genres than others.
- There are genres that students write in at home, and being able to bring these genres into school is exciting for them.

Since engagement is one of our primary goals, it follows that we need to make time in yearlong writing curricula for units of study in which students *can choose their own genres*.

Your writing curriculum may consist almost entirely of genre studies in which students must write in the genre being studied. While we find value in units in which we study genres deeply with children and feel there should be several of these studies in a yearlong writing curriculum in each grade, we also feel that genre studies shouldn't be the *only* kind of unit in curricula! Why? When a yearlong curriculum consists almost entirely of genre studies, it's possible some students won't write in a genre they're interested in or that meets their needs at that point in their life, for most or maybe even all of the school year. For many students, the experience of writing each day becomes about compliance, not engagement.

Assess Your Writing Curriculum

Take a close look at your writing curriculum to see how many units are genre studies and how many are units in which students can choose genres. If the balance is weighted heavily toward genre studies, we suggest you make some revisions to your curriculum.

In **Action 5.6,** we suggest ways to look at this balance in the curricula across grades in your school, too.

Identify Units of Study in Which Students Can Choose Genres

If you realized you need to make revisions to your writing curriculum, the next step is to identify and learn about units of study in which students can write in genres of their choosing. These units fall into two categories: *craft* and *process* studies.

- In a craft study, the focus is usually on one aspect of an author's craft (genre studies are actually a kind of craft study).
- In a process study, the focus is on teaching students how to navigate a part of the writing process.

Figures 3–2 and 3–3 list just a few examples of craft and process studies.

Craft Study	Focus of the Study
Illustration (primary grades)	Students study the craft of making illustrations in books.
Text features (upper grades)	The class studies text features and how they enhance texts.
Author	Students study the writing of one author, learning about craft from a writer they love.
Text structure	The class studies different ways writers structure texts.
Detail	Students study different kinds of details and the ways they're written.

Craft Study	Focus of the Study
Voice	The class studies the techniques writers use to give their writing voice.
Punctuation	Students study the kinds of punctuation writers use and the different purposes for punctuation.

Figure 3- 2

Process Study	Focus of the Study
Launching writers' notebooks (upper grades)	Students learn how to keep a writer's notebook, a tool writers use in the rehearsal stage of the writing process.
Reading like a writer	Students practice noticing and studying the different kind of craft moves that writers make.
Planning	Students learn strategies for planning individual pieces of writing.
Revision	Students study revision tools and strategies.
Collaboration	The class studies how to have effective partnerships, peer conferences, or response groups.

Figure 3-3

Make Time for Craft and Process Studies

The final step is to make room in your curriculum for craft and process studies. Here are some ways to do this:

- Look for gap weeks in your yearlong calendar, such as when you're planning to finish a genre study a week or two before a school break.
- Shorten your current units to make room for new ones.
- Swap out some genre studies and replace them with craft and process studies. When you've already got several genre studies of narrative or informational writing in your curriculum, consider switching out one of them for a unit that allows for genre choice.

Further Reading

You'll find descriptions of how to do these craft and process studies—and more—in Katie Wood Ray's *Study Driven* (2006) and Matt Glover's *Craft and Process Studies* (2019).

Some professional books focus on one kind of craft study. For example, in *Wondrous Words* (1999), Katie Wood Ray discusses how to do a study on reading like a writer. Dan Feigelson's *Practical Punctuation* (2008) is about how to do punctuation studies in the primary and upper grades, and Katie Wood Ray's *In Pictures and In Words* (2010) talks about illustration study.

Further Reading

In his book *Joy Write: Cultivating High-Impact, Low-Stakes Writing* (2017), Ralph Fletcher extends the discussion about engagement and writing workshop curriculum by arguing that in addition to the writing that students do in units of study, they also need time for "greenbelt writing," that is, playful, highly engaging, low-stakes writing.

You may be teaching in a school where you're in charge of determining the units of study in your curriculum and you can make these revisions on your own. If you aren't, begin a conversation with administrators and colleagues about the importance of including units in which students can choose their own genres (see Action 5.3 for guidance on how to do this).

Action 3.6: Help Students Choose Engaging Genres

Imagine you're at the local bodega or grocery store, and there are many flavors of ice cream available. How do you choose? Do you go for your favorite? Do you say to yourself, *One potato, two potato, three potato, four . . .* ? Or do you walk away from the freezer, overwhelmed by the choices? And what if you don't really like ice cream all that much in the first place? Maybe you'll just select the flavor your friend chooses or the first one you see—or since you don't really care, maybe you won't choose a flavor at all.

In this scenario, maybe you're the kind of person who has a great strategy for choosing a flavor, and you're usually satisfied with the ice cream you choose. But if you're a person who has trouble when there are lots of choices, then having someone give you tips about navigating the process might help you be more successful in finding a flavor you love or might even turn you into someone whose favorite food is ice cream.

Students will sometimes be in units of study in which they can choose to write in any genre. However, just because they can make this choice doesn't mean they'll always make good choices or even know how to make them. While genre choice makes engagement possible, engagement isn't automatic or guaranteed, and many students will need you to help them (Glover 2009, 2019).

When children don't know how to choose genres—usually because they've rarely or never had this opportunity—they typically do these things:

- They continue writing in whatever genre they wrote in most recently. For example, students who were just in an informational book writing unit may continue to write informational books, not because they love the genre, but because they're used to writing informational books and aren't sure what else to write.
- They choose whichever genre they've written most for the past couple of years. Basically the child thinks, *Hmmm, I'm not sure what to write. . . . Since I've written lots of personal narratives in writing workshop, I'll just make another one.*
- They write in the genre a lot of their friends are choosing to write in, even if this genre isn't one that especially interests them.

In each situation, there's a good chance students will choose (or default to) a genre that won't be engaging for them to write in.

Instead, your goal should be for students to be intentional in selecting genres. Children who are successful in choosing genres—and who are highly engaged because of their choices—often choose genres for these reasons:

- They choose a favorite genre. This is probably the most common reason children give for their choice. When asked to explain, they'll say, "I just love writing fantasy stories!" (or graphic novels or poetry). When students love a genre, they're much more likely to be engaged.
- They choose an intriguing genre they haven't tried before. Often this genre will be one students enjoy reading, such as fantasy, but haven't tried writing yet.
- They choose a genre based on a friend's recommendation. Other students' enthusiasm for a genre is contagious.
- They choose a genre because it fits their purpose for writing. Over time, as students have more and more experience with writing in various genres, they get a sense of what purposes these genres can serve for them and then choose to write in them when they have similar purposes.
- They choose a genre because the stakes are low. Some students prefer to learn about a genre when it's not the focus of a unit of study and there's less intensity around it. A child once said to Matt, "I chose this genre because I'm not good at it, and I thought it would be easier to get better at it when we weren't studying it." This child articulated she learned best when the pressure on her to perform was lower.

Video 3.5
Minilesson: Genre possibilities

Teach Minilessons on Genre Possibilities

It's important to give minilessons that introduce students to the wide range of genres they can choose, since many of them are unaware of the variety of genres they can write in. This type of minilesson serves the same function as book talks in reading workshop. See Figure 3-4 for some options.

Teach Minilessons on Choosing a Genre

Writers choose genres for several reasons (Ray 1999). Explaining these reasons can be the focus of one or more minilessons:

- Writers start with a topic and then decide which genre best fits the topic.
- Writers start by choosing a genre and then decide upon a topic. They might choose a genre because it's one they love or one they're intrigued by either because they enjoy reading it or see others who enjoy writing in it.
- Writers sometimes start with a purpose for writing and then decide on a genre that best fits that purpose. For example, a writer who wants to be funny might choose to write a series of humorous vignettes, while a writer who wants to work for social justice might choose to write arguments.

Video 3.6
Minilesson: Choosing a genre

GENRE OPTIONS FOR STUDENTS

Primary Grades	Upper Grades	
Realistic animal stories	Feature articles	Dystopian fantasies
Magical creature stories	Arguments	Public service announcements (PSAs)
Personal narratives	TED talks	Realistic fiction
Informational books	Cookbooks	Poems
Reviews	Graphic short stories	Songs
Poems	Personal narratives	Profiles
Original fairy tales	Historical fiction	Comics
Superhero stories	Historical narrative	Comedy sketches
Science fiction stories	Fantasy fiction	Brochures
How-to picture books	Reviews	Infographics
Literary nonfiction	How-to feature articles	Advice writing
Persuasive letters	Literary nonfiction	Photo-essays
	Science fiction	

Figure 3-4

Ask Students About Genre Choice in Conferences

When students are in a unit of study in which they can choose the genre they write in, writing conferences will give you the opportunity to ask them about genre choice. Two questions you can ask are "What genre are you writing in?" and "Why did you choose this genre?"

In some conferences, you'll learn students have made a good choice and are engaged, so you'll focus these conversations on helping students with other aspects of writing. However, sometimes you'll learn students are unsure of what genre to choose or haven't made a good choice. In these situations, you'll help students find genres that appeal to them or make a better choice.

Video 3.7
Conference: Genre choice

Ask Students to Talk About Their Genre Choices in Share Sessions

Students' choice of genre is a great focus for share sessions. When students name the genres they've chosen to write in, they help classmates imagine the range of genres that are possible to use. As students share, you can chart their choices for them to refer to the next time they begin a writing project.

In these shares, ask students *why* they chose the genres they're writing in. Their classmates' explanations will help them understand that there are reasons why they, too, might choose different genres.

WHAT GENRES ARE WE WRITING?

Alyssa	Fantasy story
Kevin	Feature article
Syeda	Opinion
Terrence	Poetry
Haskell	Review
Edward	Poetry
Molly	Fantasy Story
Raymond	How-To Feature Article
Danya	Science Fiction story
Anzia	Graphic short story
Tiffany F.	Poetry
Jemal	Fantasy Story
AJ	Feature article
Tiffany S.	Play
Meredith	Realistic Fiction Story
Kaelyn	Cook book
Evie	Fantasy Story
Harrison	Poetry
Natalie	Opinion
Jackson	Fantasy Story

Figure 3–5
Chart of Student Genre Choices

Action 3.7: Value and Teach into Illustration

When Carl started coaching baseball, he had players who were more excited about some skills than others. Some loved hitting; others, fielding. Their love for one aspect of the game was their entry point into becoming highly engaged baseball players. Over time, Carl's players became skilled at other aspects of the game, too—after all, you have to both hit and field to play baseball! But it was their initial joy in one aspect of the game that started them on their baseball journey.

Many of the genres your students write in are composed of text *and* illustrations. If you teach in the primary grades, your students usually make picture books. Illustrations in picture books aren't decoration—they're integral to the composing process and help convey meaning, sometimes even more so than the text.

Even if you teach in the upper grades, many of the genres students write in include illustrations. Graphic novels, of course, are an obvious example. And this is true in many other genres, too, such as memoir, argument, and poetry. And just like in picture books, illustrations are an important compositional tool.

Since many students love to draw, or find drawing easier than writing, valuing and teaching into illustrations gives many primary students an entry point into writing that will help them become engaged writers (Ray 2010). This is also important for older children who find writing difficult and don't know where to start. By giving children another entry point, we value the skills they already have as a composer, skills that will help them become engaged in the overall process of writing.

Also, by supporting composition thinking in illustration, we become better equipped to support compositional thinking as students write text, too. For example, we can help a child who has detailed illustrations to elaborate both in their oral language and in their writing.

Unfortunately, it's common practice to teach students *out* of illustration as soon as possible. This is true even in the primary grades, where generating text quickly becomes the main goal of composition, and illustration becomes decoration or something students add before publishing. In the upper grades, students are rarely encouraged to illustrate their writing, except to make covers for their pieces before they publish them.

The goal of this action is to help you think about how to teach *into* illustration, in any grade. While our main focus is helping students be more engaged in writing, it will also be a way for you to help students become stronger writers, too.

Include Texts with Illustrations in Your Stacks of Mentor Texts

When you gather a stack, or collection, of mentor texts for a unit of study, include several that have illustrations. If you're a primary teacher, you've probably already got this covered. Since most of what your students will compose across the year will be picture books, most of your mentor texts will be picture books.

If you're an upper-grade teacher, however, you will probably need to do some searching. Here are a few tips:

- Some authors illustrate the stories in their memoirs, such as Jon Scieszka in his book *Knucklehead* (2008).
- Almost every feature article you'll find in magazines such as *Ask* or *Highlights* will include multiple illustrations. This is also true of the op-eds (opinion pieces) you'll find in magazines such as *Time for Kids* and the short fiction in *Cricket*.
- Many collections of poems are illustrated.

Teach Illustration Techniques

By teaching lessons on illustration techniques, you communicate to your students you value their interest in this important part of written composition. And not only do you help students get better at illustrating, but you also set up follow-up conversations about how to do parallel work in their writing.

For example, a lesson in how illustrators use facial expressions and body posture to convey emotion helps students communicate important information to readers (and is the perfect precursor to lessons on how to convey characters' emotions in writing). And when students are writing in nonfiction genres, a lesson on how illustrators use multiple illustrations to show different aspects of the topic helps students convey important information (and sets up a lesson on how writers give information in text by listing several examples).

Teach a Unit of Study on Illustration

In Action 3.5, we made a case for including craft and process studies in your yearlong writing curriculum, in part because these kinds of studies increase engagement through choice of genre.

One kind of craft study is illustration study (Ray 2010; Glover 2019), which focuses on the wide range of techniques illustrators use. This is an especially powerful unit for primary students. In fact, when Matt works with primary teachers, he tells them he can't imagine teaching writing to kindergartners without having an illustration study early in the year. He finds this unit not only has a dramatic effect on students' engagement and their ability to compose illustrations but also helps expand students' oral language (students can talk with more detail when their illustrations are more

Further Reading

Are you wondering how to teach illustration techniques if you're not an artist yourself? In Martha Horn and Mary Ellen Giacobbe's book *Talking, Drawing, Writing* (2006), the authors show us how to teach basic illustration techniques to children. Katie Wood Ray's book *In Pictures and In Words* (2010) examines the link between the thinking that illustrators do with pictures and authors engage in with words.

Action 3.8

Talk About Yourself as an Engaged Writer is in the Online Resources.

detailed). This unit also sets up many of the important writing lessons that you'll give as the year unfolds, because so many illustration techniques parallel writing techniques. Matt suggests returning to this unit again in first or second grade.

Another kind of illustration study, using illustrations and text to create meaning (Glover 2019) focuses on how pictures and text work together. It's a great unit to do with children in the upper grades.

Support Students When They Are Unsure of How to Draw Something

Video 3.8
Minilesson: How to draw something you don't know how to draw

Just like you teach students strategies for spelling unfamiliar words, teach them the strategy of shape, parts, and color for when they want to draw something but don't know how:

1. Think of the *shape* for the biggest part of the object you want to draw. For example, if you want to draw a firetruck, start with a rectangle; if you want to draw an elephant, start with an oval.
2. Think about the *parts* of what you want to draw. For a firetruck: a ladder, a hose, and windows. For an elephant: legs, a head, some eyes.
3. Think about the *colors* of what you want to draw. While you don't need to be overly concerned about accuracy of color when you work with very young children (if there's any time you should be able to draw a blue horse, it's when you're five), it's important to teach into the intentionality of color and how it helps communicate important details about someone's or something's appearance.

What do I do with students who want to spend all their time drawing?

There are students who will happily spend all of writing workshop drawing, instead of drawing *and* writing (this describes Carl's daughter Anzia when she was in first grade). Likewise, there are some students who want to spend a great deal of time coloring their illustrations.

Teach these students how to manage writing time to give attention to composing illustrations and text. For example, teach them to talk to a writing partner at the start of independent writing to help them think about how they'll use this time. Keep in mind this will take a while for some students—for example, over the course of first grade, Carl's daughter's books were initially composed almost entirely of illustrations, but by the end of the school year, they had an appropriate balance of illustrations and text.

Great writing teachers know
a lot of stuff about writing.

4

Develop a Repertoire of Teaching Points

Why Is Developing a Teaching Repertoire So Important?

Great writing teachers know a lot of *stuff* about writing:

- They know about craft techniques writers use.
- They know about strategies writers use to navigate the writing process.
- They know about the purposes writers write for and the genres that writers write in to realize these purposes.

For you to teach writing well, it's essential to have this extensive repertoire of teaching points for several reasons:

- When you're teaching minilessons written by someone else, knowing a lot about writing will help you understand and improve upon those lessons.
- Differentiating instruction in small groups and writing conferences depends on having many teaching points at your fingertips, more than the number of minilessons in your units of study.
- To revise units of study written by someone else, you need to be knowledgeable about alternate teaching points you could swap for ones in these units.
- When you project, or design, your own units, you need to know about teaching points you could include in each unit.

Chapter 4

ACTIONS

4.1 Gather Stacks of Published Mentor Texts

4.2 Mine Your Stack for Craft Teaching Points

4.3 Mine Your Stack for Convention Teaching Points

4.4 Mine Process Texts for Teaching Points

4.5 Expand Your Teaching Repertoire by Reading Professional Books (see Online Resources for this action)

What Can You Do to Develop Your Teaching Repertoire?

There are two important sources of information about writing you can tap to develop your repertoire. You can learn about craft techniques and conventions by studying published mentor texts. And you can learn about strategies writers use to navigate the writing process by studying your own writing process (Ray 2002, 2006; Glover and Berry 2012).

In this chapter, we describe actions that will help you tap these two sources. Use the chart in Figure 4-1 to identify and prioritize which actions to take first.

Action	When to Take It
4.1 Gather Stacks of Published Mentor Texts	• If you have only a few mentor texts for each unit of study, sometimes even just one or none. • If you aren't sure how to decide which mentor texts to include in your stacks.
4.2 Mine Your Stack for Craft Teaching Points	• If you don't know that much about the craft of writing. • If most of your craft knowledge comes from the minilessons in your units. • If you have trouble finding more than one or two craft techniques in a mentor text.
4.3 Mine Your Stack for Convention Teaching Points	• If you teach conventions by telling students rules instead of showing them examples of how writers use conventions.
4.4 Mine Process Texts for Teaching Points	• If you teach students a few tried-and-true strategies for moving through each stage of the writing process, but they don't always work for every student. • If you rarely share with students how you move through the stages of the writing process yourself.
4.5 Read Professional Books (in Online Resources)	• If most of your knowledge about teaching writing comes from unit-of-study guides.

Figure 4-1

Action 4.1: Gather Stacks of Published Mentor Texts

Developing your repertoire of craft and convention teaching points begins with gathering a stack of four to six published mentor texts for each of your genre studies, craft studies, and some process studies. These texts will be an important source of teaching points (C. Anderson 2022b; Ray 2002, 2006; Glover and Berry 2012; Meehan and Sorum 2021). In this action, you'll learn about criteria for selecting published mentor texts (C. Anderson 2022b) that will help you gather just-right mentor texts for each unit.

Learn to Use the All, Most, Some Process for Craft Studies

Imagine your grade-level team is planning a unit on informational books. As you begin to gather texts for your stack for the unit, you may feel overwhelmed if there are many all-about books in your classroom or school library. How do you narrow these choices down to just a few?

The answer to this question is to use several criteria for selecting texts and decide whether you want *all*, *most*, or *some* of your texts to reflect these criteria. Using the All, Most, Some Form (**Online Resource 4.1**; see also Figure 4-2) will help you apply the criteria to the selection process.

CRITERION 1: ENGAGING TOPICS

Students will be more interested in studying a unit's mentor texts when they're about engaging topics. You may decide *all* of the texts in your stack should have engaging topics. But you might decide *most* of the texts will have engaging topics, in case you find one that meets all of the other criteria but the topic isn't that engaging.

CRITERION 2: AGE-APPROPRIATE QUANTITY AND COMPLEXITY OF TEXT

In general, the amount and complexity of text in each mentor text should represent an appropriate writing challenge for students. You may decide *all* of your texts should reflect this criterion. But, again, you may find a text that meets all of the other criteria except this one—such as a high-interest book

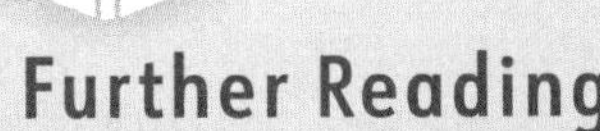

Further Reading

To learn about sources of mentor texts, elementary teachers should read Carl's *A Teacher's Guide to Mentor Texts, Grades K-5* (2022b), and secondary teachers should read Allison Marchetti and Rebekah O'Dell's *A Teacher's Guide to Mentor Texts, Grades 6-12* (2021). Katie Wood Ray's book *Study Driven* (2006) discusses sources for all grade levels.

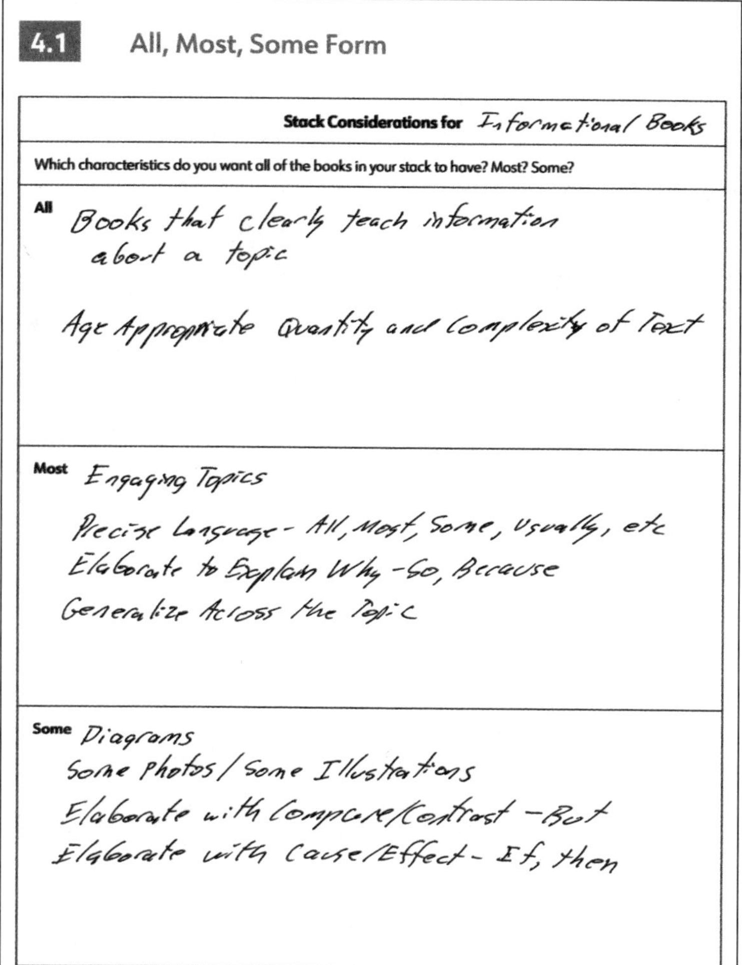

4.1 All, Most, Some Form

Stack Considerations for Informational Books

Which characteristics do you want all of the books in your stack to have? Most? Some?

All
Books that clearly teach information about a topic
Age Appropriate Quantity and Complexity of Text

Most
Engaging Topics
Precise Language - All, Most, Some, Usually, etc
Elaborate to Explain Why - So, Because
Generalize Across the Topic

Some
Diagrams
Some Photos / Some Illustrations
Elaborate with Compare/Contrast - But
Elaborate with Cause/Effect - If, then

Figure 4–2

on LEGOs that contains wonderful illustration techniques but has more text than most of your students can generate—so you might decide *most* texts should fit this criterion.

How complex should the texts be? By text complexity, we mean students' ability to comprehend texts when they're read aloud, *not* when they read them independently. With this in mind, you'll probably decide *all* of the texts in your stack should be ones students are able to comprehend when they're read aloud. At the same time, you may also decide that *some* or *most* of these texts should be ones students can read independently, since you'll read challenging texts aloud during immersion and this will give students needed support with them (see Actions 6.1–6.3).

CRITERION 3: GENRE

With the example of the informational all-about book unit, this criterion might seem superfluous. However, there are some nonfiction books, like *Bat Loves the Night*, by Nikola Davies, that fit into the category of literary nonfiction because they're beautifully written but less informational. You might decide, then, that *none* of the texts in your stack will include nonfiction books in this genre category (and perhaps you'll include a separate unit of study on literary nonfiction in your curriculum). Or maybe you'll decide *most* texts in your stack will be informational, but you'll include one to two examples of literary nonfiction.

This criterion is especially important to think about when you teach a craft study in which students can choose their own genres. For example, in a punctuation study, it doesn't matter which genres will be in your stack, as writers use punctuation in every genre. For this unit, you would probably select *some* as your criterion, as some texts in your stack could be nonfiction, some could be short fiction, some could be opinion pieces, and so on.

CRITERION 4: CRAFTING TECHNIQUES AND CONVENTIONS

For this criterion, you'll consider genre-specific craft techniques (if you're doing a genre study) or craft techniques that cross genres (if you're doing another kind of craft study).

Your state, district, or school standards will help you decide which craft techniques to include and whether you want all, most, or some of the mentor texts in your stack to include them. For example, if one of the standards is that students include an introduction in their nonfiction writing, you may decide *all* of your all-about nonfiction mentor texts will have an introduction, since every student is expected to learn to write one.

Your knowledge of the genre you're teaching, or the aspect of craft your unit is focused on, will also help you make decisions. For example, you might decide that *all* of your informational all-about mentor texts will have chapter headings, *most* will have labels on the illustrations, and *some* will have glossaries. And if you decide to put a craft technique in the *all* or *most* category, you would expect most of your students to try it out; if you include craft techniques in the *some* category, some, but not all, students, will try it.

My unit-of-study guide recommends several mentor texts. Is this action relevant for me?
When you have a list of recommended mentor texts, this action can help you evaluate them. If the list contains only a few mentor texts, this action will help you think about how to add more texts or decide whether you'll need to substitute texts for one or more of the ones on the list.

Can I include my own writing in my stack? How about student writing?
We don't usually put our own writing and student writing in our stack of texts to study with students. But we do use our own writing and student writing daily throughout the unit. We even show students our writing and student writing at the end of an immersion day so they can see what this writing looks like when it's created by someone who isn't a published author.

In some units, published texts are hard to come by (for example, if you're teaching literary essay). In these units, most of the texts in your stack will consist of examples that you and your colleagues have written.

Do I need stacks for process studies?
There are several process studies that require stacks of texts. For example:

- For a unit on reading like a writer, you'll need a stack for studying craft moves.
- In a unit on finding topics, you'll need a stack that includes authors' notes so the class can see how the writers found their topics.
- In an independent genre study, groups of students will need their own stacks of texts.

Practice Using the All, Most, Some Form

Now it's time for you to gather a stack of mentor texts, most likely for your next unit of study, and use the All, Most, Some Form to help you make selections. While you can do this yourself, you'll find working with several colleagues, discussing each of the criteria together, and then sorting through texts will give you a richer and more productive experience.

If your next unit is on a craft study you don't feel that knowledgeable about, you may need to read about the unit first before you start the process of gathering texts (see "Further Reading" on the next page). Or you could gather a large stack of texts to familiarize yourself with the kind of writing students will be doing and then decide upon the criteria you'll use to decide which ones to include in your stack.

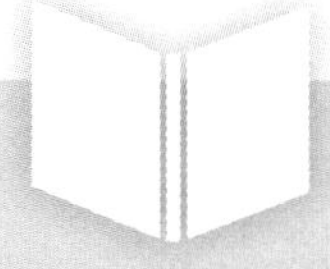

Further Reading

You'll find information about craft studies in books such as Matt's *Craft and Process Studies* (2019) and Katie Wood Ray's *Study Driven* (2006). Dan Feigelson's *Practical Punctuation* (2008) and Katie Wood Ray's *In Pictures and In Words* (2010; illustration study) describe how to do a study of one aspect of craft. There are many books on teaching genre studies, including

Carl Anderson's *Magical Writing: Teaching Fantasy Writing in Grades K–6* (2024)

Katherine Bomer's *Writing a Life* (2005; memoir) and *The Journey Is Everything* (2016; essay)

Karen Caine's *Writing to Persuade* (2008)

M. Colleen Cruz's Writers Read Better series (2018, 2019; nonfiction and narrative)

Ralph Fletcher's *Making Nonfiction from Scratch* (2015)

Georgia Heard's *For the Good of the Earth and Sun* (1989; poetry), *Awakening the Heart* (1999; poetry), and *Finding the Heart of Nonfiction* (2013)

Christopher Lehman's *Energize Research Reading and Writing* (2012)

Amy Ludwig VanDerwater's *Poems Are Teachers* (2018)

Action 4.2: Mine Your Stack for Craft Teaching Points

Once you've gathered a stack of mentor texts, the next step is to read through them, looking for craft lessons (C. Anderson 2022b; Ray 2002, 2006; Glover and Berry 2012). Katie Wood Ray (2002) writes it's possible to find over one hundred teaching points in a single mentor text. With a stack of four to six mentor texts, imagine the possibilities!

How do you mine a stack of mentor texts to identify craft lessons? This action will walk you through a process that will make this task productive—and enjoyable.

See What Jumps Out at You

Start by reading through your stack of texts to see which craft techniques jump out at you. For example, as you read, you may notice an interesting lead, a fun comparison, or text that's written in bold typeface.

If you're reading through a picture book, use sticky notes to bookmark the craft techniques you find and to jot down what you notice about them. If you're reading a text that isn't a picture book, do likewise, or make marginal notes (Figure 4-3.).

Of course, you'll notice the craft techniques you included in the All, Most, Some Form, so annotate these craft techniques as you read through your stack, too.

By doing this work with colleagues, you'll collectively identify more craft techniques than you will on your own.

What should I jot down about a craft technique? When you find an interesting craft technique, jotting down these kinds of notes will help you analyze it and be prepared to teach students about it:

- Write down the name of the craft technique if you know it. If you don't, give it a name yourself.
- Describe what you notice about how the author crafted their writing. Be as specific as you can.

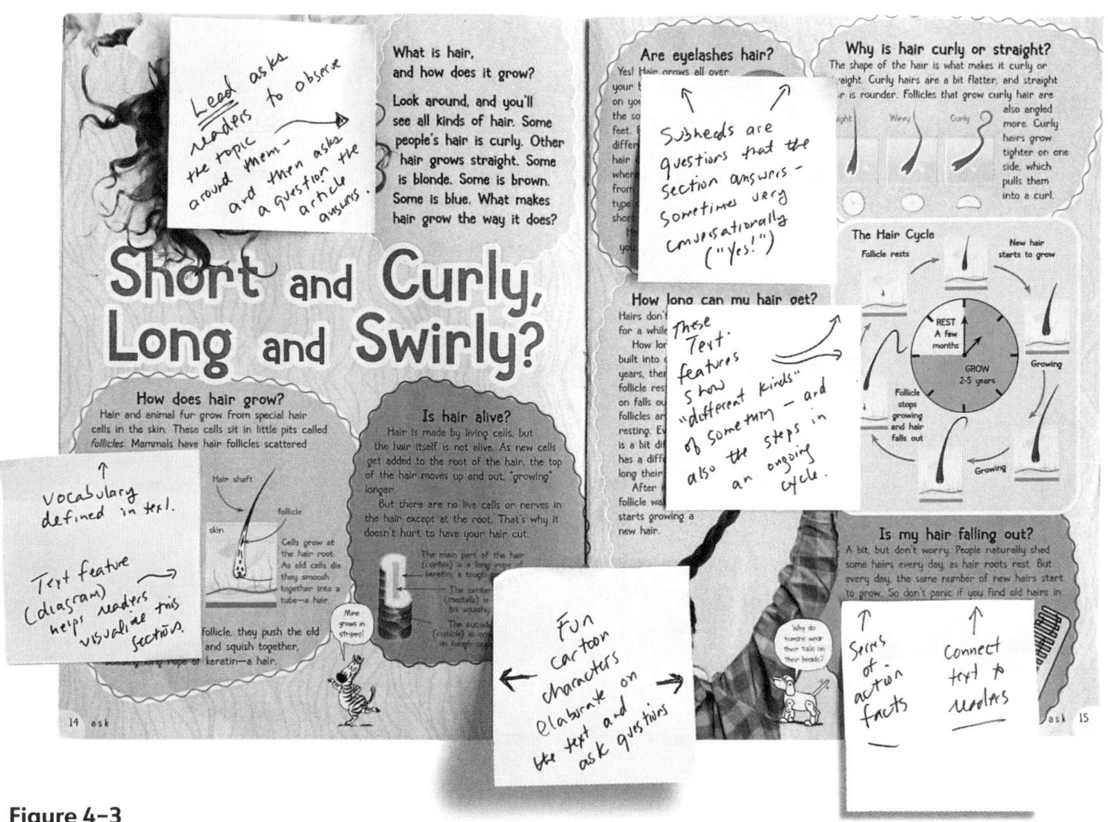

Figure 4-3

Video 4.1 Craft techniques that jump out at you in a primary text

Video 4.2 Craft techniques that jump out at you in an upper-grade text

Video 4.3 Using the qualities of writing to analyze a primary mentor text

- Jot down why you think the writer used the technique.
- Note where else you've seen an author use the technique.

You can watch Carl and Matt do this work in Videos 4.1 and 4.2.

Use the Qualities of Writing as Lenses

To find more craft techniques, reread the texts in your stack, this time using four qualities of writing—focus, structure, detail, and voice—as your guide, one at a time. Reading in this systematic way will help you see craft techniques that you didn't see during your first read-through. To help you with this process, use the Guide to Analyzing a Mentor Text for Craft Techniques and Conventions (**Online Resource 4.2**).

ONLINE RESOURCE

If the idea of doing this kind of analysis is daunting to you—after all, many of us didn't receive instruction in the qualities of writing in our own educations—watch the videos of Carl and Matt analyzing mentor texts systematically in Video 4.3 and Video 4.4. As they discuss each text, they explain each quality of writing and discuss craft techniques they find that are connected to that quality of writing.

Study One Section in Depth

Another strategy for finding craft teaching points is to study one part of a text closely. If you're studying a picture book, do a close reading of one page. If you're reading a text that isn't a picture book, read one section or even one paragraph.

For example, read the excerpt from the feature article "Short and Curly, Long and Swirly?" (*Ask* staff 2022, 14) in Figure 4–4 and see what craft teaching points jump out at you.

Did you notice these craft techniques?

- The subheading is written as a question.
- The author uses topic-specific vocabulary and define words they think readers may not know (*follicles*).
- The author uses descriptive facts ("Mammals have hair follicles scattered all over their bodies.").
- The author uses action facts ("As new cells grow at the base of the hair follicle, they push the old cells up.").
- The author enhances the text with a diagram.

What other craft techniques did you notice in the excerpt?

In Videos 4.5 and 4.6, watch Carl and Matt do this kind of analysis.

How does hair grow?

Hair and animal fur grow from special hair cells in the skin. These cells sit in little pits called *follicles*. Mammals have hair follicles scattered all over their bodies. That's something all mammals share: we're animals with hair.

Hair starts out as a column of skin cells packed with a protein called keratin. Keratin is the same stuff that makes fingernails, claws, and horns.

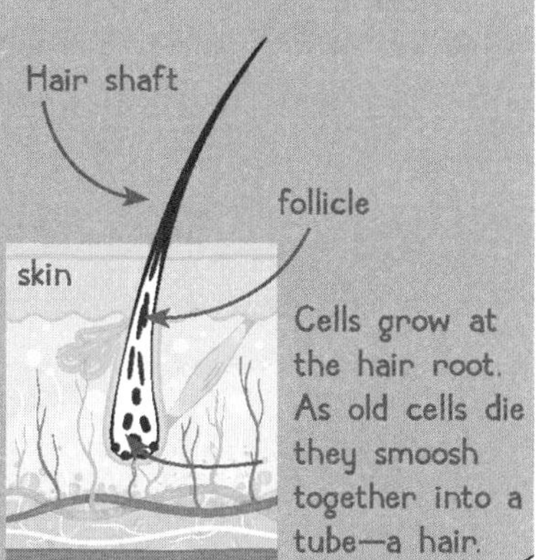

As new cells grow at the base of the hair follicle, they push the old cells up. These cells die and squish together, building long rope of keratin—a hair.

Figure 4–4

Video 4.4 Using the qualities of writing to analyze an upper-grade mentor text

Video 4.5 Analyzing one section of a primary text

Video 4.6 Analyzing one section of an upper-grade text

Further Reading

These resources can further develop your knowledge of author's craft:

- Ruth Culham's *The Writing Thief* (2014)
- Ralph Fletcher's *Pyrotechnics on the Page* (2010), *What a Writer Needs* (2013), and *Focus Lessons* (2019)
- Ralph Fletcher and JoAnn Portalupi's *Craft Lessons* (2007) and *Nonfiction Craft Lessons* (2001a)
- Penny Kittle's *Micro Mentor Texts* (2022)
- Lester L. Laminack's *Cracking Open the Author's Craft* (2007)
- Barry Lane's *After the End* (2016)
- Katie Wood Ray's *Wondrous Words* (1999)
- Mathew Salesses' *Craft in the Real World* (2021)
- Stacey Shubitz's *Craft Moves* (2016)

Action 4.3: Mine Your Stack for Convention Teaching Points

Like a multitool pocketknife, mentor texts have many uses. You can use them to teach crafting techniques *and* use them to teach your students about writing conventions (C. Anderson 2022b; Marchetti and O'Dell 2021).

There are several times in a unit of study when you can teach students about conventions.

- When students are editing their writing toward the end of a unit of study, you'll focus almost all of your instruction on conventions (as well as on strategies writers use to edit their writing).
- Throughout a unit, when students are drafting, you might decide to teach students about conventions (such as spacing) they need to learn to do automatically as they write.
- Also, you might decide to do a unit of study on conventions and devote most of your instruction in the unit to grade-appropriate conventions.
- If you have a gap of a few days or a week between units, you could teach conventions minilessons while students work on independent projects.

Traditionally, teachers have taught students about conventions by giving them rules: *Start every sentence with a capital letter. Separate items in a series with commas. The possessive of a plural noun is formed by adding an apostrophe when the noun ends in* s *and by adding both an apostrophe and an* s *when it ends in a letter other than* s.

Explanations about how conventions work make much more sense when students see examples of how writers use them in mentor texts. Also, when students love the writing of an author they admire, they'll be more interested in trying out the conventions they use.

This action will give you several strategies for finding convention teaching points in mentor texts.

There are several categories of conventions your students may need to learn about:

- conventions that help readers know when words and sentences begin and end
- conventions that help readers navigate complex sentences

- conventions that help writers elaborate within sentences
- conventions that help readers move from section to section in a piece of writing

Before you read through your stack, looking for these different kinds of conventions, it's important to assess which categories are relevant to your students. And it's important to see whether all, most, or some of your students need to learn about them, to help you decide whether to address them in minilessons (if all or most of your students need to learn about them) or small-group lessons or conferences (if some of your students need to learn about them).

Conventions That Help Readers Read Words and Sentences

Writers use conventions to help readers identify where words and sentences begin and end:

- capitalizing the first word of a sentence
- putting spaces between words in a sentence
- using end marks (periods, question marks, exclamation marks)
- putting a space after an end mark

Read through your students' writing to see if you need to address this category of conventions. If you are a teacher of primary-grade students, it's likely this will be a high-priority category. The best way to teach these conventions is in writing conferences or small groups, when you can listen to students compose sentences orally and coach them to use one of these conventions as they write them.

If you're a teacher of upper-grade students, it's better to assess *after* they've edited their writing—when students are able to identify and correct errors with this category of conventions, they don't need you to teach them about them. (Note: When upper-grade students don't put periods at the end of sentences, creating run-ons, it's not usually because they don't know that periods end sentences. Rather, it's usually because their sentences are getting more complex, and they aren't always sure where one sentence ends and another begins.)

If your students need to learn about this category of conventions, then read through your stack of mentor texts, annotating where you find good examples of them.

Conventions That Help Readers Navigate Complex Sentences

As students grow as writers, they write more complex sentences. Where emergent writers often write simple sentences (*I went to the park.*), more experienced writers write more complicated ones (*My dad threw the ball to me, and I threw it back to him.* and *When the Webb telescope blasted off on top of an Ariane 5 rocket, scientists all over the world were excited about the discoveries it would soon make.*).

When writers write more complicated sentences, they use punctuation marks to help readers navigate the parts they contain and help them understand each part's relationship to the other parts. For example:

- In a compound sentence, a comma usually separates the two independent clauses when there is a subject in each clause: *I wanted to play in the baseball game, but I was too tired.*
- A comma usually separates a dependent clause from an independent clause: *When British soldiers marched on Concord, Paul Revere rode from town to town to warn the residents.*
- Quotation marks signal a line of dialogue: *"I'd like to help you get better at fielding ground balls," my dad said.*
- A semicolon separates two related independent clauses without using a coordinating conjunction (*and, or, so, yet*): *I went swimming at the beach; my sister lay on a blanket and read a book.*

To decide which of these kinds of conventions your students need to learn—and thus which ones you need to find good examples of in your mentor texts—read through your students' writing and assess the kinds of sentences your students are composing. Then ask yourself how well they are using punctuation to help readers navigate these sentences. For example, you may see that students put a period instead of a comma at the end of a dependent clause (creating a sentence fragment). While they understand that a mark of punctuation goes after a dependent clause, they need to learn to use a comma, not a period! When you teach them this, you'll want to show them an example of a correctly punctuated sentence from one of your mentor texts.

TIP

When you teach a lesson about a convention, it's powerful to show students the convention in a mentor text *and* demonstrate how you use the convention when you write.

Conventions That Help Writers Elaborate Within Sentences

Another category of conventions writers use are punctuation marks that signal elaboration within sentences. For example:

- We can use a comma (a multipurpose punctuation mark) before a descriptive clause at the end of a sentence: *"It's good to see you," my grandma said, kissing me on the cheek.*
- A comma separates a list of specific items in a series: *I made a sandwich with salami, tomato, and swiss cheese.*
- We can use a dash to elaborate on a detail: *Saturn's rings are very thin—they're only about thirty feet thick.*
- We can use commas to punctuate appositives, phrases that give information about a noun: *Dr. Martin Luther King, the most prominent leader of the twentieth-century movement for civil rights in the United States, was born in Atlanta.*

As you read through your students' writing, look to see if some of them are trying to use punctuation to elaborate in one or more of these ways but still need some support to do so correctly. Also, look to see if you have students who have written sentences that could be elaborated on further—and would benefit from learning how to use punctuation to help them.

Once you've done this assessment, search through your stack of mentor texts for good examples of these conventions.

What about standards for language conventions?

Your state's standards for conventions can also help you decide which conventions to find examples of in your mentor texts. However, you'll have students who aren't yet ready to learn about some of the standards and some who already use the conventions spelled out in the standards; you'll need to take this into account when you decide which of these conventions to teach.

Further Reading

The examples we've given in each of these categories aren't comprehensive. Nor does every convention fit neatly into each of these categories—for example, the convention of capitalizing proper nouns.

To deepen your knowledge about conventions, read Constance Weaver's *Teaching Grammar in Context* (1996), Jeff Anderson and Whitney La Rocca's *Patterns of Wonder: Inviting Emergent Writers to Play with the Conventions of Language, Pre-K-1* (2021) and *Patterns of Power: Inviting Young Writers into the Conventions of Language, Grades 1-5* (2017), Jeff Anderson's *Patterns of Power: Inviting Adolescent Writers into the Conventions of Language, Grades 6-8* (2021), and Dan Feigelson's *Practical Punctuation* (2008).

Conventions That Help Readers Move from Part to Part

Like parents who hold their children's hands when they cross the street, writers use conventions to signal to readers when they're moving from one part to another in a piece of writing:

- In simple picture books, writers start a new page when they write a new part.
- In more complex texts, writers indent when they start a new paragraph.
- Within paragraphs, writers use bullets to signal that they are listing information.

When you read through student writing, look to see if your students are signaling to readers when new parts begin in their writing. Do primary-age students squish all of the parts of their writing together on just one page? Do upper-grade students write one long block of text, instead of separating the parts?

If you discover students need to learn about this category, look through your stack of mentor texts for grade-appropriate examples of these conventions.

Action 4.4: Mine Process Texts for Teaching Points

When Carl was seventeen, he was visiting a friend who had a bootleg album of the Beatles writing and rehearsing songs. Carl was amazed to hear that the first drafts of classic songs such as "Get Back" and "Let It Be" didn't sound very polished, and the Beatles made a lot of revisions as they gradually turned them into finished songs. This helped Carl realize it was OK that the first drafts of the papers he was writing in high school weren't that good, because by revising them, like the Beatles, he could make them a lot better.*

Students will learn about what writers do in each stage of the writing process when they see process texts. These texts—artifacts from each part of the writing process—can be written or made by you, your colleagues, or your students, and they are an important source of teaching points about the writing process (Glover and Berry 2012; Ray 2002, 2006; Roberts and Roberts 2016). See Figure 4-5 for some examples of process texts.

In your units of study, you'll teach process lessons to show students how to navigate stages of the writing process.

In a genre or craft study, *some* of your teaching will focus on process. You'll usually need one or two process texts, your own and a colleague's or a student's, that show students what writing looks like at each stage of the writing process. And just like you teach students craft techniques by showing published mentors, you'll teach them about what writers do at each stage of the writing process by showing them process texts at that stage.

In a unit of study that focuses on one aspect of process, such as keeping a writer's notebook or revising, *most* of your teaching will focus on process. To be

*You can have the same experience that Carl did with the Beatles by watching Peter Jackson's documentary *The Beatles: Get Back* (2021).

Stage of the Writing Process	Types of Process Texts
Rehearsal	Heart maps (brainstorming topics) Lists of topics to write about Sample writers' notebooks Plans for drafts
Drafting and revising	Drafts with revisions visible Mentor texts with craft techniques annotated on them Videos of model peer conferences
Editing	Drafts with edits visible Videos of model editing conferences

Figure 4–5

prepared, you'll need three to four process texts—an example of your writing plus examples from colleagues and students—that show what writing can look like at the stage of the writing process that's the focus of the unit.

While this action focuses primarily on helping you write your own process texts, if you read it with colleagues, you'll be able to share all of the ones you write with each other. This action will also help you think about how to gather student process texts.

Write Your Own Process Texts

Writing your own process texts has many benefits:

- When you share your writing with students, they'll see you as a writer, which will give you more credibility as a writing teacher.
- Going through the writing process yourself will remind you of the challenges your students are facing day to day in writing workshop, giving you more empathy for and understanding of what they're going through.
- Your process texts will be the source of many process lessons you'll teach.

TIP

Writers do some things in the process of writing that don't involve composition, like annotating mentor texts and collaborating with each other. By showing students one of our annotated mentor texts, or a video of two students having a peer conference, we can help them envision how to do similar work.

But what if I don't feel that confident about writing for my students?

If the idea of writing for students makes you anxious, remember that the purpose of doing this *isn't* for you to compose a world-class piece of writing! What's important is showing students the process of writing. The writing you do will be a bridge between the writing students are composing and the published mentor texts you show them. With younger students, where the gap between published writing and student writing is large, your writing should be at a level closer to the writing your students are doing. With older students, when the gap between published and student writing is smaller, your writing should be at a level closer to published texts.

Do I need to write process texts for every unit?

Optimally, it would be great to have process texts for every unit. Given the demands on your time, writing them can sometimes be a challenge! Here are some ways to make this possible:

- In some units, you might start but not finish a process text. For example, even if you're able to write part of a draft, you'll be able to mine that writing for the strategies you used to plan and get started.
- You can reuse process texts in subsequent units this school year or next school year. For example, reuse process texts you write in a genre study of informational nonfiction writing in any craft or process unit in which students have choice of genre later that year or if you teach the same unit the next school year.
- When you do craft or process units of study in which there is choice of genre, you might choose to write process texts in a genre you're going to do a study of later in the year.

DECIDE WHAT KIND OF WRITING TO MAKE

First, decide the kind of writing you're going to create:

- For a genre study, write in the same genre as your students, as there are some aspects of process that are influenced by genre (for example, in realistic fiction, you might revise your draft to show character change).
- In craft units of study, you can write in a genre of your choice, just as your students do. (Note: You might intentionally choose to write in a genre that would open up possibilities for students, such as fantasy, rather than what they might be required to write more often, such as personal narrative.) You'll teach process lessons in these units that will be applicable to writing in any genre.
- Likewise, in process studies, you can write in a genre of your choice. During the study, you'll mostly show your writing from the stage of the writing process that is the focus of the study.

WRITE!

Now it's time to write your process texts.

One of the challenges of writing them is you're going to approximate writing in the way that students in your grade write. This is especially important if you're a primary teacher, since to write like a primary student, you'll usually need to write a book, using the same kind of paper that your students use and writing a bit above their level!

Before you start writing, you may already know there are strategies you want to teach your students, so you'll want to use those strategies yourself as you write, so you can show students what it looks like when an experienced writer uses them. For example, reading Action 3.1 may have inspired you to teach one or more of the strategies the action contains for choosing engaging topics, and you may have already tried them yourself and included them in lessons.

To help you think about which strategies to use as you write, write them down in the "Strategies I Want to Teach Students"

column on the Writing a Process Text Chart (**Online Resource 4.3**; see also Figure 4–6).

As you go through the writing process, make the strategies you use visible:

- Make a list of possible topics.
- Make a plan for your draft.
- Show the revisions you make by writing on sticky notes or writing in the margins.
- Show the editing work you do.

And as you write, notice the small, easy-to-miss process moves that you make. For example, as you draft, do you stop and reread what you wrote before writing more? Do you read your writing aloud or silently as you revise and edit?

4.3 Writing a Process Text Chart

Stage of the Writing Process	Strategies I Want to Teach	Strategies I Discovered I Use
Rehearsal (or prewriting) • choosing a topic • gathering information about a topic • planning	• writing territories • brainstorming subtopics • finding sources & taking notes • plan with flowchart	– I got ideas for subtopics from skimming sub heads in articles I used for research.
Drafting • getting started and restarted • studying a mentor text for craft ideas	• reading plan before writing each day • use mentor text for craft ideas	• I reread what I had written so far before writing each day.
Revising • tools that writers use to revise (carets, arrows, footnotes, sticky notes, etc.) • ways to make different kinds of revisions • using a mentor text to get revision ideas	• using carets • using arrows & footnotes • revising by adding details (phrases + sentences)	– I tried out a different lead (but still kept the first).
Editing • self-editing • peer editing	• editing by reading aloud • editing with a partner	– I used Google to check spelling of words.
Publishing • formatting a final draft • using a mentor text for formatting ideas	• getting formatting ideas from mentor texts	– I got other formatting ideas from the mentor texts, like "pull quotes"

Figure 4–6

STUDY YOUR PROCESS TEXTS

Finally, after you've gone through all the stages of the writing process, reread your work and ask yourself, *Besides the strategies that I planned to use in each stage of the writing process, what other ones did I discover that I use?* As an experienced writer, you probably use process strategies without even realizing it anymore, so rereading your writing with this question in mind will help you become aware of strategies you use unconsciously.

Here are some aspects of your process to pay attention to:

- What strategy did you use to find your topic?
- How did you decide on the genre (if it's a craft study or a process study)?
- Did you consider and try out other genres before settling on the one you chose?

Further Reading

In her book *Living and Teaching the Writing Workshop* (2006), Kristen Painter gives clear and gentle guidance for doing your own writing and connecting it to your teaching.

Video 4.7 Discussion of primary process text

Video 4.8 Discussion of upper-grade process text

- Did you start with one topic and then switch to another? (This is a really common move and is helpful for students to see.)
- Did you start with a topic and then broaden it? Did you narrow it?
- How did you plan your piece?
- If you wrote a picture book, how did you decide where to put your illustrations and words on each page?
- If you created more sections than you needed, how did you narrow them down?
- Did you make any revisions as you drafted?
- What kinds of revisions did you make after you finished your draft?
- What kinds of revision tools did you use—sticky notes, flaps, footnotes, marginal notes?
- As you drafted and revised, what decisions did you make to meet your audience's needs and expectations?
- What kinds of editing strategies did you use?

When you realize you used a strategy at a stage of the writing process, write it down in the corresponding box in the "Strategies I Discovered I Use" column on the Writing a Process Text Chart.

After you've written your process text, and recorded the strategies you used, you've now got a bank of strategies you can teach students and examples of those strategies you can show. See **Online Resources 4.4** (Primary Process Text) and **4.5** (Upper-Grade Process Text) for examples of process texts written by the two of us. In Videos 4.7 and 4.8, we talk about these texts.

Write Process Texts with Colleagues

Try this action with colleagues, as part of the planning process for a unit of study. By sharing your work with each other, you'll have several sets of process texts to show students. Since it's likely you'll each find out someone else used some strategies you didn't, this is also a way to collectively build your repertoire of process strategies.

Gather Student Process Texts

Showing process texts written by your students is also valuable, since they are by definition on the level of other students in your class.

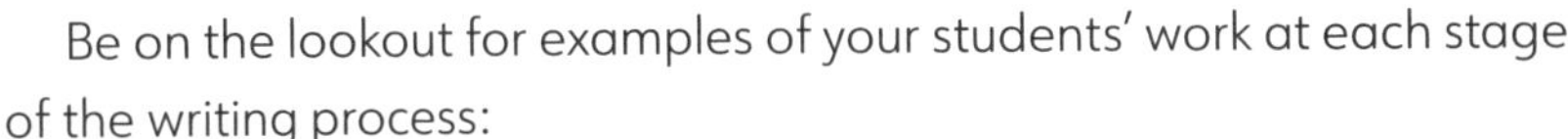

Be on the lookout for examples of your students' work at each stage of the writing process:

- During a unit of study, look for when students use strategies you've taught.
- Look for strategies your students try or even invent that you haven't taught!
- Save student process texts to use in the future. While it's best to use student-written process texts when the authors are in your class—since they'll be able to explain how they used the strategies to their classmates—you can save student-written process texts to use in other school years, too.

Action 4.5

Expand Your Teaching Repertoire by Reading Professional Books is in the Online Resources.

The only person who can truly know what your students need to learn tomorrow is you.

5

Become a Curriculum Decision-Maker

Why Is Being a Curriculum Decision-Maker So Important?

When Matt drives, he checks his GPS app beforehand to see the best route to his destination. But when he's driving near his home in Cincinnati, where he knows the roads well, he sometimes ignores the suggestions the app makes and takes a different route because he knows there will be school buses on one of the roads at that time of day, and he may get stuck behind them, or because a train is likely to block his progress on another. In fact, sometimes Matt doesn't check his GPS at all, preferring to draw upon all he knows about driving in the area to plot his route.

A plan for a unit of study maps the journey you'll take your students on to study an aspect of writing. You may be using someone else's plan for a unit—one that's commercially available or has been created in-house in your school district. Or you may *project*, or design, your own units (Ray 2006; Glover and Berry 2012).

Chapter 5

ACTIONS

The goal of this chapter is to help you become a curriculum decision-maker, someone who can think through an existing unit and improve it as well as someone who can design their own units.

There is one overarching reason to develop your skill as a curriculum decision-maker: *The only person who can truly know what your students need to learn tomorrow is you*. After all, it's *you* who was with your students today, talking with them about their writing in conferences and reading their writing. And it is *you* who can take what you learn about your students each day and make decisions about what just-right step should come next (Hertz and Mraz 2018; Meehan and Sorum 2021; Roberts and Roberts 2016; Tomlinson 2014).

When you're a curriculum decision-maker, there are some other benefits:

- You'll deepen your knowledge base about writing.
- You'll be a teacher who reads and uses curriculum products with a critical lens rather than as a passive consumer.
- You'll have an insider's understanding of your units and how the lessons work together to achieve your goals for students.
- You won't be powerless when commercial curriculum products are compromised by unjust state and national pressures and laws.

Assuming the identity of curriculum designer may be a major shift in the way you see yourself and your role as a teacher. Curriculum written by others is *everywhere* in education; you probably had many teachers who relied on it when you were a student, and today it's used in every subject area in every grade in schools around the world. And if you know and respect the authors of units of study, whether they're colleagues in your district or members of professional development organizations, it may be hard to imagine you can do the same curricular thinking as they do.

However, having worked with many teachers who have successfully become curriculum decision-makers, and who have learned how to do this work thoughtfully and effectively, we know that you can, too.

What Can You Do to Become a Curriculum Decision-Maker?

Take This Action . . .	When You Realize . . .
5.1 Revise Existing Units	• Your students have needs as writers that aren't addressed in the units of study you use. • Your students are interested in aspects of writing that aren't addressed in the units of study you use. • You want to learn how to make thoughtful, evidence-based revisions to the units of study you use.
5.2 Project Units of Study	• There is a unit of study you would like to do with students, but there is no guide for it. • Your school gives you the option of projecting your own units, but you aren't sure how. • You want to create units that are custom-made for the needs of your students. • You enjoy designing units and want some guidance in how to do this effectively.
5.3 Talk to Your Principal About Being a Curriculum Decision-Maker	• You need help in initiating a conversation with your school's leadership about how to support you as a curriculum decision-maker.
5.4 Improve Your Teaching When You Closely Follow a Unit	• Even though you closely follow units of study written by someone else, you would like to teach them in ways that are as responsive as possible to your students' needs.
5.5 Project a Yearlong Writing Curriculum	• You want to create a yearlong road map for your students to meet their needs and interests. • The expectation in your school is you should create your own yearlong writing curriculum, but you need guidance with this. • You and your colleagues are on a grade-level curriculum mapping team and want some guidance about how to do your work well.
5.6 Assess Students' Curricular Experiences in Your School	• You and your colleagues want to think about students' experience as writers across the grades in your school, not just in your individual grades.

Figure 5–1

Action 5.1: Revise Exiting Units

One of the most important questions to think about while you're teaching in a unit is *Why did I teach today's minilesson?* Ideally, if someone asked you this question, you would be able to say something like this: "Yesterday, I did the minilesson suggested in the unit guide on writing narrative leads because that was something I saw my students needed to learn—the leads they were writing were simplistic, and they needed to learn how to craft them to really hook readers! Today, the unit guide suggested I should teach a lesson on writing dialogue. However, as I've been reading student writing, I've noticed most students are already writing dialogue—some of them quite a bit of it. So I decided it would be better to do a minilesson on mixing character actions and thoughts into the dialogue they're writing."

A response like this shows the teacher is familiar with the unit, pays close attention to what students are doing in their writing, and makes evidence-based decisions to teach some of the lessons in the unit as well as revise the unit by swapping out some lessons for others. Taking this stance—that you have the agency to assess the appropriateness of the minilessons in your unit guide and make revisions to them when necessary—is important because different classes have different needs, and authors of units of study, no matter how knowledgeable they are about teaching writing, can't write units that meet the exact needs of these classes (Harris 2019; Roberts and Roberts 2016; Meehan and Sorum 2021).

However, becoming a teacher who assesses and revises units can present several challenges:

- You may lack confidence in your ability to make thoughtful changes, and think, *Who am I to make changes when the authors of the unit are more knowledgeable about the unit than I am?*
- You may be unsure of why and how to make changes.
- You may have supervisors who want you to follow a unit closely (see Action 5.3 for help with talking with them).

This action will help you envision how to make three kinds of thoughtful, evidence-based changes: revising existing lessons, adding (and subtracting) lessons, and changing the sequence of lessons.

Know the Unit

Before you revise a unit, it's important to start by becoming thoroughly familiar with it. Read it from beginning to end! Designers of a unit, whether they're the authors of a commercially available unit, or a school or district team who created the unit, put a lot of thought into creating it, and it's important you understand its flow and logic.

Knowing the unit's lessons will also help you assess students as it unfolds. As your students write, you'll be asking yourself, *What do my students already know about the topics of upcoming lessons?*, which will help you decide if you need to revise them.

Knowing the unit well will also help you make your case if you are asked by colleagues or supervisors to justify revisions. Speaking knowledgeably about an existing unit will help you show that you carefully considered the changes you're making.

Make Revisions to Individual Lessons

What you learn about your students during a unit will sometimes lead you to make changes to one or more of its lessons. That's because you'll realize that while the topic of a minilesson is appropriate, the lesson itself is either too challenging for many students or not challenging enough.

For example, take the aforementioned minilesson on dialogue. Say the lesson in your unit guide suggests you teach your class about how characters sometimes go back and forth several times in a conversation. However, in the days preceding the minilesson, when dialogue was the focus of several conferences, students said, "But I can't remember what people said!" And as you've read through other students' writing, you've noticed very little dialogue. In response, you could decide to revise the focus of the dialogue minilesson to how to generate dialogue in the first place.

Or maybe you've noticed many students already are including back-and-forth dialogue in their writing, making the planned minilesson redundant. In response, you might decide to revise the lesson to focus on adding character thoughts and actions into dialogue.

When you decide to revise an existing minilesson, how can you make it more or less challenging for your students?

- For craft minilessons, look at the unit's mentor texts for examples that will provide an appropriate challenge for students.
- For process lessons, teach a strategy you used while writing your process text instead of the one taught in the unit.
- You could use a professional book such as Jen Serravallo's *The Writing Strategies Book* (2017) to find an alternative minilesson.

Add (and Subtract) Lessons

Sometimes, you'll decide to add or subtract minilessons. If through conferring with students and reading their writing, you learn many of your students have a need not addressed in the unit, you might want to add a lesson. For example, if in several conferences, you taught students how to write topic sentences for the sections of their feature articles, but the unit doesn't address this, you might want to add a lesson on it.

Another reason why you might add a lesson is in response to student noticings during immersion or whole-class text study, when students become interested in craft techniques and conventions that aren't addressed in the unit's minilessons. For example, your students notice several voice techniques in the unit's mentor texts—capitalizing all the letters in a word, making a word bigger than others in the sentence, and so on—yet there are no minilessons on these techniques.

When you decide to add a minilesson to a unit, insert the new minilesson in an appropriate place in the flow of the unit. For example, you should teach a minilesson on writing topic sentences when students are drafting or revising, while you should teach a minilesson on using commas to separate items in a series when students are editing.

Since you don't want units to run over time, if you add minilessons to a unit, you should subtract others from the unit plan. To make thoughtful decisions about which minilessons to remove, ask yourself these questions:

- Given what I've learned about students as the unit has unfolded, which upcoming minilessons are the lowest priority?
- Which upcoming minilessons focus on topics most of my students have demonstrated they can already do?
- Are there any upcoming minilessons that seem too challenging for most students?

TIP

When you decide not to teach minilessons, you aren't throwing them away! These lessons still remain in your teaching repertoire and could be the focus of writing conferences or small-group lessons.

Move a Lesson to a Different Place

Finally, upcoming lessons may seem out of place. As you confer and read student writing, you may decide to move up a minilesson to address a need that is coming up frequently. Or maybe you'll decide a minilesson is better placed later on in the unit, since the lessons that currently follow it better address the needs you're seeing now.

Use the Unit Revision Tool

Use the Revising a Unit Tool (**Online Resource 5.1**; see also Figure 5–2) to help you think through the revision process. It gives you a place to record the lessons you teach and to note the reasons for changes you make.

You can also use this form to help you justify changes you've made to units when you're in conversations with colleagues or supervisors.

5.1 Revising a Unit Tool

Minilesson from the Unit of Study	Revision (Modified the Lesson, Swapped with a Different Topic, Deleted the Lesson, Extended the Lesson Across Additional Days)	Rationale
1.		
2.		
3.		
4.		
5.		
6.		
7.		
8.		
9.		
10.		
11.		
12.		
13.		
14.		
15.		

page 1

28.		
29.		
30.		

page 2

Figure 5–2

Action 5.2: Project Units of Study

To project, or design, units of study (Glover and Berry 2012; Ray 2006), follow these steps:

1. Give the unit a name, defining its focus.
2. Gather a stack of mentor texts, and mine them for craft teaching points.
3. Write a process text, and mine it for process teaching points.
4. Set a primary goal for what you'll be teaching in the unit and then choose secondary ones.
5. Draw upon your knowledge about how units of study are structured and the writing process to arrange the minilessons in a logical order.

In this action, we'll walk you through this process, so you can design your own units of study with confidence. As you project a unit, you'll draw from what you've learned from doing actions in previous chapters. The projecting process will also help you think through and prepare for a unit you have

TIP

Try this action with colleagues. If the process is new for you, you'll give each other support as you learn the steps. Once you're familiar with the process, you'll learn from each other's ideas and thoughts, which will help you craft better units.

taught before, since it will help you deepen your knowledge base about the unit even further.

To work through the steps of the process, you should have a unit in mind you want to project. Use the Projecting a Unit Form (**Online Resource 5.2**; see also Figure 5-3) to write down your ideas each step of the way.

5.2 Projecting a Unit Form

Unit of Study: ______

___ Genre ___ Craft (choice of genre) ___ Process (choice of genre)

Number of weeks: ___ Number of days of immersion: ___ Number of minilessons: ___

Type of Writing Celebration: ______

Primary goal(s)

1.
2.
3.
4.
5.
6.

Secondary goals (qualities of writing, writing habits, aspects of process, community of writers, conventions, editing)

1.
2.
3.
4.
5.
6.

Figure 5-3

Name the Unit

The first step is to name the unit. This will help you decide upon the unit's focus (see Figure 5-4). Once you've selected the unit's name, write it down on the Projecting a Unit Form.

Gather Mentor Texts and Mine Them for Teaching Points

If you're designing a craft or genre study, these actions will help you gather a stack of mentor texts and find craft and convention teaching points in it:

- Action 4.1: Gather Stacks of Published Mentor Texts
- Action 4.2: Mine Your Stack for Craft Teaching Points
- Action 4.3: Mine Your Stack for Convention Teaching Points

As you find teaching points in your stack, record them on the Projecting a Unit Form.

Video 5.1 Naming a primary unit of study

Write Your Own Process Text and Mine It for Teaching Points

Whether you are doing a genre, craft, or process study, write your own process text for the unit.

- Some of the lessons you'll give in a craft study will be about aspects of process—how to find a topic, plan a piece, revise, edit, and so on.
- In a process study, you'll need examples of writing from the stage of the writing process that is the focus of the study. In a unit on keeping a writer's notebook, you'll need sample notebooks; in a revision study, you'll need examples of drafts with revisions.
- A genre study includes both craft and process teaching points, so writing a process text in the genre you're studying will allow you to find important process teaching points.

Video 5.2 Naming an upper-grade unit of study

Name of Craft or Process Study	Focus of the Study
How to Keep a Writer's Notebook	Students learn about strategies for using a notebook to find and develop topics before drafting.
Genre Study	The class studies the craft moves writers make in a genre.
Collaboration Study	Students learn how to use writing partnerships, peer conferences, or both to get feedback on their work in progress.
Illustration Study (primary grades)	The class studies the craft of making illustrations in books.
Text Features Study (upper grades)	Students study text features and how they enhance texts.
Reading Like a Writer	The class practices noticing and studying the different kind of craft moves that writers make.
Voice Study	Students study the techniques writers use to give their writing voice.
Revision Study	The class studies the different ways that writers revise their drafts.
Punctuation Study	Students study the interesting ways that writers use punctuation.

Figure 5–4

Video 5.3
Discussion of primary mentor texts

Video 5.4
Discussion of upper-grade mentor texts

Video 5.5
Discussion of primary process text

Video 5.6
Discussion of upper-grade process text

Action 4.4: Mine Process Texts for Teaching Points will help you think about writing a process text for a unit and how to mine it for process teaching points.

As you find teaching points in process texts, record them on the Projecting a Unit Form.

Set a Primary and Several Secondary Goals

Now that you've mined your mentor and process texts for teaching points, narrow down your list of possible lessons. To help you do this, you first need to set a primary goal for the unit as well as several secondary ones.

Your primary goal is the aspect of writing that is the focus of the unit and comes right out of its name.

Video 5.7
Discussion of goals for primary unit

- In a craft study, your primary goal will be to study the craft of ________________. For example, in a voice study, your primary goal will be to study the craft of getting voice in writing.
- In a genre study, your primary goal will be to study the craft and process of writing ________________. For example, in a memoir study, your primary goal will be to study the craft and process of writing memoir.
- In a process study, your primary goal will be to study the process of ______________. For example, in a writer's notebook or revision study, your primary goal will be to study the process of keeping a writer's notebook or the process of revision.

Video 5.8
Discussion of goals for upper-grade unit

Since students will usually be working through the entire writing process one or more times in a unit, your primary goal won't always be applicable to what students will be doing each day. For example, in a memoir study, your students will spend several days finding topics, planning their drafts, and revising and editing them, and on these days, you'll probably teach them strategies for navigating each of these stages of the writing process. Or in any craft study, you might decide to include one to two days of whole-class text study (Action 6.4). Since the teaching on any of these days is separate from your primary goal, you'll address secondary goals on these days (the process of finding topics for days devoted to topic choice, the process of reading like a writer for whole-class text study days, and so on).

Once you know your primary and secondary goals, write them down on the Projecting a Unit Form.

TIP

Remember, when you're finding teaching points, don't limit them to ones you will definitely teach in minilessons. Also record any teaching points you might teach only to an individual child or small group. You'll narrow them down to minilessons later, but your goal right now is to have more teaching possibilities than available days of minilessons.

Select and Arrange Minilessons in Logical Order

To arrange your minilessons, first, figure out how many days you have to work with:

- Decide the number of weeks you'll devote to the unit (on average, units run for three to six weeks).
- Then look at your calendar to see how many days are actually available during that time. Are there holidays or field trips? Do you not have writing workshop on one day each week?

Next, schedule these important components of units of study:

- Decide how many days of immersion to have at the beginning of the unit (see Actions 6.1–6.3). We recommend two to four days.
- Designate the last day of the unit as a writing celebration.
- If you're doing a genre or craft study, decide how many days you'll devote to whole-class text study (see Action 6.4). We recommend one to two.

Once you've made decisions about these components, see how many days are now available for minilessons. For example, in a five-week unit with twenty-two days available, devoting two days to immersion, one to a writing celebration, and one to whole-class text study would mean you would now have eighteen days when you could teach minilessons.

Now it's time to select minilessons for the days of the unit in which many of your students will be in these stages of the writing process:

- finding topics
- developing topics
- planning drafts
- drafting
- revising
- editing
- publishing and celebrating

Look at your calendar and figure out how many days you think most of your students will be in each stage. In **Online Resources 5.3** (Sample Primary Unit Calendar) and **5.4** (Sample Upper-Grade Unit Calendar) you'll find sample calendars with days plotted.

Finally, plug in teaching points you generated from studying your stack of mentor texts or your process text:

- Start by choosing minilessons connected to your primary goal and to the appropriate stage of the unit. For example, if your primary goal is to study the craft and process of argument writing, look at your list of craft and process lessons and select the ones that seem most relevant, based on

TIP

When you project your own unit, you need to be as open to making revisions to it as the unit unfolds as when you're using a unit designed by someone else! Action 5.1 is just as applicable to revising units you've projected as it is to revising units written by others.

Further Reading

For more information about projecting units, read Matt Glover and Mary Alice Berry's *Projecting Possibilities for Writers* (2012).

Video 5.9
Selecting and arranging primary minilessons

what you've learned about your students so far. As you write these lessons down on the Projecting a Unit Form, place them in the part of the unit where you imagine students will be drafting and revising, and put them in an order that makes logical sense to you.

- Then select minilessons that are connected to your secondary goals, and assign them to the appropriate parts of the unit. For example, for the goal of studying the process of finding topics, choose lessons about topic choice, and assign them to the days when students will be choosing topics. And for the goal of studying the convention of using commas, select teaching points about commas you came up with from studying your stack, and assign them to days at the end of the unit when students will be editing their writing. As you write these lessons down on the Projecting a Unit Form, put them in an order that makes the most sense to you.

Video 5.10
Selecting and arranging upper-grade minilessons

One of the hard things about selecting minilessons is that there will be many great teaching points you aren't going to be able to do as minilessons, given the number of days you have to do a unit! However, you'll still be able to do these lessons in writing conferences and small groups, when you discover you have students who need them.

TIP

Once you've finished projecting a unit, if you have a unit-of-study guide for the unit, read through it to see if the authors of the unit have ideas for lessons you may have overlooked.

Action 5.3: Talk to Your Principal About Being a Curriculum Decision-Maker

When Matt was a principal, at one point he had twenty-two kindergarten classrooms in his school. There were twenty-two kindergarten classes in the morning and twenty-two more in the afternoon.

As the school's instructional leader, Matt didn't expect the teachers in the forty-four classes to give the same minilesson on the same day. In fact, he didn't even expect each teacher would teach the same lesson to their morning and afternoon classes.

Why? Because he wanted his teachers *to respond to the needs of the students in front of them*. He expected teachers to assess their students' needs by observing them closely, talking with them, and reading their writing. Sometimes students in different classes would have a similar need and would receive the same minilesson. Other times students in classes had different needs and didn't receive the same minilesson.

Matt also expected his teachers to project or modify writing units of study. Matt felt his teachers were best equipped to project units, since they spent every day with their students and knew them intimately as writers.

Does the leadership of your school share the same instructional approach as Matt? If so, when you read through the two previous actions in this chapter, you knew you had the agency to make revisions to an already existing unit or project your own units of study.

But what if you don't have this kind of agency, and you're expected to follow lessons in existing units as written? What can you do to create a professional space in which you can be a curriculum decision-maker? The starting point is to talk with your principal and other members of your school's leadership team. This action will help you envision how to have this conversation.

Start by Talking About Beliefs and Actions

In many schools, there's a misalignment between the professed *beliefs* of a school and the *actions* teachers are empowered to take. Sometimes school leadership doesn't realize there is a misalignment. Other times leadership does realize there is one but isn't sure how to change the situation.

As a starting point, initiate a conversation about the school's beliefs. Use some of these conversation starters as entry points to the conversation (to make the discussion about the school or district, not your principal, each of the conversation starters begins with "Does the school . . ."):

- Does the school or district believe students learn and grow at different rates? That students start and end the school year in different places?
- Does the school or district believe that since classes are made up of students with different needs, it follows that different classes will have different collective needs?
- Does the school expect teachers to assess their students and make instructional decisions based on what they learn?
- Does the school believe students learn by trying things out, evaluating how it goes, and making changes for next time? If so, does the school believe teachers learn similarly?
- Does the school or district think all schools are exactly the same, with the same needs? If not, does that also apply to classrooms in a school?

Ask questions like these from a place of honest curiosity. Doing so can lead to meaningful conversations. In Matt's experience, he was thrilled when a teacher wanted to talk about foundational educational beliefs.

The more challenging part of this conversation comes when you shift toward asking questions about actions. Assuming your principal's responses to questions about beliefs were in the affirmative, *you* know there is misalignment about beliefs and the actions you're empowered to take in your classroom. Asking about actions begins a conversation about this misalignment and opens up a space to talk about how to address this misalignment. Use some of these conversation starters to initiate a discussion about actions:

- Since the school believes different classes need different things, why should all teachers teach the same sequence of minilessons in a unit?
- Since the school believes teachers should make decisions informed by what they learn about students, does that apply only to writing conferences and small-group lessons? Shouldn't it also apply to minilessons?
- Since we agree that different schools need different things, why doesn't that apply to different classrooms?
- Since the school believes it's important teachers know their students as writers, why shouldn't they make important instructional decisions about units of study?

While there is no guarantee a conversation about beliefs and actions will result in the change you want, if you don't initiate this conversation, there will be no change. Moreover, this conversation may be one you'll need to return to over time with your principal and the leadership team, and it may require some patience on your part to see it through.

Explain Specific Decisions to Your Principal

To help your principal feel comfortable with you revising or projecting units, it helps to give specific examples. For example, pick a lesson from a unit you want to change, or a lesson in a previous unit that you did change or wanted to change. Then you could do one or more of the following:

- Explain the rationale for the change you want to make or did make.
- Point to data that supports the change you want to make. For example, you might say, "From looking at their writing so far in the unit, I found over half of my students can already do what the next minilesson teaches, so I don't think I should teach it."
- Show your principal writing samples that are evidence for the type of change you want to make.
- Invite your principal into your classroom so they can watch the lesson you changed or swapped in, so you can have a conversation about how it went.
- Explain you don't expect the principal to trust you blindly because "teachers always know best." Explain you want to share the thinking behind your decisions and would like their support to help you better meet your students' needs.
- Suggest a series of periodic conversations to talk about how your unit decisions are going.

To get your principal's support with projecting units, you could discuss a plan for a unit that you (or you and your colleagues) projected and explain the thinking you did as you designed it. Stress how you kept standards and the school's curricular goals in mind as you projected the unit.

By discussing concrete examples of curricular decision-making, you'll demonstrate how you think through a unit, make data-driven decisions, and evaluate how lessons go. Hopefully, your principal will trust you're making thoughtful, effective decisions.

TIP

When you have several like-minded colleagues, having these conversations as a group with your principal will show there's a deeper level of interest in and commitment to your becoming curriculum decision-makers than if you initiate separate conversations.

In fact, your principal will probably be thrilled you're thinking deeply about your students and about how to teach units in a way that's best designed to meet their needs.

Action 5.4: Improve Your Teaching When You Closely Follow a Unit

While we strongly advocate that you become a curriculum decision-maker, we realize you may be in a situation where either you are required to follow a unit plan exactly as it's written or, in some cases, you'll choose to do so.

How can you be the best writing teacher possible when you're closely following a unit written by someone else? There are several ways.

Check That the Requirement to Follow a Unit Isn't a Myth

Matt remembers a teacher who said to him, "We have to follow this unit lesson by lesson."

The principal, who was in the room, stood up and said, "That's not what I meant by following the unit." What the principal actually wanted was for teachers to meet the unit's goals and follow the *general* sequence of its lessons—he assumed they would make changes when lessons didn't meet students' needs. In that school, it was a misunderstanding that all teachers in a grade had to teach the same lessons in the same sequence at the same time.

If you believe you're expected to follow a unit's sequence of lessons faithfully, confirm this with your literacy coach or principal.

Read the Unit's Mentor Texts Before You Start

The best way to familiarize yourself with a genre or craft unit is to read the mentor texts for the unit *before you start reading through the lessons*. Since the goal of the unit is for students to learn to write texts in a genre, or to incorporate in their writing a quality of writing exemplified by the mentor texts, reading them will help you envision what your students will be learning. Then, as you read through the lessons, they will make more sense because you'll understand what the ultimate goal is and how each one is designed to take students one step toward that goal.

If you're using a commercial unit of study, mentor texts may be bundled with the unit. If not, units usually include a list of suggested mentor texts. Likewise, if you're following a unit written by teachers in your school or district, it'll probably contain a suggested list of possible mentor texts.

If published mentor texts are provided or suggested, see Action 4.1 for advice on evaluating the texts. After doing this action, you may decide to supplement or replace the provided or suggested texts with different ones, another way of enhancing a unit that you're following closely.

Write a Process Text

Another way to prepare yourself for teaching well in the unit is to do the kind of writing students will be doing in it. In a genre study, write in the genre you'll be studying with your class. In units that are craft and process studies in which students have choice of genre—such as an illustration or revision study—write in a genre of your choice, just as your students will be able to do.

You can do this writing in two ways. You could do all the writing before you start the unit, or you could do it as the unit unfolds, keeping ahead of your students by a lesson or two.

As you write, try out each lesson you'll be giving during the unit. Doing so will give you a feel for what students will experience. And when a minilesson asks you to show your writing, you'll have an example on hand.

Add Immersion to the Beginning of the Unit

Spend several days at the beginning of a unit *immersing* students in the mentor texts that they'll be studying and learning from in the unit (see Actions 6.1 and 6.2). That is, for several days, have students read and discuss the unit's mentor texts. Immersion makes teaching and learning throughout the unit more effective by giving students a clear vision for what they will be writing.

If a unit doesn't include immersion days, then add several to the beginning of the unit. Doing this won't alter the sequence of lessons in the unit.

There is no advantage to *not* showing students examples of what they'll be doing in the unit. Helping students have a vision for what they'll be writing will be invaluable right from the start.

Prepare to Differentiate in Your Conferences and Small-Group Lessons

To teach a unit well, you need more teaching points in your repertoire than the number of minilessons it contains. While some writing conferences and small-group lessons will focus on the same teaching points you'll give in your minilessons, others will focus on different aspects of craft, process, and conventions.

That's because your students will sometimes have needs that are different from those you address in your minilessons, and your job in writing conferences and small-group lessons is to differentiate your instruction to meet those needs.

How do you develop your repertoire of teaching points so that you can be prepared to differentiate?

First, to find more craft lessons, reread the unit's mentor texts, and this time, look for craft teaching points that aren't addressed in the unit's minilessons. In fact, you may have already noticed some interesting craft moves when you read the mentor texts to familiarize yourself with the unit! (If you need help finding more craft teaching points, see Action 4.2.)

Second, to develop your repertoire of process teaching points, reread the process text you wrote before starting the unit or are writing as the unit progresses. As you read, name the strategies you used at each stage of the writing process. You'll probably find you used some that weren't addressed in the unit's minilessons—and that you can teach some of your students when you meet with them in conferences and small groups. (To help you find process teaching points in your writing, see Action 4.4.)

When Necessary, Modify a Lesson

What if you think one of the unit's lessons isn't appropriate for your students? For example, perhaps there's a lesson on an aspect of writing your students already know how to do (such as a lesson on how to use headings in an informational book when most of your students are already using them in their writing). Or perhaps a minilesson is too challenging. In either case, modify the lesson so that it becomes appropriate.

If your students already know how to do the lesson, you have several options:

- ***Teach a more advanced version of it.*** For example, show your students how to write engaging, catchy subheadings.
- ***Make the lesson inquiry-based.*** For example, show students the subheadings in the mentor texts, but ask them what they notice about them. By doing this, you'll give students practice with reading like a writer.
- ***Shift the focus of the lesson to the effect on the reader.*** For example, after you show students several subheadings in the mentor texts, ask, "Why does the author do this? What does it do for us as readers?" Too often students see craft techniques as something to try out without thinking about the impact on the reader. Considering audience is another skill that will benefit students beyond the content of a lesson.

- ***Focus on the process of using a craft technique.*** For example, explain that writers often brainstorm several subheadings before settling on one, and demonstrate this yourself with your own writing. When you do this, students learn that writing involves experimentation, and writers don't get it right the first time they try something.

If you feel that a lesson is too challenging, *show students a simpler example* than the one highlighted in the minilesson. For example, show your students one-word headings in a mentor text, instead of ones that are short, catchy phrases.

Action 5.5: Project a Yearlong Writing Curriculum

When you project a yearlong writing curriculum, you may feel like a kid in a candy store, wide-eyed as you consider the many wonderful units you could include. Over the past several decades, educators have written about units that focus on many aspects of writing (see Action 4.5). And of course, since you can project your own units, you are not limited to published units.

SOME POSSIBLE UNITS OF STUDY	
Genre studies	personal narrative * memoir * realistic short fiction * fantasy short fiction * historical fiction * mystery * poetry * all-about nonfiction books * feature articles * literary nonfiction * opinion * reviews * argument * essays * literary essays * TED talks * public service announcements
Craft studies	illustration study * text features study * things writers do to make writing interesting * using structure as a crafting tool * detail study * punctuation as a crafting tool * author study
Process studies	launching writing workshop * keeping a writer's notebook * how to read like a writer * finding and developing independent writing projects * how to have a good writing partnership * how to have good peer conferences * planning study * revision study * editing study * how to make good paragraphing decisions

Figure 5–5

To project a quality writing curriculum for the school year, you'll need to answer two questions:

1. Which writing units will you include in the curriculum?
2. What order will you put these units in?

Decide Which Units You Could Include

There are several criteria for identifying possible units, such as the standards for your grade level and connections you can make with other content your students will be studying.

STANDARDS

Start by looking at your local or state writing standards to see which ones you can address by choosing certain units. For example, standards usually require students to learn about writing texts in certain categories, such as informational, narrative, and opinion or argument, so we suggest you include genre studies that fit in these categories.

Since most standards don't specify which genre within a text type students must study, that decision is up to you or your school. For example, if the standards state that students should learn about narrative writing, you can satisfy that requirement by choosing a unit that focuses on personal narrative, realistic fiction, fantasy, historical fiction, or biography.

Many state and local standards focus on other aspects of writing besides genre. For example, the standards may say students will learn to plan and revise their writing. In many cases, you can satisfy standards like these *within* units. Or you could decide to include units on these standards, such as a unit of study on revision.

TIP

We suggest that you plan your yearlong curriculum *before* the school year starts for several reasons:

- You'll be able to give students (and their parents) a preview of where you're going to take them as writers during the school year.
- When you know your units ahead of time, you'll have time to gather stacks of mentor texts (especially harder-to-assemble stacks).
- You'll have more time for projecting units.
- If you're on a curriculum team, you'll be able to publish the curriculum for your colleagues.

GENRES THAT AREN'T MANDATED BY STANDARDS

There are high-engagement genres that don't neatly fit into the text categories that are usually required by the standards. Poetry is one of these and is a genre we suggest be a strong contender when projecting writing curricula in all grades!

And there are other genres that teachers should consider in upper grades, such as TED talks and digital genres such as blogs.

OTHER ASPECTS OF WRITING

While we value genre studies, we suggest you also include several units that focus on other aspects of craft (such as illustration study or how to use punctuation to create voice) or on aspects of process (such as keeping a writer's notebook, reading like a writer, or revising).

Including these kinds of craft and process studies in your curriculum will give you more time for studying these aspects than you can in a genre study. And since students can choose which genres to write in in these units, they're often highly engaged during them.

Further Reading

Two resources on parallel reading-writing units are M. Colleen Cruz's Writers Read Better series (2018, 2019) and Ellin Keene's *The Literacy Studio* (2022).

CONNECTIONS BETWEEN READING AND WRITING UNITS

Sometimes, a reading unit will suggest a parallel writing unit. For example, you might choose to include a study of realistic fiction in your writing curriculum because you have a reading unit on character.

One of the advantages of parallel curriculum is you can make connections between what students are learning about in reading units and what they're learning in writing. And sometimes you'll be able to use texts you're using in reading as mentor texts in a writing unit.

This kind of reading-writing unit matching will sometimes make a lot of sense, but not always—especially if it leads to forced, superficial curriculum choices.

CONNECTIONS BETWEEN SCIENCE, SOCIAL STUDIES, OR UNITS OF INQUIRY AND WRITING

Likewise, you can sometimes have parallel content area and writing units. For example, if students are going to study the solar system in science, you might simultaneously have them study informational books in writing workshop and write about features of the solar system.

When you decide to parallel a writing unit with a content area unit, you'll narrow the range of what students can write about. This has its advantages—in the example of the solar system writing, the students would be able to draw from all they've learned in the science unit. However, because limiting choice may decrease engagement for some students, we recommend that, whenever possible, students write more than

TIP

As you work through this action, we suggest you have a stack of blank index cards. As you identify possible units, write the name of each one on a card. Then, once you decide which ones will actually be in the curriculum, you can experiment with their order by moving the cards around on your desk or tabletop until you find a sequence that makes the most sense.

one piece in such a unit, writing the first several pieces on topics of their choosing before moving to the content area topic. If this isn't possible, we recommend you follow the unit with one in which students have more choice.

THE DEMANDS OF HIGH-STAKES TESTING

If your students will take a standardized test during the school year that requires them to write in a certain genre, you'll probably want to do a unit that focuses on that kind of writing. You can do this in a genre study or as part of a test-prep unit.

Decide How Many Units You Want to Project

You may want to project every unit in your curriculum, which means that you can do any unit of study you want to do.

However, you might decide you want to project some units but rely on district or commercial unit-of-study guides to help you with others. If you prefer to go this way, then some of your unit choices will come from the menu of units that are available.

Put Your Curriculum Together

Now it's time to decide which units you'll do and the order you'll do them in.

DECIDE ON THE NUMBER OF UNITS

Given that units of study take between three and six weeks, you'll have time during the school year for six to eight units. If your list of potential units includes this number of units already, you're in good shape.

If you have more units on the list than you have time to do them in, you'll have to make some difficult choices. Start by sorting your list of possible units into ones you must do (for example, the ones you've included to meet standards) and ones that are optional. To help you decide about the optional units, consider which ones will best meet your students' anticipated needs as writers as well as ones that will create the most student engagement.

DECIDE ON THE ORDER OF YOUR UNITS

While there are no hard-and-fast rules about how to order units, consider these criteria as you think about their sequence:

- Start the year with a unit you think will invite high student engagement. You could do the same after a long break.
- Save more challenging units until later on in the school year.

- Spread out units that will invite the highest student engagement across the year. Strategically place them after units you think will be less engaging.
- If you have writing units that parallel reading or content area units, position them in the same place on the calendar.
- Try *not* to place two challenging units or two low-engagement units next to each other.
- Units that will help students with the writing they'll be doing on standardized tests should go before these tests.

WRITE IT DOWN

Once you've selected which units to include, and their order, then the last step is to make a formal curriculum plan. Your school or district may have a template that they want you to use, or you can fill out the Curriculum Planning Form (**Online Resource 5.5**; see also Figure 5–6).

5.5 Curriculum Planning Form

Grade: 1

Unit of Study	Type of Unit (Genre, Craft, Process)	Unit Length
Launching WW/Reading Like a Writer	Process/Process	5 weeks
Illustration Study	Craft	5 weeks
Poetry	Genre	4 weeks
How To Books	Genre	5 weeks
How To Use Punctuation in Interesting ways	Craft	4 weeks

page 1

Figure 5–6

Action 5.6: Assess Students' Curricular Experiences in Your School

No matter how well constructed your curriculum is, reaching the ultimate goal—that by the time students graduate from your school, they'll have grown significantly as writers and have met the writing standards of their exit grade—depends on their curricular experience not just in your class but in all their classes during their time in the school.

The last action is one you do with colleagues to assess students' curricular experiences across *all* the grades in your school. This might be a process you initiate, inviting colleagues and the leadership team to join you. Or this process may already be ongoing in your school, and this action can help guide it.

Use the Unit Data Form

First, use the Unit Data Form (**Online Resource 5.6**; see also Figure 5-7) to gather information about all of the units in each grade. Once you have this data collected, you can study the data through various lenses to help you size up students' overall writing experience.

On the Unit Data Form, you'll record every unit in each grade's writing curriculum. In addition to recording the name of each unit, generate other important data by writing in the appropriate symbol to represent each unit's type:

G = genre study

C = craft study

P = process study

R = writing study that parallels a reading unit

I = writing study that parallels a content area unit

5.6 Unit Data Form

Grade K	Grade 1	Grade 2	Grade 3	Grade 4	Grade 5

Grade K	Grade 1	Grade 2	Grade 3	Grade 4	Grade 5
# of Units	# of Units	# of Units	# of Units	# of Units	# of Units
Craft	Craft	Craft	Craft	Craft	Craft
Process	Process	Process	Process	Process	Process
Genre	Genre	Genre	Genre	Genre	Genre

Narrative	Narrative	Narrative	Narrative	Narrative	Narrative
Info	Info	Info	Info	Info	Info
Opinion	Opinion	Opinion	Opinion	Opinion	Opinion
Poetry	Poetry	Poetry	Poetry	Poetry	Poetry

School Data

Total Units:

Unique Units:

Most Repeated Units:

Genre Studies:

Process Studies:

Craft Studies:

Narrative:

Informational (Info):

Opinion:

Poetry:

Figure 5-7

Analyze the Data You've Collected

Study the data you've collected by analyzing it through several lenses.

HOW MANY UNITS ARE THERE IN EACH GRADE?

The number of units in each grade's curriculum directly impacts student learning. We recommend teaching six to eight units each year that last between three and six weeks. If there are fewer units, students won't have the opportunity to study many aspects of writing. If there are too many units, students won't be able to do in-depth studies of the aspects of writing that are the focus of the units.

KEY QUESTIONS

- How many units are there in each grade?
- Are there in general too few or too many units across the grades in the school?
- Are there particular grades where there are too few or too many units?
- Are there the exact same number of units in every grade? This may indicate there is an artificial constraint impacting unit length, rather than the needs of particular units.

WHAT IS THE BALANCE OF GENRE, CRAFT, AND PROCESS STUDIES?

See if one type of unit is over- or underrepresented across the grades. For example, if most units are genre studies, students won't get many opportunities to study other aspects of writing.

KEY QUESTIONS

- What is the aggregate number of genre studies? Craft studies? Process studies?
- Are any of these types of units overrepresented? Underrepresented?

HOW MANY UNITS PROVIDE CHOICE?

Since choice of genre and topic are closely linked to student engagement, tally the number of units in which students get to make these important decisions.

When students rarely get to choose genres, it's often because curricula overemphasize genre studies. And when students rarely get to choose their own topics, it's often because too many units are linked to content area classes.

As part of your analysis, look to see where units that give kids choice of genre and topic are placed in curricula. If they're put toward the end of the school year, as a reward after a series of less-engaging units, there's a danger these units won't actually get done if preceding units go on for longer than planned.

KEY QUESTIONS

- How many units give students choice of genre? Topic?
- Where are units that give students choice of genre and topic placed in each grade's curriculum?

WHAT GENRES ARE STUDIED?

While state, district, and school standards usually say that students should learn how to write in three text types—narrative, informational, and opinion or argument—these categories don't include every genre that you can study with students. For example, one of these genres is poetry, which can sometimes fit into any of these categories and sometimes not.

Look to see if the focus on text types defined by the standards is inadvertently excluding some high-engagement

KEY QUESTIONS

- How many studies across the grades fit into the text types that the standards require students to learn about?
- How many genre studies are outside of the standard text types?

KEY QUESTIONS

- How many units are repeated across the grades?
- How many times are units repeated?
- When units are repeated, how are they projected to be more challenging for students?

KEY QUESTIONS

- How many writing units are connected to reading units?
- How many writing units are connected to content area classes?
- Why are the writing units connected to these other classes?

genres like poetry and is therefore hindering students from exploring these genres.

HOW OFTEN ARE UNITS REPEATED?

Note how many times various units are repeated across grades.

You *should* see that units are sometimes repeated. When students encounter a unit for a second or even third time, they'll have the opportunity to get better at the aspect of writing being studied. And teachers can project units to be more challenging as students move to higher grades (in line with standards that get progressively more challenging). For example, in a study of feature articles in sixth grade, students might write about topics they already know about, while in the same unit in seventh grade, they might write about topics they'll need to research, giving them the opportunity to develop research skills.

However, when units are repeated too many times, students lose the opportunity to study other aspects of writing. For example, consider a school where students study personal narrative in every grade! These students are missing out on the opportunity to study other narrative genres, like realistic or fantasy fiction, that would still teach them about how to write narratives but would at the same time offer new challenges and probably be more engaging.

HOW OFTEN ARE UNITS TIED TO READING OR CONTENT AREA CLASSES?

While it's a good idea to tie some units to reading or to what students are studying in content area classes, this should be done thoughtfully, not reflexively. If too many units are connected in these ways, there are many units that will probably not be considered because they don't logically connect to what students are studying in reading or a content area class. For example, it would make no sense to connect a unit of study on revision to a study of the water cycle that students are doing in science if students don't have a piece of writing on the water cycle to revise!

Make Sense of What You Learn

The point of analyzing the data you gather on the Unit Data Form is to help you identify trends in your school's curriculum across the grades. For example, you may identify trends that go across your school that should be addressed, such as repeating some units too many times. Or you may identify issues specific to one or several grades that should be addressed, such as an overreliance on genre studies.

AREAS FOR FURTHER SCHOOLWIDE STUDY

As you continue to try to improve the curricular experience of students across your school, these are other areas you can analyze and discuss:

- What mentor texts are teachers using across the grades? Are there some that students see over and over again in multiple grades? Or do students rarely encounter mentor texts again, missing the opportunity to learn even more from them?
- Are newly published mentor texts added and some older, perhaps less relevant ones retired?
- What strategies are students learning in each grade to help them navigate each stage of the writing process? Do they learn about the same ones year after year and not learn others that could expand their repertoire? Or do they learn a whole new set of strategies every year and rarely get the chance to get better at them by using them again in subsequent years?
- What craft techniques are taught across the grades? Are the same ones repeated year after year, or do students learn new ones?
- What language conventions do students learn across the grades? Are the conventions matched to the level of sentence complexity in student writing (for example, in K–1, beginning a sentence with a capital letter and ending with a period, question mark, or exclamation mark; in upper grades, using internal punctuation to separate the parts of the complex sentences they're writing)?

By teaching your students how to learn from other writers, you'll equip them to keep learning about writing even when they're no longer your students.

6

Help Students Learn from Mentor Authors

Why Is Helping Students Learn from Writers So Important?

How will students learn what they need to know to write well? The answer is you'll introduce them to a wide variety of writers who *collectively* will teach them a great deal about writing. In fact, by teaching your students how to learn from other writers, you'll equip them to keep learning about writing even when they're no longer your students (C. Anderson 2022b; Marchetti and O'Dell 2015, 2021; Ray 1999, 2002, 2006; Rief 2018).

The writers you'll introduce to your students will include

- *published authors*, from whom students will learn about craft and conventions,
- *you*, from whom students will learn about how to navigate the stages of the writing process, and
- *their classmates*, from whom they'll learn how people their age approximate the work of experienced writers so they feel comfortable diving in themselves.

This chapter will help you envision how to introduce students to these writers and will show you a variety of ways to help students learn from them.

How Can You Help Students Learn from Writers?

Action	When to Take It
6.1 Plan for Immersion	• If your students need a vision for what they're writing in units. • If you usually begin units by teaching students how to find topics so they can quickly start writing drafts. • If your students often keep writing in the same genre(s) they wrote in during the previous unit, for a week or more into a new unit. • If your students aren't excited when you start units.
6.2 Do Whole-Class Immersion	• If you want to create a sense that your class is on a shared journey in a unit of studying. • If you want students to learn from each other about how to respond to mentor texts as readers and writers.
6.3 Do Small-Group Immersion	• If you want students to learn how to immerse themselves in mentor texts. • If you want to confer with students about immersion.
6.4 Teach Students to Read Like Writers in Whole-Class Text Study	• If the primary source of information about the craft of writing and conventions in your classroom is you. • If you want students to know how to learn about craft and conventions from other authors.
6.5 Prepare to Use Mentor Texts in Craft and Convention Lessons	• If you don't always have mentor texts at your fingertips, especially when you're in writing conferences. • If you're not always sure about which text you should use to teach students.
6.6 Teach with Process Texts	• If most of the strategies you teach about how to navigate the writing process come from outside sources—professional books, unit guides, and so on. • If you want to know how to use your own writing to teach students about the writing process.

Action	When to Take It
6.7 Use Students as Writing Mentors	• If some students feel how mentor authors write is too much of a stretch for them. • If your students will benefit from seeing what writers at their age or level can do. • If you would like to build up your low-confidence writers.
6.8 Help Students See Mentor Authors as Real People (in Online Resources)	• If your students see the authors of mentor texts as being different kinds of people than them. • If your students know little or nothing about the mentor authors you study. • If you want students take on identities as writers just like the authors of mentor texts.

Figure 6–1

Action 6.1: Plan for Immersion

One way to become better at something is to study what more skilled people do. For example, throughout his time as a Little League baseball player, Carl's son Haskell watched Major League Baseball games on television to see how great baseball players played the game. As part of running track, Matt's daughter Molly watched skilled runners compete in races to see what it meant to run at an elite level. And you have probably watched more skilled teachers to help you imagine how you could be more like them.

To create this experience for your students, at the beginning of a unit of study, you should devote several workshop periods to *immersion*. The idea that learners need to be immersed in the concept or skill they are learning comes from Brian Cambourne's "principles of learning" (1988). During immersion, students learn from experienced writers by reading and discussing writing by these authors that's like what they'll be composing in the unit:

- During a craft or genre study, you'll read and discuss texts from your stack of published mentor texts for the unit (Ray 2006; Glover and Berry 2012).
- During a process study, you'll read and discuss samples of your writing and students' writing from the stage of the writing process that's the focus of the study (Ray 2006; Glover 2019).

See Figure 6–2 for more tips on what mentor texts to use.

Type of Study	Kinds of Texts You'll Immerse Your Students In
Genre study	Published texts that are good examples of the genre being studied
Any craft study (structure, detail, voice, punctuation as a crafting tool, illustration study, etc.)	Published texts in various genres that contain excellent examples of the kind of craft the unit focuses on
Keeping a writer's notebook	Sample writers' notebooks (yours and students')
Revision study	Drafts with revisions visible (yours and students')
Editing study	Drafts with edits visible (yours and students')
Collaboration study	Transcripts or videos of writing partnerships or peer conference conversations you've made of your students or of you and colleagues; videos of authors talking about collaboration
Study of how to confer with a teacher	Transcripts or videos of conferences

Figure 6–2

Why should we devote time to immersion?

- Students will come to know the aspect of writing or stage of the writing process they'll be studying just well enough to give it a shot themselves. What advantage would there be to keeping what students will be doing a mystery?
- When students read the relevant and interesting texts you've chosen, they'll get excited about the writing they'll be doing in the unit and will be more engaged.
- During immersion, students respond to texts first as readers. By naming the kinds of responses they're having, you'll help students understand they can elicit similar responses from their own readers.

UNIT OF STUDY CALENDAR

	Monday	Tuesday	Wednesday	Thursday	Friday
Week 1	Immersion				
Week 2					
Week 3					
Week 4					

Figure 6–3 Immersion Happens at the Beginning of a Unit of Study

- As students start reading texts during immersion, they begin to read like writers and notice the writer's craft or process moves or the conventions they use. Because you'll read some texts aloud, some of this noticing will happen aurally. And when they see the texts, they'll notice many things about how authors write texts.
- Immersion gives you your first opportunity to engage your students in conversations about how the mentor texts are crafted (in a craft study) or about the moves that writers make in the writing process (in a process study). Because of these conversations, students will have ideas about the things they can try out as writers, right from the start of the unit.
- Immersion across units supports students' incremental growth in noticing what writers do.

Decide How Many Days to Devote to Immersion

There are several rules of thumb for deciding how many immersion days to include in a unit:

1. In a genre or craft study, include two to four days, and in a process study, one to two.
2. When the kind of writing students will be doing is new for them, devote more days to it. For example, in kindergarten, *everything* students will be learning about will be new, so students need more days of immersion in

TIP

When you launch writing workshop at the beginning of the year, your goal is to get students writing immediately. In this case, we recommend you *not* do any immersion days in the launching writing workshop unit, but instead begin with teaching your students about finding ideas for writing so they can get started right away.

every unit. And in upper grades, when students study genres of writing or stages of the writing process that are new, such as argument or historical fiction or keeping a writer's notebook, they'll likewise need more immersion days.

Conversely, when a unit of study involves students doing a kind of writing they have done in previous school years, schedule fewer immersion days.

3. When the kind of writing students will be doing is challenging, plan for more immersion.
    - For example, if you're doing a genre study of literary nonfiction in a primary grade, students will need more days of immersion.
    - If you're doing a study in the upper grades of how to keep a writer's notebook or about revision, students will benefit from studying notebooks or revised drafts for several days before doing this work themselves.

Some factors may limit the number of immersion days you can include in a unit. For example, if a unit is three weeks long, you'll include one, maybe two periods of immersion.

It's wise to err on the side of more immersion. Students will *always* benefit as writers from reading and studying texts.

Mark the Immersion Days for the Unit on Your Calendar

Now that you've decided how many days of immersion you'll have in the unit, make it official and mark them on your calendar.

What if my unit of study guide doesn't include any immersion days?
Just because immersion isn't included in your guide doesn't mean you can't do any. Fortunately, it's easy to add several immersion days at the beginning of a unit!

- If you're projecting a unit, use the Projecting a Unit Form (see Action 5.2) to write down your immersion plans.
- If you are revising a district or commercial unit of study that doesn't include immersion, add immersion days on the Revising a Unit Tool (see Action 5.1).
- If you are closely following an existing unit, include several immersion days when you enter the unit's lessons in your plan book.

Action 6.2: Do Whole-Class Immersion

Video 6.1 Whole-class immersion in primary

Video 6.2 Whole-class immersion in upper grades

Immersion days are different from the regular writing workshop. On these days, there is no minilesson, independent writing time, or share session. Instead, the whole period is devoted to reading and responding to mentor or process texts.

One immersion method is *whole-class immersion* (Ray 2006). When you do this, you'll read texts aloud to your class and then give students the opportunity to respond first as readers and then as writers. This action will take you through the steps of whole-class immersion.

Prepare for Immersion

Since whole-class immersion involves reading mentor craft or process texts aloud, take some time beforehand to familiarize yourself with them. Practice reading them aloud so you'll read them well when you read them to students.

Explain the Purpose of Immersion

Gather students together and explain these things to them:

- If the text you're reading is the first one you're sharing, let students know what unit you're starting: "Writers, today we're going to be starting a new unit. You'll be studying and writing short fantasy fiction." Then explain to students the purpose of immersion: "Since you'll soon be writing short fantasy stories yourselves, we're going to spend a couple of days immersing ourselves—that is, reading and starting to study the mentor texts for this unit. Reading and learning from mentor texts is something experienced writers do all the time, and so of course you'll be doing the same thing!"
- Even if you're reading a second or third mentor text, keep reminding students of the purpose of immersion. Since your ultimate goal is for students to do immersion themselves in the future, it's worth repeating this message.

Wait a second—I thought students should write every day in writing workshop?
Immersion days—when students read texts instead of writing texts—can seem counterintuitive. However, for experienced writers, reading texts like the ones they're about to write is actually part of the rehearsal stage of the writing process, and it's important that you—and students—understand this.

- In some units, you'll want students to figure out what the new genre is, so you'll say, "Today we're going to start a new unit. You'll be writing in the same genre that is in this stack. As we read the texts, let's describe this genre and figure out how it works."

How do I respond when my students say, "Writing workshop feels more like reading workshop!"?

Explain that when you're reading texts similar to ones you're soon going to be writing yourself, you're actually doing the work of writers.

What if students don't like a mentor text?

Even though you try to select mentor texts you think will be relevant and interesting, sometimes they'll fall flat. If this happens, consider removing the text from your stack next year, as students won't be as motivated to learn from a text that doesn't interest them.

Read the Text Aloud

Read the mentor or process text as you would any read-aloud text, with feeling and in an animated way. Remember that your enthusiasm will be contagious!

When you finish reading the text, be quiet for a couple of moments, so students have time to feel the impact of the text.

When possible, give students the opportunity to see the text as you read it aloud. This can be as simple as showing students the pages of a picture book or writer's notebook as you read it. You can also project the text using your document camera. And in the upper grades, give students copies of the text, so they can follow along as you read.

Give Students the Opportunity to Respond as Readers

After you read, give students time to respond to the *content* of the writing. For example, if you've read a nonfiction book, students will want to talk about some of the cool facts they learned or make connections to similar things they've seen or experienced. Or if you've read excerpts from a writer's notebook (in a study of keeping a writer's notebook) or a text with revisions (in a revision study), students will still want to respond to the content of these process texts.

Students can respond in several ways:

TIP

In a revision study, as you read your writing or student writing aloud, make sure to display it so students can both see and hear the revisions.

- They can turn and talk to a classmate and afterward share what they discussed with the class.
- Older students can write about their responses in their writers' notebooks and then share either with a classmate or the whole class.
- You can conduct a "choral reading" (Ray 1999, 81). That is, ask one student to start by sharing their response. As soon as that student finishes, another student can chime in, without your calling on them. When students are especially moved by a text, a choral reading can go on for several minutes!

After students share, name the kinds of responses you're hearing, then tell students that the pieces they write in the unit will elicit the same kinds of responses from their own readers.

Invite Students to Respond as Writers

Finally, nudge students to put on their writing hats and discuss what they noticed about how the mentor author wrote the text. This initiates a conversation about craft or process that will continue and deepen throughout the unit.

To support this conversation in a craft study, prompt students with these questions:

- What do you notice about this kind of writing?
- What are some of the interesting things you noticed the author of this text did *as a writer*?
- On what page (or part) of the text did you see something interesting the author did as a writer?
- What are some of the things the author of the text did as a writer that you especially liked?

In a process study, prompt students with these questions:

- What are some of the interesting things that the author did in this stage of the writing process?
- On what page (or pages) did you notice the writer used some strategies? What do you notice about these strategies?
- How can you describe the work you see the writer doing at this stage of the writing process?

Don't be discouraged if students initially respond in superficial ways! This may happen when they don't have much prior experience with talking about texts as writers or if they're encountering a kind of writing for the first time. If you give students repeated experiences with responding as writers across the school year, they'll gradually get better at reading and talking about the mentor or process texts like writers.

As students share what they've noticed, chart their ideas. When you return to the text later in the unit and study it more closely, add to the chart. During the unit, students will refer to the chart and try things on it as they write. (See Figures 6-4 and 6-5.)

Informational Nonfiction Books

- Have lots of facts
- Illustrations on most pages
- Illustrations can have labels that tell the name of things
- Several facts on each page
- Titles are fun, and can have exclamation marks at their end
- Illustrations sometimes "zoom in" on something
- Fun beginnings
- Jokes and riddles on some pages
- Some books have glossaries
- There are diagrams on some pages

Figure 6–4 Primary Immersion Chart

Short Realistic Fiction

- Has a main character with a problem
- Titles give hints about what the story is about
- Characters are described with a couple of details
- Lots of dialogue
- Stories sometimes have illustrations
- Settings described with a couple of details
- Interesting similes
- Authors sometimes skip time
- Main character solves their problem, sometimes with help

Figure 6–5 Upper-Grade Immersion Chart

TIP

At the end of an immersion period, show your own writing or a student's piece from a previous year. If we read only published texts, students might start to think, *These published authors are pretty skilled, and I'm not sure I can do that.* Showing our writing and student writing will make the writing for the unit seem much more achievable to students.

TIP

You can save the conversation about what students notice about the mentor texts as writers until the last day of immersion. Devote ten to fifteen minutes at the end of this period to asking students, "What are some of the interesting things that you noticed the authors of the texts did as writers?" Students will respond by naming some of the things the mentor authors did either in most of the texts or in a specific text.

Action 6.3: Do Small-Group Immersion

Another way of doing immersion is to have students read and respond to mentor texts in small groups. When they're in charge of immersion, students get practice with doing it themselves, a skill they'll use throughout their lives. Also, small-group immersion gives you the opportunity to coach students by conferring with the small groups as they read and respond to the texts.

Video 6.3 Small-group immersion in primary

Plan for Small-Group Immersion

First, decide how many groups you'll have. Small-group immersion works best with groups of two to four students. Then decide who will be in each group. If you have already established writing partnerships where students talk to their partner regularly, it's best to use those. In the early grades (K–1), partnerships work better than small groups.

In all grades, you can have groups read different texts. Each group might read a single text or choose to read one or more from a basket of texts.

In the upper grades, students in every small group might read the same text. This will require you to make copies.

Video 6.4 Small-group immersion in upper grades

Provide groups with sticky notes so that they can mark pages they find interesting and annotate them.

Teach Your Students How to Do Small-Group Immersion

Before you do small-group immersion for the first time, explain to students how this will go:

1. Groups will first need to decide how to read a text. Will one group member read the entire text aloud, or will group members take turns?
2. After the group finishes reading, they should first respond as readers.
3. Finally, group members or partners will discuss what they noticed the author of the text did as a writer. Before doing so, the group might skim through the text and put sticky notes on parts they found interesting as writers.

Should I do small-group immersion with emergent readers?

Small-group immersion will make most sense for emergent readers when there are a lot of visual elements to notice in texts. For example, if you're doing an all-about nonfiction unit, choose mentor texts that have interesting text features students can notice and discuss.

Students can use the Small-Group Immersion Guide (**Online Resource 6.1**) to help remind them of these steps.

TIP

If you have five to ten minutes left at the end of an immersion period, you can do some topic choice work with the class. Reading mentor texts will probably give students ideas for topics they can write about, so having students share their ideas will give them a head start with finding topics they can write about in the unit.

Confer into Small-Group Immersion

Your role during small-group immersion is to confer with groups to teach them how to do immersion better. Focus on one of these things in each conference:

- ***Help students decide the best way for them to move through the immersion process.*** For example, you might help a group decide on how to read a text together.
- ***Name the kinds of reading responses students are having to a text and nudge them to respond in other ways.*** For example, point out that students are responding as readers to a memoir by recalling their own similar experiences, and suggest they can also talk about the life lesson(s) they think the author is trying to get across in the text.
- ***Teach students to talk about what the author of the text did as a writer.*** For example, you might teach a group that has identified several parts they think are written in interesting ways how to name exactly what the writer did in these parts. Do the same thing if students are studying a process text together and have noticed places where the writers used certain strategies.

PUTTING IT ALL TOGETHER: BALANCING WHOLE-CLASS AND SMALL-GROUP IMMERSION

However many days you decide to devote to immersion in a unit, decide upon the balance you want between whole-class and small-group immersion.

See Figure 6-6 for a sample three-day immersion plan. Remember, this is just one way immersion can go.

Day 1	Day 2	Day 3
Introduce unit of study and give overview of period. (5 minutes) Introduce and read aloud first text and discuss students' responses as readers and writers. (15–20 minutes) Introduce and read aloud second text and discuss students' responses as readers and writers. (15–20 minutes)	Give overview of period. (5 minutes) Introduce and read aloud third text and discuss students' responses as readers and writers. (15 minutes) Introduce fourth text. Students then read text in small groups and discuss their responses as readers and writers. As groups meet, confer with them. (20 minutes) Conduct whole-class discussion about what students noticed about fourth text. (5 minutes)	Give overview of period. (5 minutes) Students browse through a collection of mentor texts, selecting one or more texts to read and respond to as readers and writers. (30 minutes) Conduct whole-class discussion about what students noticed in small groups. (10 minutes)

Figure 6-6 Sample Immersion Plan

Do a Whole-Class Share

After groups have read their mentor text(s) and responded as readers and writers, bring them back together as a class to share what they noticed, and add what they say to the class chart. If students have read different texts, have them name the texts and authors as they talk, so other students are aware of them so they can choose those texts if there's another small-group immersion experience.

Action 6.4: Teach Students to Read Like Writers in Whole-Class Text Study

When the players on Carl's baseball team were little, they attended a Mets or Yankees game as a team each season. Since they saw themselves as baseball players, the kids did more than just enjoy being at the game—they noticed what moves the players made at bat or on the field, moves they could try themselves. This started the first time the team went to a game, when Carl and the other coaches asked the players, "What do you notice about what the batter is doing? What did you notice about how the shortstop made that play? What do you see the outfielders doing?" Very quickly, players started to notice all sorts of things themselves and would point them out to each other. Then, at practice the next week, they came wanting to try some of the moves they noticed. Today, Carl's players do this on their own, when they watch games live or on television, and bring what they learn to practice and games.

Just like Carl's players had a guided experience with what could be called reading like a baseball player, your students need the same kind of experience with reading like a writer. Another place for them to get this experience is in *whole-class text study*, when, with your support, your class will spend time studying a text together, noticing the craft moves and the conventions the writer used (Ray 1999, 2006; C. Anderson 2022a and 2022b).

Whole-class text study is important for several reasons:

- Students get a guided experience with reading like a writer.
- Students get the experience of constructing knowledge about craft and conventions themselves (Chavez 2021).
- These conversations help create a community of writers in your classroom who study writing together.
- Students will learn about studying craft and conventions from each other as they hear what classmates notice and have to say about texts.
- Students build a class repertoire of craft techniques and conventions they can try in their writing.
- Students' enthusiasm for trying new craft techniques and conventions is greater when they feel they've discovered them themselves.
- Helping students develop their skill with reading like a writer will help them learn more from the mentor texts you use in your teaching and the ones they find and learn from themselves.

Further Reading

This action has its roots in the writing that Katie Wood Ray does about whole-class craft study in her book *Wondrous Words* (1999). Also, Carl discusses whole-class text study in his book *A Teacher's Guide to Mentor Texts, K–5* (2022b), which includes videos of himself doing this work with primary and upper-grade students.

Envision What Whole-Class Text Study Entails

During whole-class study, you'll suspend the daily structure of writing workshop to devote most, if not all, of a period to the study. If you finish before the end of the period, students can continue working on their writing independently.

In a unit of study, you might devote one or several days to this kind of study. You could do this on the days just before

In this unit of study, whole-class text study happens for two days, before students start drafting.

	Monday	Tuesday	Wednesday	Thursday	Friday
Week 1	Immersion			Process lessons on finding topics, gathering information, planning, and so on	
Week 2	Process lesson	Whole-class text study		Drafting	
Week 3	Drafting				Revising
Week 4	Revising	Editing		Getting writing ready for celebration	Celebration

Figure 6–7 Sample Unit Calendar

students start working on drafts or while they're drafting or revising. If you're doing several days of study, you could do them consecutively or spread them out. See Figure 6–7 for a sample schedule.

Reread a Mentor Text

Bring students together as a class so you can reread a mentor text from the current unit. If students are new to whole-class text study, select a mentor text that has easy-to-notice craft moves and conventions or text features in the text.

Before reading the text aloud, explain to students that writers notice the ways other writers craft their texts and use conventions and then try these moves themselves. Today, they're going to do this together as a class so they'll be better able to do it themselves.

If it's possible for you to give students a copy of the text, do so. Students should also have a pencil. Tell them that as you read the text, they can underline or put checks or stars next to parts they think are well written.

If you can't give students a copy of the text, project the text using a document camera or a scanned version of the text. Tell students that as you read, they should be on the lookout for well-written parts or interesting features they like.

TIP

You can watch Carl lead whole-class text study in videos in the Heinemann Blog post "Teach Students to Read Like Writers During Whole-Class Text Study" (Anderson 2022a).

Have Students Share What They Noticed

When you finish reading the text, ask students to share the parts they liked for several minutes. If they have a copy of the text, they can read the part they liked aloud. If the text is projected, have them tell you which part or page you should return to, and then they can read the part aloud.

Having students share like this does several things. First, students hear well-written sections of the text again. And as they share, you'll learn which parts they're drawn to and will want to discuss. (Note: As students share, put checks on your copy next to the parts they choose so you can keep track of them.)

Select Craft Techniques and Conventions to Discuss

After students have shared, decide which parts of the text to discuss. If your class is new to whole-class text study, choose parts you think your students will more easily be able to discuss as writers. For example, students will usually be able to talk about italicized words (young children might describe them as words with slanted letters) and bold words (or words with big, thick letters). Also consider discussing parts students were obviously excited by when they shared them with the class.

Discuss Several Craft Techniques and Conventions

The discussion part of a whole-class text study is its most important part. Here you'll nudge kids to talk about the parts of the text they liked *as writers*. To do this, reread one of the selected parts, and then ask, "What did you notice the author did *as a writer* when she wrote this part?"

For students who are new to whole-class text study, this discussion can be challenging:

- ***Some students will respond as readers instead of as writers.*** For example, a student might say, "The author wrote an interesting beginning." When this happens, say, "So, what do you notice about what the author did *as a writer* in this interesting beginning?"
- ***Some students will describe parts in very general ways.*** For example, a student might say, "I think the writer used a lot of punctuation in that sentence." When this happens, say, "Hmm, that sentence has a lot of punctuation . . . say more about that." That may be enough to nudge the student to say, "Well, the writer used a lot of commas in that sentence . . . there's, like, a list of things, and the commas go between them."

After students discuss a craft technique or convention, ask them to speculate about why they think the author used it, as this will help them imagine reasons they could use the technique themselves. Ask students to give the craft technique or convention a name, to help them remember it. (Of course, craft techniques and conventions have names, and students may know them.) Also, ask students if they've seen the crafting technique before in other texts.

Expect that students may find this step challenging the first time they do it. To help them, model how to talk about a part by picking one you like and talking about it as a writer. As the year progresses, students will gradually get better and better at discussing craft techniques and conventions.

To keep track of what you discuss with them in whole-class text study, use the Whole-Class Text Study Chart (**Online Resource 6.2**; see also Figure 6–8) to record what they say. You can post a larger version of this chart in your classroom for students to reference.

Invite Students to Try Out What They Noticed

Finally, end whole-class text study by nudging students to select one or more craft techniques or conventions to try themselves. You could list each of the things you discussed and say, "Who is going to try bold words in their writing? Who is going to try the 'three dots' [ellipsis]?"

6.2 Whole-Class Text Study Chart

Craft Technique	What did we notice about how the writer wrote this technique?	Why do we think the author used this technique?	What name can we give this technique?	Have we seen other authors use this technique?	What are some examples of how we've tried or could try this in our own writing?

This chart is based on the work of Katie Wood Ray (1999).

Figure 6–8

If there's still time for independent writing in the period, students can try out things they noticed immediately. Or you could start the next period with a minilesson on how to try out a new craft technique or convention. Model this yourself by choosing one of the things your class discussed and trying it as you write in front of your students.

It's also helpful for students when you make a folder-size version of the chart for students to refer to when they write.

Action 6.5: Prepare to Use Mentor Texts in Craft and Convention Lessons

Video 6.5
Craft minilesson in primary

Video 6.6
Craft minilesson in upper grades

We find that teachers are often amazed that we have just the right mentor texts to teach with in minilessons, small-group lessons, and especially writing conferences. "It's like magic!" we hear teachers say, over and over. "How do you do this?"

The answer is that having just the right published mentor text to teach with isn't magic; it's preparation. Because many of the lessons you're going to teach students are going to be about craft techniques and conventions, you'll need to have mentor texts at your fingertips for these lessons. You'll also need to know how to select which mentor text to teach with as well as the steps for teaching with it (C. Anderson 2022b).

There are two things you need to do to be ready to teach with mentor texts. The first is to put together a *stack* of four to six mentor texts for each unit of study. For more on this, see Action 4.1. The second is to know how to use your stack when you're teaching a minilesson or small-group lesson or having a writing conference.

Minilessons

When you teach a craft or conventions minilesson, you already know what you're going to teach ahead of time. As you prep the lesson, ask yourself, *Which text in my stack contains a great example of what I want to teach?*

Once you've selected the just-right text, think through *how* you're going to teach with the text:

- ***How will you make the text visible?*** You could project the text using a document camera, or from your laptop or tablet onto an interactive whiteboard. If possible, make copies of the text for students.
- ***How will you annotate the text?*** If you're using a document camera to project the text, have a pencil or marker to highlight parts of the text you're showing the class. If you're projecting the text from your laptop or tablet onto an interactive whiteboard, be familiar with your device's annotation functions.

Video 6.7
Craft small-group lesson in primary

Video 6.8
Craft small-group lesson in upper grades

Small-Group Lessons

The preparation for small-group lessons is similar to the preparation for minilessons. However, if you plan on sitting at a table with students where you don't have the ability to project the text, make the text visible to them either by showing them pages from a picture book or giving them a copy of the text that contains the craft technique or convention you're teaching.

Writing Conferences

Unlike minilessons and small groups, when you know what you're teaching beforehand and have already selected which mentor text to use, when you begin conferences, you don't know what you'll be teaching students—or which mentor text you'll show them. This means you'll need to prepare differently for conferences—and be ready to think on your feet—so you'll be able to teach one of a wide variety of craft techniques and conventions. Remember, because one text contains many, many craft techniques and conventions, having four to six texts will make it possible to teach students about almost anything that comes up in a conference!

When you confer, have your stack of mentor texts with you. If you're moving from student to student, carry them with you; if you're working at a conferring table, place the texts next to you.

Before you can teach, you'll first discover what the student is doing as a writer. Start each conference by asking an open-ended question, such as "How's it going?" or "What are you doing as a writer today?" As the child talks

Video 6.9 Craft writing conference in primary

Video 6.10 Craft writing conference in upper grades

Video 6.11 Process minilesson in primary

Video 6.12 Process minilesson in upper grades

about what they're doing, you'll often find out they're working on a crafting technique or trying to use a convention. For example, they may be trying to write a lead or punctuate the dialogue they're writing. (To help you get better at supporting student talk in conferences, read Action 7.2.)

Once you know the focus of a conference, select a text from your stack to teach with by asking yourself, *Which text in my stack contains a great example of what this student is trying to do as a writer that's at their level?* Then make this text visible to the student by placing it in between the two of you. To highlight what you're teaching, point to the part of the text with your finger or underline it with a pencil as you teach. In Chapter 8, "Teach Clearly and Precisely," you'll read about how to describe craft techniques and conventions to students.

Action 6.6: Teach with Process Texts

While you'll use mentor texts to teach students about the craft of writing and conventions, they can't help you teach how to navigate the stages of the writing process. Usually, you won't know much, if anything, about how the authors planned their writing, nor will you have copies of the authors' drafts that would help you see their revisions and edits. How will you help your students have mentors for navigating the stages of the writing process?

The answer is *you're* going to be their mentor for process (Painter 2006; Ray 2002, 2006). You'll do this by teaching with your own process text, that is, a piece that you write or have already written (see Action 4.4). When you write a process text, you go through the entire writing process, so you'll be able to explain to students how you navigated each stage and talk about the strategies you used.

Choose a Process Text

First, you must decide what kind of process text you'll teach with. This will depend on the unit of study you're doing:

- In a genre study, the decision is easy: you'll teach with a piece you wrote in the genre that's the focus of the study.
- If you're in a craft or process study, you can teach with a piece in any genre, since students will be writing in a variety of genres, and what you'll

be teaching isn't genre-specific. However, consider teaching with a piece in a genre your students are familiar with, so that when you share it with them, they won't be sidetracked by the newness of the genre and will be able to concentrate on the process moves you're teaching.

You may already have a process text you can use in a unit. It could be one you wrote the previous year when you did the unit, or you might reuse one that you wrote for a unit you did earlier in the year. If you projected the unit you're doing, you'll have the process text you wrote as part of that work.

Of course, you can also write a new process piece for a unit! You might write it before you start the unit or as the unit progresses.

Video 6.13 Process small-group lesson in upper grades

Teach with Your Process Text

How you'll teach with your process text will differ when you're using it in a minilesson or a small-group lesson or a writing conference.

When you teach about the writing process in a minilesson or small-group lesson, you already know what stage of the writing process you'll be teaching about and the strategy you want the students to learn. As part of the process of prepping the lesson, ask yourself, *How can I use my process text to teach this?*

Just like you do when you use a mentor text to teach craft, you'll need to think about how you're going to make your process text visible to your students and how you're going to annotate it during the lesson.

You have to be ready to think on your feet when you have a process conference with a student (C. Anderson 2018). To be prepared, have your process text with you when you're conferring. Then, when you know you're going to be teaching about an aspect of process, you'll have your process text at your fingertips so you can bring it out, put it between you and the student, and say, "Let me show you how I . . ."

Video 6.14 Process writing conference in primary

Video 6.15 Process writing conference in upper grades

What if I want to teach students about a writing strategy I don't use myself?

You will sometimes teach students about strategies you don't personally use. Sometimes, you'll find an example of how another writer used the strategy in a professional book on teaching writing, and you can show your students that writer's work. Or you could try the strategy yourself, as a writing exercise, and then show students the result.

Can I demonstrate a strategy instead of showing a process text?

Yes, you can do a demonstration in front of your class or in a small group or conference. In Action 8.5 we discuss how to give a good demonstration lesson.

Action 6.7: Use Students as Writing Mentors

One day, Matt was having a conference with Sasha, a confident fourth-grade writer, about a feature article she was writing about jaguars. As he talked with Sasha and looked at her writing, Matt discovered she was writing precise action facts about what jaguars do. He decided to help Sasha add to her repertoire of nonfiction details by teaching her to write explanation facts so she could explain why jaguars do what they do.

For a moment, Matt thought about how to teach Sasha. He could show her a mentor text, one of the feature articles from *Highlights* or *Ask* magazine in his stack of published mentor texts. Or he could show her the feature article he had written himself.

Instead, Matt decided to use one of Sasha's classmates as a writing mentor. Just before working with Sasha, Matt had conferred with Travis, a low-confidence writer. While Travis hadn't yet used explanation facts in his article about Minecraft, as Matt talked with him, he discovered that Travis included many of these kinds of facts when he talked about playing the video game.

So Matt asked Travis to join him and Sasha. Matt said, "Sasha, Travis told me that the best building material to use in Minecraft is diamond. Listen as Travis explains why he thinks this is true."

Matt then looked at Travis, who began, "Well, diamond is the best because it's really tough and sturdy. It's difficult for other people to break apart." Matt then asked Travis to give explanations for some of the other things he knew about the video game.

Matt looked at Sasha and said, "Do you see how Travis explained *why* as he talked about Minecraft? As he talked, he used a kind of nonfiction detail called an explanation fact." Sasha nodded. Matt continued, "Travis is now adding explanation facts to his writing, and I'd like for you to be just like Travis and try doing this in your writing, too."

After the conference, Sasha got to work and began to add some explanation facts to her article. And Travis? He beamed all the way back to his seat. His teacher later told Matt it was the first time she had seen him smile in writing workshop that year.

By using Travis as a writing mentor, Matt helped Sasha learn about an important kind of nonfiction detail. And Matt also helped build Travis' confidence as a writer—something you want to do for all of your students, but especially for your students who, like Travis, are low-confidence writers.

Using students as mentors is a tremendously powerful and often underutilized teaching technique (Eickholdt 2015). Whenever teachers tell us they have a low-confidence writer, the first question we ask is, "How often have you used the child to be the mentor for someone else?" We've seen the impact it has had on a student when we (strangers in the classroom whom the child didn't really care about) have used them to be the mentor for another. Imagine what happens when it's you who decides to bring them over to be a mentor!

Envision *How* You Can Use Students as Mentors

Students can mentor each other in a lot of different ways. The more ways you can envision students mentoring each other, the more likely it is you'll see that each of your students has strengths in some aspects of writing. Look at these examples:

- ***The ways they move through the writing process:*** Students may have strengths in how they use their writer's notebook to brainstorm ideas or gather information for drafts or in how they plan, revise, and edit their writing.
- ***The ways they craft their writing and use conventions:*** In response to the teaching you do with mentor texts, students will be trying out craft moves and conventions in their writing.
- ***The ways they talk about their writing:*** Some students (like Travis) will have strengths in how they talk about their writing that aren't yet appearing in their writing.
- ***The ways they collaborate:*** Students may have strengths in how they talk to each other in partnerships and peer conferences, such as how they listen to each other or ask questions.
- ***The ways they talk to you in conferences:*** Some students are skilled at talking to you about what they're doing as writers in conferences or at responding to your teaching.

Look for Ways Students Can Mentor Each Other

There are many times when you will discover a student could be a good mentor.

- ***During writing conferences:*** Since you start writing conferences by trying to discover what students are doing as writers, conferences are an important time for you to identify ways students can mentor each other. In fact, you'll sometimes be able to use a student from a conference you had earlier in the period as a mentor, like in the conference with Sasha.

Video 6.16 Using a student as a mentor in a primary writing conference

Video 6.17 Using students as mentors in primary small-group immersion

- ***While reading student writing:*** As you read writers' notebooks, and drafts with revisions and edits, look for process strengths. And as you read student drafts, look for craft moves and conventions they are trying with some success.
- ***In conferences with partnerships and peer conferences:*** As you confer with students when they're trying to help each other as writers, look for strengths in how they collaborate.

Imagine *When* You Can Use Students as Mentors

There are many opportunities to use students as mentors:

- ***In writing conferences:*** Invite another student into a conference to talk about their work or to demonstrate a craft technique or writing strategy. When you confer with students who are working together in a partnership or peer conference, you can invite another pair of students to demonstrate a collaboration skill.
- ***During minilessons and small-group lessons:*** Showing student work is a great way of teaching a minilesson or small-group lesson and positioning students as mentors for their classmates. Show a craft move or process strategy a student used, or have a student explain the work they did or a partnership demonstrate how they work together in a particular way.
- ***At share sessions:*** Tell your class you've learned that some of them have special skills as writers that everyone can learn from, and then have these students share their work.

Prioritize Using Low-Confidence Writers as Mentors

It's easy to overuse the most experienced and confident writers as mentors and to have them talk about and show their writing again and again. Unfortunately, this kind of overuse implicitly communicates the message that only some of the students have strengths.

Since low-confidence writers benefit greatly from being used as mentors, it's important to look for ways to do so. In fact, you'll probably find it beneficial to use low-confidence writers more often than you use confident writers.

Here are some tips for using low-confidence writers:

- Like with Travis, you can highlight the moves they make when they talk about what they're going to write, even if they can't yet make these moves in their writing.

Action 6.8

Help Students See Mentor Authors as Real People is in the Online Resources.

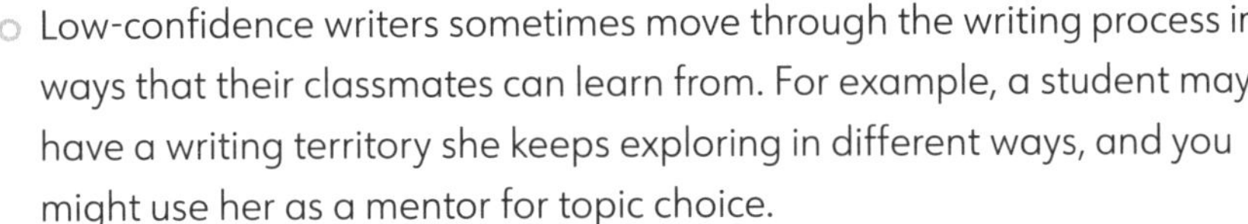

- Low-confidence writers sometimes move through the writing process in ways that their classmates can learn from. For example, a student may have a writing territory she keeps exploring in different ways, and you might use her as a mentor for topic choice.
- Some low-confidence writers are good at responding to their classmates' writing, and you can use them as mentors for collaboration.
- Sometimes low-confidence writers do things in conferences that other students should hear about. For example, a student who diligently tries what you teach in conferences is a good model for students who don't always do this.

Track Ways Students Can Mentor Each Other

Here are two ways to record how your students can mentor each other:

1. When you discover a way a student can be a mentor, record it on the Student Mentoring Form (**Online Resource 6.3**). You can then refer to this form as you confer or if you want to use a student as a mentor in a minilesson.
2. Put up a "Ways We Can Mentor Each Other" chart. When you discover a way a student can be a mentor, ask them to put their name on a sticky note and then put it on the chart in the corresponding section. When students in the class need to have a peer conference, they can refer to the chart for ideas for who can help them. (See Figure 6-9.)

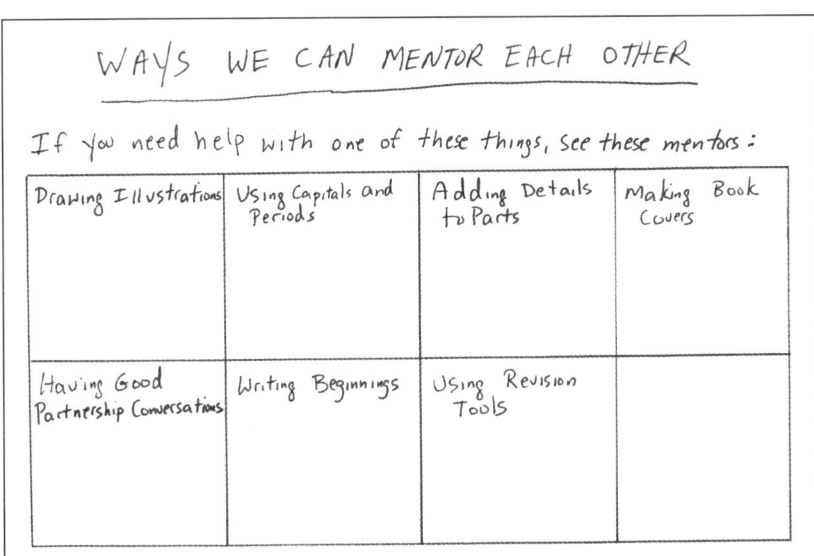

Figure 6-9 "Ways We Can Mentor Each Other" Chart

It's important to welcome all students into your classroom, whoever they are as learners, and to know how to differentiate instruction for them.

7

Individualize Instruction

Chapter 7
ACTIONS

7.1 Make a Plan for Conferences and Small Groups

7.2 Focus Conferences on What Students Are Doing as Writers

7.3 Make Responsive Teaching Decisions

7.4 Give Individualized, Meaningful Feedback

7.5 Stop Suggesting and *Teach*

7.6 Sharpen Your Follow-Through Moves

7.7 Be Purposeful About Forming Small Groups

Why Is Individualizing Instruction So Important?

When Carl looks down the street in front of his Brooklyn home, he sees the Statue of Liberty in New York Harbor, which has historically welcomed all sorts of people to the United States. In a very real sense, you play a similar role in your classroom, as it's your job to welcome all sorts of writers into your classroom:

- Students who like to write and those who don't.
- Students who've had extensive experiences with writing and those who haven't.
- Students who can easily generate text and those who are low-productivity writers.
- Students who enjoy writing in some genres but not others.
- Students who know a lot about craft and those who still have a lot to learn about it.
- Students who write drafts with few convention errors and students who write drafts with many of them.

- Students whose first language is English and students for whom English is a second or third language.
- Students who have special needs as learners.

It's important to welcome all students into your classroom, whoever they are as learners, *and* to know how to differentiate instruction for them (Tomlinson 2014). In writing workshop, there are two powerful ways you can individualize instruction:

- Most important, you can lead effective *writing conferences* (C. Anderson 2000, 2008, 2018; Kaufman 2000; Feigelson 2022; Abraham and Matthusen 2021).
- You can supplement your conferences with *small-group lessons*, when you work with two to five students who have similar needs (Serravallo 2021; Slaughter 2009).

This chapter will help you individualize instruction by giving you ideas for improving your conferences and small-group lessons. Since conferring is the most effective method for individualizing instruction, most of the actions focus on this teaching method.

How Can You Get Better at Individualizing Instruction?

Action	When to Take It
7.1 Make a Plan for Conferences and Small Groups	• If you would like to give students frequent individualized instruction. • If you are unsure of the balance between conferring and small-group lessons. • If you overemphasize small-group work at the expense of conferring.
7.2 Focus Conferences on What Students Are Doing as Writers	• If your conferences usually focus on that day's minilesson. • If you want to get better at figuring out what students' needs are in conferences.

Action	When to Take It
7.3 Make Responsive Teaching Decisions	• If you reflexively tend to get behind the first thing students tell you they're doing as writers in conferences. • If you see multiple directions you can go in conferences but have trouble deciding which one is the most important.
7.4 Give Individualized, Meaningful Feedback	• If your feedback is often superficial, even rote. • If you aren't sure what feedback is most important to give students.
7.5 Stop Suggesting and *Teach*	• If you realize your efforts to individualize instruction in conferences are falling flat because you're making suggestions instead of teaching.
7.6 Sharpen Your Follow-Through Moves	• If your students aren't following through after conferences.
7.7 Be Purposeful About Forming Small Groups	• If you want to group students thoughtfully for small-group lessons.

Figure 7–1

Action 7.1: Make a Plan for Conferences and Small Groups

How much individualized instruction does a student need? We believe each student should have individualized teaching, in either a writing conference or a small group, *every full week of school.*

You're more likely to meet this goal if you make a weekly plan for conferences and small groups in which you figure out the balance between one-on-one and small-group instruction.

As you plan, prioritize conferring. After all, writing workshop is called the "conference method for teaching writing" (Fletcher and Portalupi 2001b), not the "small-group approach":

- In conferences, you're able to talk with students individually and learn about their needs.
- Conferences offer the most differentiated teaching.

Video 7.1 Writing conference in primary

Video 7.2 Writing conference in upper grades

Video 7.3 Small-group lesson in primary

Video 7.4 Small-group lesson in upper grades

- Conferences are the most effective time to support students with the more challenging aspects of writing, such as focus and elaboration.
- As you confer, you'll discover many students have similar needs, information that will help you form small groups.
- Conferences help you develop the relationships that are key to helping students learn from you.

At the same time, small-group lessons should be part of your teaching. You may choose to teach a small-group lesson when

- several students missed an important minilesson;
- some students have a similar need but not enough to justify addressing it in a minilesson;
- you want to give students extra support with what you've been focusing on with them in conferences;
- some students may be ready to learn about aspects of writing their classmates aren't ready for yet; or
- some students need help with skills most of your class can do already.

And—most importantly—you teach small-group lessons when you aren't able to confer with all students individually each week, even if you devote all of independent writing time to conferring. Given that an experienced teacher can usually confer with three to five students a period, that means they can have fifteen to twenty-five conferences per week. If your class size is larger, teaching some small-group lessons will make it possible for you to see every child weekly.

Figure Out the Balance of Conferences and Small Groups

Let's assume you're usually able to confer with three to five students in thirty minutes of independent writing time. (If not, see Action 8.2: Keep Conference Length in the Goldilocks Zone.) The question of how many small groups you'll need to see each week is then a math problem related to your class size. Here are a few scenarios to help you decide the balance that will work for you:

1. ***You have fifteen to twenty students in your class.*** In this scenario, you can do most of your teaching in conferences. And, if you invite another student who has a similar need to listen to your teaching point in some conferences, essentially forming an informal small group, you'll be able to see more students. See Figure 7–2 for a sample schedule.

Total conferences: 15–25
Students invited into informal small groups: 5
Total students seen: 20–30

Monday	Tuesday	Wednesday	Thursday	Friday
3–5 conferences	3–5 conferences In two of the conferences, you invite another student to participate.	3–5 conferences	3–5 conferences In two of the conferences, you invite another student to participate.	3–5 conferences In one of the conferences, you invite another student to participate.

Figure 7–2 Sample Schedule for a Class of Fifteen to Twenty Students

2. ***You have twenty to twenty-nine students in your class.*** In this scenario, you can see each student if in addition to your writing conferences, you have two formal small groups of four to five students each and several informal small groups. See Figure 7–3.

3. ***You have thirty to thirty-five students in your class.*** In this scenario, you can work with each student if you have three formal small groups and several informal small groups in addition to your conferences. See Figure 7–4.

Total conferences: 13–19
Students invited into informal small groups: 4
Students in small groups: 8–10
Total students seen: 25–33

Monday	Tuesday	Wednesday	Thursday	Friday
3–5 conferences In two of the conferences, you invite another student to participate.	Small group: 4–5 students 2 conferences	3–5 conferences	Small group: 4–5 students 2 conferences	3–5 conferences In two of the conferences, you invite another student to participate.

Figure 7–3 Sample Schedule for a Class of Twenty to Twenty-Nine Students

Total conferences: 12-16 Students invited into informal small groups: 6 Students in small groups: 12-15 Total students seen: 30-37				
Monday	**Tuesday**	**Wednesday**	**Thursday**	**Friday**
3–5 conferences In two of the conferences, you invite another student to participate.	Small group: 4–5 students 2 conferences In one of the conferences, you invite another student to participate.	Small group: 4–5 students 2 conferences In one of the conferences, you invite another student to participate.	Small group: 4–5 students 2 conferences	3–5 conferences In two of the conferences, you invite another student to participate.

Figure 7–4 Sample Schedule for a Class of Thirty to Thirty-Five Students

There are several things to consider about these scenarios:

- First, these scenarios are a projection of how things *could* go in your classroom, not how they *should* go. For example, even if you have fifteen to twenty students, you might decide to do one or two small groups some weeks.
- Each time you see a small group during a week, you decrease the number of conferences. The implications of this are that if your class size is twenty to twenty-nine, you'll be able to have a one-on-one conference with each student roughly every two weeks, and if your class size is thirty to thirty-five, it will be roughly every two and a half weeks. Given that class size is out of your control, there's little you can do about this. Over the course of the year, you'll still have plenty of conferences with students—likely many more than you had with your teachers when you were a child!
- Finally, things won't always work out as neatly as in these scenarios. The important thing is the intent to see each child every week in some way. By carefully considering the balance that's right for your classroom, you'll be able teach with that intention—and simultaneously maximize your conferring time.

TIP

If you have a large class, you may decide it's more realistic to try to individualize instruction for each student every six days instead of every five.

Make Your Weekly Plan

As part of planning for the week, when you think about which minilessons to teach each day, make a plan for conferences and small groups. Use the This Week's Conferences and Small Groups Form (**Online Resource 7.1**; see also Figure 7-5) to help you do so.

Here are some things to consider as you plan your small groups:

- Form small groups with students you conferred with the previous week.
- To help you think about how to group students, read Action 7.7: Be Purposeful About Forming Small Groups.
- You might decide to add a small group midweek, for example, when several students were absent for a key minilesson.

7.1 This Week's Conferences and Small Groups Form

In addition to the number of conferences and small groups, you could also write in the names of the students you are planning on conferring with and putting in small groups each day.

	Monday	Tuesday	Wednesday	Thursday	Friday
Number of small groups/students		One SG: Wyatt, Kamara, Ben T., Sara		One SG: Dash, Tunde, Kayla, Ruby	
Number of individual conferences/students	1. Alyssa 2. Tara 3. Tunde 4. Danya	1. 2.	1. 2. 3. 4.	1. 2.	1. 2. 3. 4.
Number of individual conferences where I will invite another student to join (impromptu small group)	1. 2.	1.	1. 2.	1.	1. 2.

Figure 7-5

What about students who need extra support?
Some students need extra support, meaning you will need to see them twice a week, perhaps for two conferences or a conference and a small group. To fit this in, start by considering that your effective class size is your actual number of students plus the number of students who need extra support. So if you have a class size of twenty, and you have five who need extra support, think of your class size as twenty-five when you are deciding how many students will get conferences each week and how many will be in small groups.

In my classroom, there is a general education teacher and a special education teacher. How should we work together?
When Carl taught middle school, he often had a special education teacher in the classroom to provide support. Carl conferred with all students, including the ones with IEPs. When he conferred with a special education student, his special education colleague joined him and sometimes supported the student after the conference was over and the student was trying the teaching point. When they had separate conferences with the child, they used one set of conferring notes so they always knew what had been taught in the most recent conference.

It's not necessary to plan conferences days ahead of time. Instead, decide which students to confer with each day (try doing this after your minilesson while students are settling into their writing) by considering these factors:

- Prioritize conferring with students who were in a small group the week before.
- Select students whose writing goals (see Action 2.6) will be best addressed at the current point in the unit.
- On some days, students will ask for conferences. (Note: You can't accommodate students who frequently ask for conferences, as you have other students to see! Suggest these students seek out other ways to get help, such as having peer conferences—see Action 9.4.)

Action 7.2: Focus Conferences on What Students Are Doing as Writers

In conferences, you give students the most individualized instruction. This is because in a conference, you learn about what they're doing as writers *right now* and then teach them how to do what they're doing even better. In fact, the purpose of the first part of a writing conference is to help you discover what students are doing as writers (C. Anderson 2000, 2018).

Video 7.5
Minilesson: How to have a good writing conference

The Three Parts of a Writing Conference

1. **Discover what students are doing as writers.**
2. Assess how well they're doing what they're doing, and decide what to teach them.
3. Teach.

To help you discover what students are doing, ask students about what they're doing *as writers*. When they're able to respond by letting you know what stage of the writing process they're in, and the specific kind(s) of writing work they're doing in that stage, they help you figure out what they need to learn.

What do you mean by writing work?

- strategies writers use to navigate each stage of the writing process, such as brainstorming a list of topics during the rehearsal stage or reading a draft out loud to look for spelling errors during the editing stage
- ways writers craft their writing, such as writing leads or developing a section of a draft with detail
- using writing conventions

Discuss Conferring with Your Class

Teach a minilesson on the student's role in a conference in which you name the kinds of things they can talk about:

- strategies they're using to navigate the stage of the writing process they're in
- ways they're crafting their writing or using conventions
- problems they're having as they write
- recent minilessons they're trying
- writing goals they're working on

Give students examples of things they could say to you in a conference. Sharing a chart of common things that students say makes this concrete. See Figure 7–6 for a sample chart.

In some conferences, students don't say that much, making it more challenging for me to discover what they're doing. Why?

- Sometimes students aren't sure of what they're supposed to talk to you about. This will happen when students are new to writing workshop. And this will apply to most students in primary classrooms at the beginning of the school year and some in upper-grade classrooms, particularly those who haven't been in a writing workshop before.
- Some students who may be feeling shy or intimidated learn that if they don't say much, you'll take over the conversation, relieving them of further conversational responsibility.
- Students who are new to writing workshop don't yet have the writing vocabulary they need to describe what they're doing. This is true of emergent bilinguals, who are learning conversational English as well as the specialized academic English necessary to talk with a teacher about their work.

Use Conversational Strategies to Support Talk

We all marvel at how great interviewers, such as Oprah Winfrey or Jimmy Kimmel, get celebrities to say so much about themselves. Through a combination of active listening and skillful questioning, they're able to nudge people to reveal things that surprise and amaze us.

To support student talk in conferences, you'll need to develop the same conversational skill set that great interviewers use. By getting your students talking in detail about their writing, you'll get the information you need to make teaching decisions that are truly responsive to students' needs as writers.

GET THE CONVERSATION STARTED

Begin conferences with an open-ended question like "How's it going?" or "What are you doing as a writer?" Then, be quiet! Give students five to ten seconds of

Kinds of Writing Work Writers Talk About	Examples of Things You Might Say
Strategies that help you in a stage of the writing process	"I'm brainstorming a list of topics." "I'm planning my book by touching each page." "I'm revising by adding on to my draft." "I'm editing by reading my book out loud."
Ways you might be crafting your writing	"I'm trying to write a lead that gets my readers wanting to read more!" "I'm writing action facts in my nonfiction book." "I'm using text evidence to support the point I'm making." "I'm writing a counterargument." "I'm using ellipses to make my writing sound more dramatic."
Ways you're using conventions	"I'm putting spaces between my words." "I'm trying to figure out where the commas go."

Figure 7–6

wait time so they can gather their thoughts about what to say to you. This shifts the responsibility in the conversation onto the student.

If students respond to your opening question by saying, "OK," or "Fine," or even with a shrug, don't give up on the conversation!

- Ask more specific questions, such as "What's going well with your writing today?" "Is there something that's a little bit hard that I can help you with?" or "Are you trying a recent minilesson?"
- Have students look at their writing and describe what they've done. This gives them some time to think and reminds them of the work they've been doing or thinking of doing.

Video 7.6 Supporting student talk in a conference

HELP STUDENTS TALK WITH PRECISION

Students sometimes use general words and phrases to describe what they're doing, such as "I'm adding detail" or "I'm revising." A powerful way to get students to talk more precisely about their work is to nudge them to *say more* (C. Anderson 2018; Feigelson 2014, 2022):

1. Start by repeating what the child just told you: "Oh, so you're revising."
2. Next, ask them to say more, inflecting your voice in a way to let the student know you're genuinely interested in learning more about what they're doing: "Hmm . . . could you say more about that?"
3. Then give the student some wait time, simultaneously looking at them with an air of expectation, until the student starts to speak more precisely: "Well . . . I'm revising by adding some analysis of the text evidence in my argument." Bingo!

SUPPORT STUDENTS' USE OF WRITING VOCABULARY

To help students develop the writing vocabulary they need to talk in conferences, try these conversational moves:

- Bring a chart to your conferences that lists what you've taught your class in recent minilessons, and have students look at it to help them think about what to say to you (Laman 2013).
- List several things the student might be doing. You could say, "Hmm . . . are you trying to add dialogue, or character thinking, or character actions in this part of your story?"
- Take a tour of the student's writing, and describe what you see them doing: "I see that you've got a *subheading* for this chapter. . . . And you're describing what penguins look like by writing *descriptive facts* and what penguins do by writing *action facts*. . . . Do you want to talk about one of these things today?" Hearing you connect writing language to their writing helps students understand these terms, and soon they'll be able to use them on their own.

Further Reading

See Chapter 2 of Carl's book *A Teacher's Guide to Writing Conferences, K–8* (2018) for more information on how to support student talk. Tasha Laman's book *From Ideas to Words* (2013) is a resource for working with emergent bilingual children in writing workshop and includes a discussion of how to confer with children who are learning to speak and write in English.

Video 7.7
Supporting precise student talk in a conference

TIP

These are two clues that students are unsure of what to talk about in conferences:

1. They respond to the question "How's it going?" by reading their draft aloud.
2. They respond by telling you what their piece is about instead of talking about what they're doing as writers.

Action 7.3: Make Responsive Teaching Decisions

When Carl coached his baseball team, he stressed that his players should have a plan when they came up to bat. He noticed many of his players were nervous when they were at the plate and swung at every pitch, good or bad, often resulting in strikeouts, weak ground balls, or pop-ups. Instead, Carl explained, they should think about what kind of pitch they liked to hit the best, wait until they got it, and then swing. By having a batting plan, players were more likely to have a successful at bat.

Likewise, you should have a plan for how to be responsive to each child's most important needs in a conference (C. Anderson 2018). Otherwise, it's too easy to respond reflexively to the first thing a child tells you they're doing or the first thing you notice when you read their writing—even when doing so isn't the best use of precious conference time.

Confer with Criteria in Mind

The most important part of your conferring plan is having a set of criteria to help you determine importance when students are talking about their writing and when you're looking at their writing.

In your next several conferences, try listening with the following criteria in mind. When the answer to one (or more) of these questions is yes, then you've found a worthwhile conference focus:

1. ***Is the student telling you about a problem that's frustrating them?*** All writers have problems, but when students encounter them, they may not have strategies for working through them and may get stuck or shut down. When students bring up a problem they're having, it's a good idea to focus the conference on teaching them a strategy for navigating it, especially when they're visibly frustrated.

2. ***Is the student telling you they're working on something they learned in a recent minilesson?*** Optimally, your minilessons address needs many students have as writers. When the minilesson the student is trying out corresponds to one of their needs, you've probably found a good focus for the conference.

3. ***Is the student telling you they're working on something connected to the focus of the current unit of study?*** When students bring up that they're trying to do something connected to one of the current unit's goals, it's a good idea to support them.
4. ***Is the student telling you they're working on one of their writing goals?*** When students tell you they're trying to do something that's connected to one of the individual writing goals you set for them (see Action 2.6), you've likely found a good focus.
5. ***Is the student excited about doing something as a writer?*** It's joyful work when you confer with a child who's especially invested in what they're trying to do as a writer. Perhaps they were inspired to try something they saw a friend doing or they're on fire about something they saw in a mentor text.

In conferences when students don't tell you much about what they're trying to do as writers, look at their writing to help you decide on the focus for the conference. Read their writing with these questions in mind to help you decide what to teach them.

Are some of these criteria more important than others?

In general, if what you decide to focus on in a conference matches one of these criteria, you're making good use of conferring time. However, we suggest you give more weight to some criteria:

- If a student is having a problem, and is visibly frustrated, prioritize helping them with it. If you don't, the student may not be able to proceed with their writing!
- Otherwise, prioritize helping students with one of their writing goals.
- Ideally, students will tell you they're trying what you taught in a recent minilesson, and that lesson connects to one of your writing goals for them (for example, a student who needs support with elaboration tells you they're working on adding dialogue to their fantasy story).
- When a student is super excited about something they're doing, consider giving them support with it, even though it may not connect to one of your goals for them.

Be Open to Probing Further

In some conferences, the first thing students tell you they're doing won't seem important. Sometimes this will be because it doesn't match one of the criteria for responsive decision-making. Other times, what they tell you does match one of the criteria (they're working on a recent minilesson, for example), but you would rather focus on something that matches another, more important criterion (a writing goal).

In these situations, probe more deeply by encouraging the student to keep talking about their writing. You may find it will be the second or third thing the student tells you they're doing that's the more important thing to work on!

Remind yourself of students' writing goals before conferences by looking at your conference record-keeping form (see Action 2.7).

To probe more deeply, ask, "What *else* are you doing as a writer?" like in this scenario.

Teacher: *How's it going?*

Student: I'm working on my ending.

Teacher [Thinks to himself, *Endings? OK, that was my minilesson yesterday, but this isn't a big priority for her right now.*]

Teacher: *What else are you doing as a writer?*

Student: I've been trying to stretch out the pages of my all-about book with lots of facts.

Teacher [Thinks to himself, *Yes! She needs to get better at elaboration!*]

Teacher: *Lots of facts . . . say more about that.*

Student: I've been trying to write descriptive facts, but it was kind of hard to do.

Teacher: *So let's talk about how you could do that better.*

Assess Your Conference Decision-Making

By rereading your conference notes, you can see which of the criteria usually influence your decision-making.

Do this by taking out your notes for the last week of conferences. Next to what you wrote for each student, jot down why you taught what you did—"problem," "minilesson," "goal," and so on. If what you taught satisfied two criteria, write them both down.

What trends do you notice in your conference decision-making? And what do these trends suggest about ways you can grow in your conference decision-making?

Here are a few problematic trends and ways to address them:

- ***Do you usually get behind that day's minilesson?*** If so, you may need to think more about students' writing goals when you confer. The best way to do that is to glance at your notes from previous conferences with the student before you begin each conference. If the minilesson connects to a goal you have for a student, that's great. If not, try asking the child, "What else are you doing as a writer?"
- ***Do you notice that in many conferences you're addressing problems students are having that are frustrating them?*** While you should address problems when they arise, if you're doing this in many conferences, it may mean you need to teach your class strategies for addressing these problems in minilessons.
- ***Is there a disconnect between students' writing goals and minilessons?*** While in general prioritizing conferring into students' writing goals is best, if you find these goals are usually different from your minilessons, it may mean there's a disconnect between your minilessons and students' needs as writers. If so, read Action 5.1 for ideas on how to make your units of study more responsive to students' needs.
- ***Do you rarely get behind students' passions?*** It's easy to overlook this criterion, especially when what students are excited about (for example, adding ellipses to their writing) doesn't seem as important as other things the student needs to learn. However, what students learn when you support their passions will help them learn about other aspects of writing (for example, as part of teaching a student about ellipses, you can also show them how to study a mentor text).

See **Action 8.6** (in the Online Resources) for more ideas about how to use conference notes to reflect on your teaching.

Action 7.4: Give Individualized, Meaningful Feedback

You've probably received some superficial feedback. When you received it, you learned the person giving it didn't seem to know much about the quality of

Video 7.8
Feedback in primary conference

Video 7.9
Feedback in upper-grade conference

your work. And you probably felt disappointed—you may have rolled your eyes inwardly because the feedback wasn't meaningful.

Helpful feedback, on the other hand, demonstrates that the person who is giving it really *sees* you and the work you've done. By giving you helpful feedback, this person is invested in helping you see what you can do and also in helping you do even better work in the future (McGee 2017).

In a writing conference, feedback has several qualities:

- It's positive.
- It names students' strengths—what children can do so far (their *partial understanding*).
- It's specific.
- It reassures students they're on the right track.
- It points them toward a next step they can take as writers.
- It energizes students and helps them be receptive to the teaching that will follow.

In this action, we'll detail several steps you can take to improve your conference feedback so that it's individualized and meaningful.

Start with Assessment

Before you can give students conference feedback, you'll look at their writing and assess it. This is what you do in the second part of a writing conference:

The Three Parts of a Writing Conference

1. Discover what students are doing as writers.
2. **Assess how well they're doing what they're doing, and decide what to teach them.**
3. Teach.

To practice assessing, read some student writing, either by yourself or with colleagues who are also working on giving helpful feedback. Use these questions to guide your assessment (use the Form for Coming Up with Helpful Feedback [**Online Resource 7.2**] to record your answers to the questions):

1. ***What aspect of writing will you focus on?*** Will you look at an aspect of process, such as how the child plans or revises their writing? Or will you look at an aspect of craft or conventions, such as how the student uses detail or punctuation?
2. As you read, ask, ***What can the child do already with this aspect of writing?*** (Hint: If you are new to looking for what children can do, you may find it challenging during your first couple of attempts. Action 2.5 will help.)
3. Next, answer the question, ***What next step(s) could this child take as a writer?***

To help you envision this kind of assessment, let's look at two student writing samples and the assessments that we made of them. First, read Raiken's informational nonfiction book in Figure 7–7, shown on the next three pages.

1. ***What aspect of writing will you study in the book?*** We are going to look at how Raiken elaborates.
2. ***What can this student already do to write with detail?***
   - In his illustrations, Raiken gives the names of parts of the school (page 2) and classroom jobs (pages 9–10).
   - In his writing, Raiken writes precisely by naming the specific kinds of specials (page 6) and classroom jobs (pages 9–10).
   - Raiken introduces details with the phrase *For example* (pages 6 and 7).
   - In the text, he includes specific number facts (pages 7 and 9).
   - Raiken develops each part about school specials by writing action facts (pages 6–7).
   - He develops his section on being a "wish well leader" by writing a mini narrative about what he does when he has this job (page 10).
3. ***What kind of next steps could this child take?*** When Raiken writes lists of examples (page 9) in his writing, he could develop them with details as he does successfully in other places in his writing.

Page 1

Page 2

Page 3

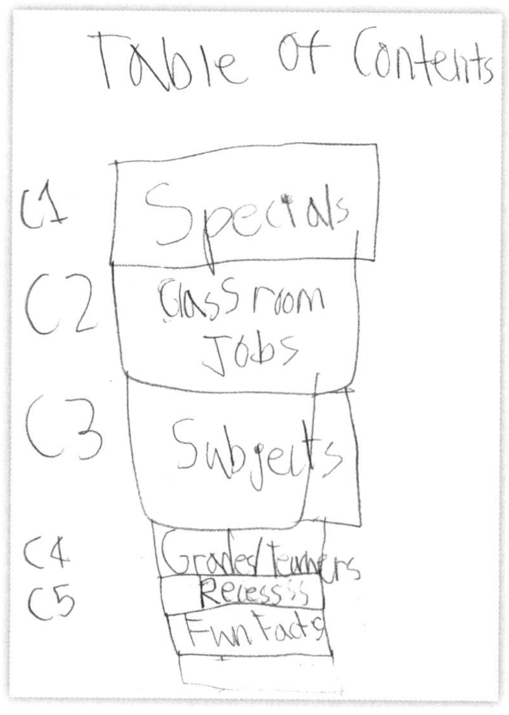

Page 4

Figure 7–7

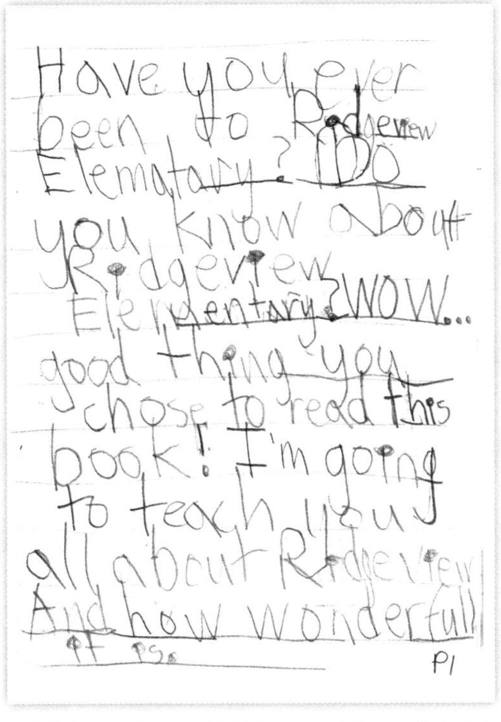

Page 5

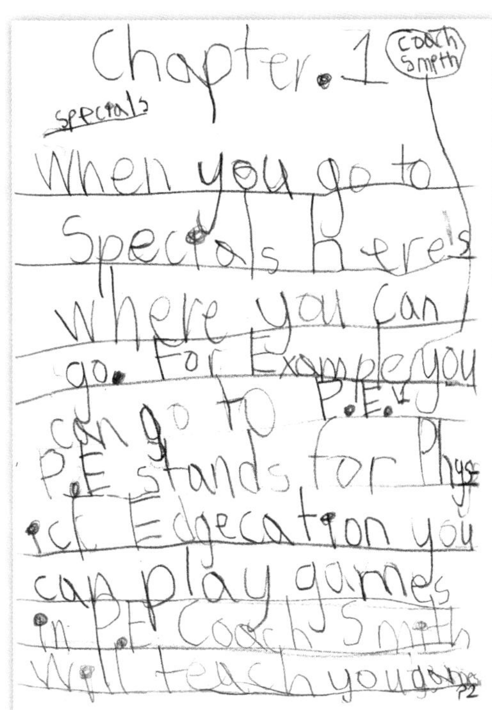

Page 6

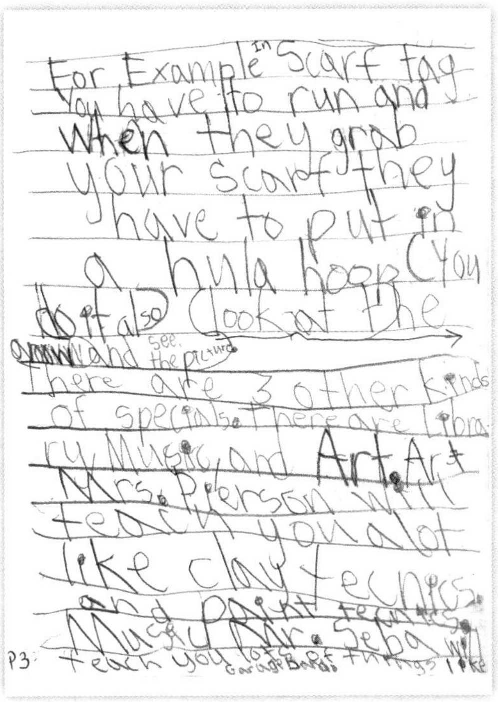

Page 7

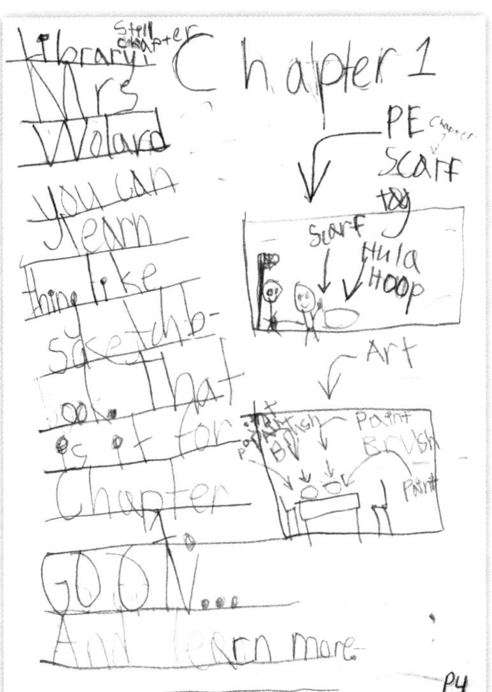

Page 8

Figure 7–7 *continued*

Figure 7–7 *continued*

Now read Dylan's personal narrative in Figure 7–8.

1. ***What kind of writing work will you study in the piece?*** We will study how this student gives her writing voice.
2. ***What does this student already do to structure her writing?***
   - » She uses exclamation marks to let readers know to read sentences with feeling.
   - » She capitalizes all the letters in some words to signal to readers to read them loudly.
   - » She uses all caps and exclamation marks together to give the ends of sentences a beat.
3. ***What kind of next steps could this child take?***
   - » She could add to her repertoire of voice techniques by learning to use the ellipsis to give the end of sentences a beat ("It was time for my favorite part . . . DECORATING!").
   - » She could also add to her repertoire of voice techniques by using the dash to give the end of sentences a beat ("Then we started whisking, melting, cutting, pouring, cracking—every single thing there is to do!").

CUPCAKE BAKING

I had just eaten lunch with my best friend Mckenna. We were playing mini bakery with her toy kitchen.

Her mom came downstairs to do the laundry and saw us playing. When she was finished doing the laundry, she asked us, "Hey, wanna bake cupcakes in the real kitchen upstairs?"

I looked at Mckenna and she looked at me at the same time. We said "YES!"

We rushed upstairs and started digging through the cabinets and drawers for every tool we needed! We were so excited about baking. After that, we set the table and her mom got all the ingredients. Then we started whisking, melting, cutting, pouring, cracking, every single thing there is to do! Once we whisked everything together, we poured the batter in the tray and popped it in the oven.

"Hey Dylan? Wanna play Lyla tag"? McKenna said.

"Yeah I do!" I said.

"I'm gonna get you guys!" said Lyla.

Lyla tag is when Mckenna's little sister Lyla tries to get us while we run around trying not to get tagged.

"Girls the cupcakes are ready," McKenna's mom said

It was time for my favorite part DECORATING! When we were baking the batter, we also made the frosting. Me and Mckenna were making all sorts of designs. Dots and swirls were our favorite designs. When we were finished decorating, we gave them a good look and almost started drooling.

"Let's eat them all!" said Lyla.

Me and Mckenna laughed. Then we each took one and stuffed them in our mouths. They were amazing! When I was finished, I looked at Mckenna and Lyla. They both had frosting all over their faces, especially Lyla. Then I realized I had frosting all over my face too, even my nose. How did I even get frosting there? Me and Mckenna both had two. Then we were stuffed.

Then we decided to just watch YouTube. After a bunch of videos, it was time for me to go home. Lyla gave me a big hug and I said bye to Mckenna.

Whenever I remember this moment, it brings me joy. That's because of one person, okay, maybe two people, but that main person is Mckenna. Mckenna is my best friend, and she always will be. Everyone should have a friend that makes them happy, just like Mckenna.

Figure 7–8

Practice Formulating Feedback

You'll give feedback in the beginning of the third part of a writing conference:

The Three Parts of a Writing Conference

1. Discover what students are doing as writers.
2. Assess how well they're doing what they're doing, and decide what to teach them.
3. **Teach.**
   - **Give feedback.**
   - Teach.
   - Coach.
   - Link.

To practice coming up with feedback, use the Form for Coming Up with Helpful Feedback (**Online Resource 7.2**) to help you think about the students whose writing we just assessed. As you write down the feedback, be sure to include what you would tell the student about their strength(s) and what next step you would describe to the student.

Here's the feedback we came up with for Raiken, the student who wrote about his school:

> **Teacher:** I see you're trying to help readers learn a lot about your school by including lots of detail in your book. It's great that you have many different kinds of details in your writing—you give the names of things in your illustrations and in your writing and you write number facts, action facts, and mini-stories. I think a next step for you is to develop lists of examples with more details.

Here's our feedback for Dylan, who wrote about baking:

> **Teacher:** I'm noticing that you give readers lots of information about where you want them to read what you wrote with feeling and expression. You do this by ending sentences with exclamation marks and also by capitalizing all the letters in some words at the end of sentences, which, combined with the exclamation mark, gives the end of these sentences a big beat! A next step for you is to learn how to use other punctuation marks that let readers know how to read your writing, such as the dash.

Give Feedback in Real Time

Now that you've practiced coming up with feedback, it's time to apply your new skills in real time: Come up with feedback as you watch the conference in Video 7.10.

When you get to the screen that says, "What feedback would you give?" stop the video. Ask yourself:

- What kind of writing work is the child doing?
- What can the child already do with this aspect of writing?
- What next step could this child take as a writer?
- What feedback would I give this child?

Once you've answered these questions, continue watching the video and compare what you came up with with what Carl said to the child.

Practice Giving Feedback in Your Own Conferences

Finally, confer with students, and pay special attention to giving feedback. Since it can be challenging to assess the feedback you give as you confer, use your smartphone to record or videotape several of your conferences and listen to or watch them afterward. Ask yourself, *How was my feedback helpful for this child? What could I do to give even better feedback?*

Video 7.10
Conference feedback

Action 7.5: Stop Suggesting and *Teach*

When we were children, our teachers gave us plenty of individualized suggestions about how to improve our writing. Teachers wrote comments all over our compositions, usually in red ink: *Tighten up your topic sentences. Always end sentences with periods. You need more details in your body paragraphs.* And so forth.

The problem we had with these suggestions was we didn't know how to do what our teachers were suggesting, which is why we wrote the way we did in the first place! What we needed from them—and didn't usually get—was *individualized teaching*. We needed our teachers to explain exactly *what* it was they wanted us to do as writers and *how* to do these things, in a way we could understand. (In defense of our thoughtful, hardworking teachers, we know they didn't get professional development in how to teach writing and were doing the best they could at the time.)

When we coach teachers, we often notice they, too, give students individualized suggestions (rather than teaching) in writing conferences: "Good writers add dialogue, so I'd like you to try this in your story!" or "Experienced writers add details to their writing when they revise, and I want you to try to do some of this right now." This doesn't surprise us—many of them had teachers like ours—and they bring this image from their childhoods of how their teachers responded to student writing into their conferences.

Helping teachers give students individualized *teaching* in conferences is some of the most important work we do with them (C. Anderson 2018, 2022b). After all, if students don't get individualized teaching, they won't learn how to write better.

Here's how to strengthen your conference teaching.

Understand *When* and *How* to Teach in a Conference

Teach right after you've given students feedback:

The Three Parts of a Writing Conference

1. Discover what students are doing as writers.
2. Assess how well they're doing what they're doing, and decide what to teach them.
3. **Teach.**
    - Give feedback.
    - **Teach.**
    - Coach.
    - Link.

A typical teaching point in a conference is one to two minutes long. In your teaching points, make these moves:

1. Start by naming *what* you're teaching: "I want to teach you that writers define important words in their nonfiction writing."
2. Next, explain *why* it's important for the student to learn what you're teaching: "Writers define important words so that readers will understand what you're writing about and won't get confused."
3. Then, *explain* what you're teaching. If you're showing the student an example (a mentor or process text), select one from your stack that shows the next step you want the student to make and describe what the author does in the text. If you're doing a demonstration, show the next step as you write and explain what you're doing.
4. Finally, describe *how* the student can do what you're teaching them by giving them a strategy: "One way you could do this work is by . . ."

Study Several Conference Teaching Points

Try these ways of studying conference teaching points:

- ***Watch videos.*** If you're a primary teacher, watch Video 7.11, and if you're an upper-grade teacher, watch Video 7.12. Each video is annotated to help you see the teaching moves.
- ***Read annotated transcripts of other conferences.*** **Online Resources 7.3** (Primary Annotated Conference Transcript) and **7.4** (Upper-Grade Annotated Conference Transcript) provide two examples.

Video 7.11
Primary writing conference teaching point

Write Out Several Teaching Points

It's helpful to write out a few teaching points word for word and then revise them to make them even better. Doing this will help you think carefully about each teaching move, and how to weave them together, without the pressure of having to do it live. (When Carl wrote *Strategic Writing Conferences* [2008], he wrote out over one hundred teaching points, which *really* sharpened his conference teaching skills. Fortunately, writing out just a couple will be enough to help you do the same!)

Use the Composing a Teaching Point Guide (**Online Resource 7.5**) to help you with this exercise.

ONLINE RESOURCE

Video 7.12
Upper-grade writing conference teaching point

Role-Play Teaching Points

Another way of practicing teaching points is by role-playing them with colleagues as part of a PD session. This may be a little nerve-racking, but the benefit is that colleagues can give you feedback. You can use the Composing a Teaching Point Guide to help you.

You could do the role-play in two ways: You could use the teaching point you wrote in the previous step, or you could more closely simulate actual teaching by doing it live. Be sure to have the appropriate materials—a mentor or process text or paper and pencil if you're doing a demonstration.

Videotape a Conference

Using your smartphone, make a video of one or more of your conferences and watch them afterward, paying special attention to your teaching points. As you watch, use the Composing a Teaching Point Guide to help you reflect on what you did.

You may find doing this to be uncomfortable—not everyone enjoys watching videos of themselves—but once you get past any discomfort you may be feeling, you'll find doing this exercise will give you a lot of insight into how well you're teaching in conferences.

Watching a video with a colleague is a way to get another pair of eyes on your work and get valuable feedback.

Ask for Feedback

Lastly, you can ask a colleague, coach, or supervisor to watch you confer. The feedback they give you afterward about your teaching points will help you identify what you're doing effectively and what you could still do better.

Action 7.6: Sharpen Your Follow-Through Moves

In baseball and tennis, a player's swing isn't over when the bat or racket hits the ball. Rather, it's over after the player completes his swing, which we call the *follow-through*. By following through, the player can hit the ball in such a way that it leaves the bat or racket with much higher velocity, which usually results in more success in a game.

One of the biggest complaints we hear teachers make about their writing conferences is that after they've tried so hard to individualize instruction, many students don't try what they teach. This is a serious problem, because students learn when they try what you teach right after conferences are over.

To address this problem, work on your conference *follow-through* moves. Consider that your teaching point in a conference is similar to the point of contact when swinging a baseball bat or tennis racket. After you teach, there are several follow-through moves you can make at the end of conferences and then five to ten minutes after the conference is over (C. Anderson 2000, 2018).

The Three Parts of a Writing Conference

1. Discover what studens are doing as writers.
2. Assess how well they're doing what they're doing, and decide what to teach them.
3. **Teach.**
    - » Give feedback.
    - » Teach.

» **Coach.**

» **Link.**

In this action, we discuss three follow-through moves you can try (Videos 7.13 and 7.14).

Video 7.13 Conference follow-through moves in primary

Video 7.14 Conference follow-through moves in upper grades

Coach

Once you've finished teaching, have the student try out what you taught them *with you* for one to two minutes. Doing this brief practice will help students get past any hesitancy they may be feeling about trying something new. If you find they have some trouble during the try-it phase, coach them. Even after just a couple of minutes, students will usually feel more confident in their ability to do what you taught by themselves and leave the conference excited to try it.

Here's the flow of what happens in the coaching part of a conference:

1. Begin by saying something like, "Before I move on to my next conference, I'd like you to try what I just taught."
2. In most conferences, you'll nudge students to do the try-it *orally*. To get them started, say, for example, "So I'd like you to talk out how you could stretch out the dialogue in this part of your story."
3. If the student has some difficulty (which is entirely normal, since you're teaching them how to do something that's a step above where they are as writers), coach them. Prompt them with the strategy you described at the end of your teaching point. For example, you could say, "It's a little bit hard to come up with dialogue, isn't it? To figure out how to stretch out the dialogue, say to yourself, 'Who started the conversation? What do I think they said? What do I think the second person in this conversation might have said in response to what the first person said? And then what did the first say? The second again?'"
4. Sometimes you'll find it effective to help the student envision how what you've taught could sound in their writing. For example, you could tell the student, "Maybe in your story, you could say, 'Mom, why can't I go outside?' or 'Mom, I really want to go outside!' or 'Mom, I just have to go outside!'" Helping students envision how what you've taught can go can give them a bit of a boost and help get them started.
5. In some conferences, it'll make more sense to have the child try what you taught by doing some writing. For example, if you teach kindergarten or first grade, have a child try out putting spaces between words by having them write a sentence and, with your support, practice putting spaces between words.

Explicitly Link the Conference to the Student's Independent Work

Students sometimes don't try what we teach because we don't make it clear we're expecting them to do so. The place to do this is at the end of conferences.

To bring conferences to a close, say something like, "It's been great talking to you today! Now I'd like you to revise your draft by adding details, just like I've taught you in this conference. I'll be back after my next conference to see how you're doing with this work." Being clear and assertive will prevent misunderstandings about what students are supposed to do when conferences are over.

Check Back with Students

The final move is to do a quick check-in with students after your next conference:

> **Teacher:** So how did adding details to your draft go?
>
> **Student** [*Points to her draft*]: I reread my draft and added details to a couple of places.
>
> **Teacher** [*Scans the draft*]: I see you added on in several places—fantastic! And I see you drew arrows from the places you wanted to add over to the margins, so you would have space to write the new details. That worked really well for you. Congratulations!

Doing quick check-ins gives students the message you expect they'll try what you teach. Of course, if you discover a child hasn't followed through, you'll have to figure out why:

- Did the student have some trouble with what you taught? If so, you may need to do some more coaching so they can be successful.
- Did the child forget or not feel like doing what you asked? In this case, make it clear you expect them to try what you taught immediately.

Occasionally, you'll discover that a child has done something unexpected because there's a bug in your teaching point. When you see this, revise your teaching point so that (hopefully) you don't see other students do this again!

For example, Carl once showed a third grader a draft where he had written the letter *A* after a sentence where he wanted to add a detail and then wrote the letter *A* as a footnote on the bottom of the page, with the added detail. When he returned to check in with the student, she said she was using the "A strategy." Puzzled, Carl looked at the child's writing and saw she had put the letter *A* after several sentences, instead of writing *A*, *B*, *C*, and so on, and then written several *A*s at the bottom of the page, with added details. Carl realized she did this because she had seen only the letter *A* on his draft and overgeneralized what he had done. Ever since, Carl has shown drafts with several different letters!

Action 7.7: Be Purposeful About Forming Small Groups

Doing small-group lessons in addition to your writing conferences makes it possible for you to provide each of your students with a differentiated learning experience each week (Serravallo 2021; Slaughter 2009).

Small groups are especially important when your class size makes it difficult—if not impossible—for you to confer with each student during the week. Some small groups will be preplanned (formal small groups), and you'll know who will be in them, when you'll teach them, and what you'll teach. Other small groups will happen spontaneously, when you're conferring and you realize another student (or more) could benefit from listening to and trying out the teaching you're about to give (informal small groups).

When planning small-group work, there are two questions to answer:

- Who should be in a small group this week?
- What should I teach in small groups?

This action will help you answer these questions with accuracy, so that the combination of your writing conferences and small-group lessons will enable you to provide effective individualized instruction for all of your students each week.

Figure Out Which Students Have Similar Writing Goals

Small groups will often include students who share the same writing goals. For example, you can group students who need support with planning their writing or some help with using end marks consistently.

To help you identify which students have similar needs, fill out the Writing Goals Across the Class Form (**Online Resource 7.6**; see also Figure 7–9). To fill out this form, reread the writing goals you wrote on your conference record-keeping forms that you keep for each student. (Actions 2.6 and 2.7

7.6 Writing Goals Across the Class Form

Student	Process Goals	Qualities of Writing Goals	Convention Goals
Alyssa	Write multiple pieces about same topic/territory	Develop repertoire of details	Consistent use of periods
Ben L.	Repetoire of Revision Tools	Writing specific details	Punctuating compound sentences
Wyatt	Editing strategies	Repertoire of transitions	Punctuating dependent clauses
Bonnie	Planning Strategies	Focus on part of topic	Punctuating multiple clause sentences
Syeda	Planning Strategies	Develop repertoire of details	Consistent use of periods
Kayla	Write multiple pieces about same topic/territory	Develop important parts	Punctuating dependent clauses
Jonathan	Repertoire of Revision Tools	Writing specific details	Punctuating compound sentences
Kamara	Editing strategies	Develop repertoire of details	Punctuating dependent clauses
Chloe	Planning Strategies	Focus on part of topic	Consistent use of periods
Dash	Planning Strategies	Focus on part of topic	Using capitalization consistently

Figure 7–9

focus on how to set writing goals for students and record them on record-keeping forms, respectively.)

Since students' growth as writers is gradual, it will take time—several months, even the entire school year—for students to meet your goals for them. This means you'll be able to use the Writing Goals Across the Class Form as a tool across several units. (Every couple of months, update the form so it reflects how students have grown as writers and how your goals for them have shifted in response.)

Decide Which Students Will Be in Small Groups

The first step is to decide who'll be in small groups and who *won't*. Look at your This Week's Conferences and Small Groups Form from last week to see who was in a small group then. You should prioritize having conferences with these students this week.

You'll form small groups out of some or all of the remaining students, depending on the size of your class:

- Some of the remaining students will get conferences, too. For example, in a class of twenty-five students, one week fifteen of them had conferences and ten were in two small groups of five each. During the next week, those ten got conferences, and a different ten went into small groups, giving the remaining five the opportunity to have more conferences.
- You may decide that some or all of the children who will get small-group teaching in a given week will be in a formal small group. From this list, group students who have a writing goal in common. Of course, it should make sense to focus on that goal when the students are in that stage of the writing process in the current unit of study. A small group on planning will make most sense when the students who are in it are getting ready to draft. And a small group on end marks will make sense either while students are drafting, so they can practice using end marks as they compose, or when they are editing.

- You can also teach some students on the small-group list in informal small groups. As you have writing conferences, bring students on your small-group list into a conference when what you're teaching matches one of their goals. Of course, it's easier to do this when you include a child who is sitting nearby to the child you're conferring with, but you could also call a child over who is sitting in a different part of the classroom.

Assess Your Individualized Work at the End of the Week

Finally, at the end of each week, look at your record-keeping form to see which students didn't have a writing conference or a small group. Try not to get down on yourself when this happens, as sometimes you'll have fewer conferences than you had hoped for in a week, or your small-group work will take longer than you thought it would. Instead, plan to see these children first thing the next week, preferably in writing conferences.

TIP

When several students have the same goal, it doesn't mean they'll be in exactly the same place as writers. For example, you may have three students who need to learn about ending sentences with periods. One may occasionally leave out periods; another might use periods to end every line, whether or not that's where sentences end; and another may use periods only to end each page. After teaching the lesson in your small group with these students, you'll coach each child, differentiating the teaching point based on what each child understands so far about using periods.

Working on the clarity and precision of your teaching is part of the lifework of being a teacher.

8

Teach Clearly and Precisely

Why Is Teaching Clearly and Precisely So Important?

Excellent writing teachers are clear and precise in how they teach. They know the content of what they're teaching, *and* they know how to translate that knowledge into beautifully specific teaching (C. Anderson 2018, 2022b; Angelillo 2008; Brunn 2010; Eickholdt and Vitale-Reilly 2022; Marchetti and O'Dell 2021).

Working on the clarity and precision of your teaching is part of the lifework of being a teacher, something you do every day. As you learn about writing and teach new lessons, you figure out how to teach them well. And even when you've been teaching a particular lesson for years, you continue to refine it, making it better and better.

What are the benefits of this ongoing work?

- When you break down a craft technique or convention, highlighting each aspect of how writers use it, students are more likely to add the technique or convention to their repertoire.
- When you describe precisely how writers use a strategy for navigating a stage of the writing process, students can make these strategies part of their writing tool kit.

Chapter 8

ACTIONS

Just like good writing, good teaching is clear and precise when it's focused and contains specific detail. The actions in this chapter will help you focus your teaching points in minilessons, small-group lessons, and writing conferences as well as teach with specificity.

How Can You Get Better at Teaching Clearly and Precisely?

Action	When to Take It
8.1 Keep Minilessons Truly Mini	• If your minilessons (and small-group lessons) regularly exceed ten to twelve minutes. • If you try to pack too many teaching points into your minilessons.
8.2 Keep Conference Length in the Goldilocks Zone	• If your conferences regularly exceed five to seven minutes. • If you teach more than one thing in your conferences.
8.3 Teach Precisely with Mentor Texts	• If you describe craft techniques and conventions in general ways.
8.4 Help Students Read Like Writers in Inquiry Lessons	• If your students need practice with reading like writers. • If you aren't sure how to help students read like writers.
8.5 Teach Precisely in Process Lessons	• If you want to get better at explaining exactly *how* writers use strategies to navigate each stage of the writing process.
8.6 Improve Your Teaching Through Study and Reflection (in Online Resources)	• If you want to improve your teaching points but aren't sure exactly where to start. • If you would like to energize your teaching by having some goals for improving your teaching.

Figure 8–1

Action 8.1: Keep Minilessons Truly Mini

Millions of people love to watch the short program in competitive figure skating. In the individual short program, skaters perform a series of seven elements—various kinds of jumps, spins, and step sequences—all in two minutes and forty seconds.

Just like in the short program, your goal with a minilesson is to keep its length within a time boundary: ten to twelve minutes. The most important reason to keep minilessons mini is that minimizing their length maximizes the time students have to write—and you have to work with students in conferences and small groups, when you can individualize instruction for them.

Also like the short program, minilessons have several elements (C. Anderson 2000; Eickholdt and Vitale-Reilly 2022):

- an *opening*, when you explain what you're teaching and why;
- *teaching*, which you'll do by discussing a mentor or process text or by doing a demonstration;
- an opportunity for students to *try it*; and
- the *closing*, when you restate the teaching point and invite students to try the minilesson in their writing that period or in the future.

One of the biggest challenges of teaching effective minilessons is including these elements seamlessly and artfully, all within the ten-to-twelve-minute time boundary. This action is designed to help you learn how to do this better.

Study Minilessons

First, read and watch several minilessons. This will help you envision the elements of a minilesson and how they flow together.

Start by reading several minilesson transcripts:

- **Online Resource 8.1:** Primary Minilesson Transcript: Using Several Techniques to Add Voice to a Text (K–2)
- **Online Resource 8.2:** Upper-Grade Minilesson Transcript: Punctuating Dependent Clauses (3–8)

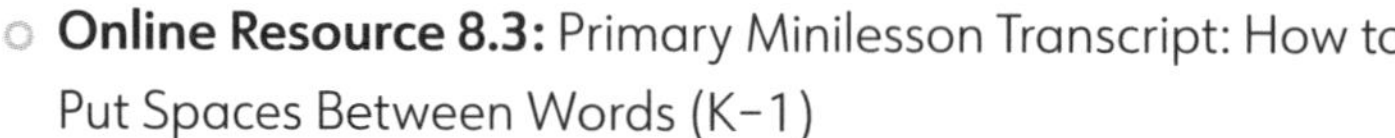

- **Online Resource 8.3:** Primary Minilesson Transcript: How to Put Spaces Between Words (K–1)

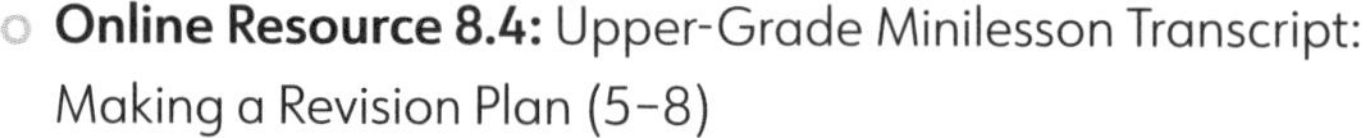

- **Online Resource 8.4:** Upper-Grade Minilesson Transcript: Making a Revision Plan (5–8)

Video 8.1
Minilesson in primary

Then watch the minilessons in Videos 8.1 and 8.2.

When you read and watch the minilessons, ask yourself, *What do I notice about this minilesson?* Jot your thoughts down. To guide your reading and watching, use the Guide for Studying a Minilesson (**Online Resource 8.5**).

Video 8.2
Minilesson in upper grades

Write Minilessons

Now that you've done a study of minilessons, write out a minilesson (or two), word for word as if you were actually giving it. By writing out a minilesson, you'll get practice incorporating the elements in a careful, slowed-down way, without the pressure of doing it live. (Note: We're *not* suggesting you do this for every minilesson during the school year! Rather, writing out one to two minilessons is an exercise that will help you improve all of your minilessons.)

Start by deciding on the topic of your minilesson. Optimally, pick one you're planning to teach soon. You could flash-draft the minilesson and try to incorporate the elements you've learned about. Or you can use the Minilesson Planning Form (**Online Resource 8.6**) as a guide to help you write it.

After you've written the minilesson, assess what you've done. Refer to the Guide for Studying a Minilesson to help you think about your lesson. If you're doing this exercise with colleagues, use the guide to facilitate a discussion about each other's work. As you reflect on your minilesson, look for what you've done well and also what you could do to improve the lesson. Unlike when you teach an actual minilesson, you can revise the written lesson to make it better. The process of revising a lesson is a valuable one, as it helps you think carefully about the elements you can improve, the first step toward incorporating these elements into your minilessons the first time you give them.

TIP

We suggest you read and watch the minilessons with colleagues and discuss what you notice about them. Collectively, you'll notice many more aspects of the lessons than you will on your own!

Record Minilessons

Now it's time to use what you've learned so far in some live minilessons. If you are doing this work during the school year, teach these lessons to your students. If you're doing this work as part of a PD workshop, teach some live minilessons with your colleagues.

Record your minilessons with your smartphone, so you can watch them later and assess your work. Use the Guide for Studying a Minilesson to help you think about what went well in your lesson(s) and what you can do to improve them further.

It's helpful to have colleagues, especially those who are also working on improving their minilessons, give you feedback. You might show each other videos of your minilessons during a PD session and discuss them. Or you could invite colleagues to watch you teach a minilesson to your class and then discuss the lesson afterward.

QUICK FIXES WHEN MINILESSONS ARE TOO LONG

If you're having trouble keeping your minilessons truly mini, see if one of these quick fixes works for you:

1. Introduce and read mentor texts with your students during immersion, not in minilessons.
2. Make sure you teach only one thing in each minilesson.
3. Use only one to three teaching methods in any one minilesson:
    - Show how one published author did something.
    - Show how several published authors did something.
    - Show your own writing.
    - Do a demonstration.
    - Show how a student did something in their writing.
    - Envision how a student could do something in their writing.
4. Remember that you won't usually write in front of students in minilessons, unless you're doing a demonstration. Writing in front of students is time-consuming and takes away from student writing time if we do it unnecessarily.

Video 8.3
Small-group lesson in primary

Video 8.4
Small-group lesson in upper grades

TIP

What we've written in this action applies to small-group lessons, too, since they are similarly structured. A key difference between minilessons and small-group lessons is that when students try the teaching point, you'll *briefly* coach each of them as they write. One reason why small-group lessons go on too long is that this coaching goes on too long.

Action 8.2: Keep Conference Length in the Goldilocks Zone

Whether it was the temperature of the porridge she ate, the size of the chairs she sat in, or the softness of the mattress she tried to sleep in, Goldilocks was a child in search of what was just right when she visited the bears' house.

Like Goldilocks, you want the length of your writing conferences to be just right. In most conferences, the Goldilocks zone, or their most effective length, is between five and seven minutes. This is the amount of time experienced writing teachers usually need to navigate the three parts of a conference (C. Anderson 2000, 2018):

1. *Discover* what a student is doing as a writer.
2. *Assess* what the student is doing.
3. *Teach* the student how to do what they're doing better.

When your conferences are too short (one to two minutes), you're checking in with students, not conferring. When you spend too little time with students, you don't have enough time to teach well. And when your conferences are too long, you'll have conferences with fewer students.

Are your conferences in the Goldilocks zone? This action will help you find out. And if they're not in this zone, this action will help you make them just right.

Assess the Length of Your Conferences and Adjust If Necessary

Start by looking at your conference record-keeping forms and counting the number of conferences you've had on days when you've spent all of independent writing time conferring (independent writing time will usually be twenty-five to thirty minutes). The average number of conferences you have on these days will tell you whether your conferences are too short or long (see Figure 8-2).

Video 8.5
Conference in primary

If you find that your conferences are too short, you've probably been checking in with students for the best of intentions—you've been wanting to see as many students as possible each workshop period. However, once you get beyond five conferences in a period, the less effective your interactions with students are, since you don't have the time to teach them well in just a few minutes. Here's what you can do to transition away from just checking in:

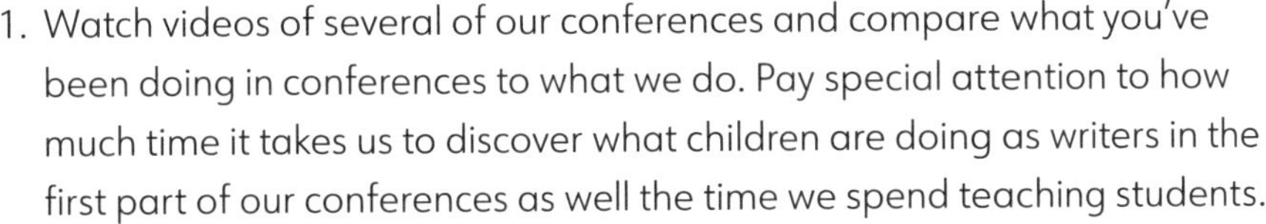

Video 8.6
Conference in upper grades

1. Watch videos of several of our conferences and compare what you've been doing in conferences to what we do. Pay special attention to how much time it takes us to discover what children are doing as writers in the first part of our conferences as well the time we spend teaching students.

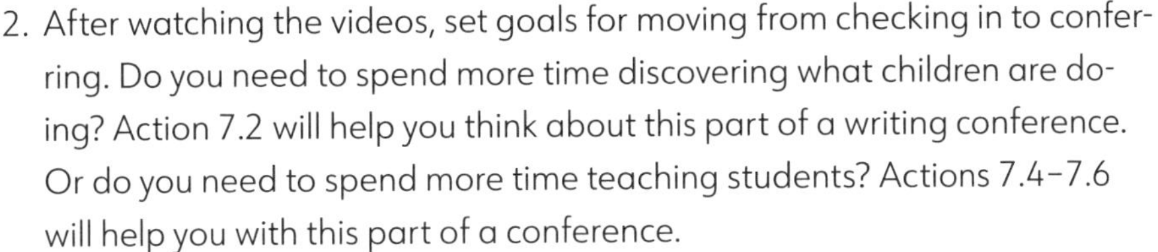

2. After watching the videos, set goals for moving from checking in to conferring. Do you need to spend more time discovering what children are doing? Action 7.2 will help you think about this part of a writing conference. Or do you need to spend more time teaching students? Actions 7.4–7.6 will help you with this part of a conference.

Average Number of Conferences You Have per Workshop	What This Average Number Reveals
More than 5	Your conferences are too short, and you're checking in with students, not conferring.
3–5	Your conference length is in the Goldilocks zone.
1–2	Your conferences are too long.

Figure 8-2

If your conferences are too long, it may be because you're spending more time than necessary in the discovery part of your conferences, trying to decide what to teach. Or it may be that you're spending too much time in the teaching part of your conferences, perhaps because you're teaching students several things.

An easy way to determine where your conferences are running long is to record a few with your smartphone. Rewatch them to see how much time you take in each part. What trends do you notice?

If you're taking too much time in the discovery part of your conferences, here are some strategies that will help you come up with a conference focus more quickly:

- Before each conference, review your conference notes for the student, especially your writing goals for them. Do this as you're walking over to the student or when you sit down next to them before you ask, "How's it going?" Starting conferences with your goals for them in mind can help you decide what to teach more quickly. Sometimes a student will bring up that they're working on a goal. If they don't, ask them how they're doing with their goals, or read their writing to see if there's an opportunity to work on a goal.
- Take a few moments to read some current student writing ahead of time to help you see what kinds of things might come up in conferences. Then, when you're conferring, you can anticipate some of the things that may come up in the conversations.

If you're taking too much time in the teaching part of a conference, you're probably overteaching in your conferences. You may be teaching more than one thing. You might be doing this because you see students have many needs and you're feeling anxious. Or you may be using too many teaching tools. For example, you might be showing students several excerpts from mentor texts, when one may be enough.

Try these strategies to prevent overteaching:

- When you decide what to teach in a conference, write down the teaching point on your record-keeping form right away. Just like starting a piece of writing with your main idea can help you focus the piece, writing down your teaching point can slow you down for a moment, and help you focus on one teaching point.
- When you're feeling anxious about things you *aren't* addressing in a conference, write them down in the goals column of your record-keeping

form (see Action 2.7). In this way, your record-keeping form can be a to-do list for each of your students. Knowing you've written these postponed teaching points down can help you feel you'll remember to focus on these things in the future.

- Limit yourself to teaching with one teaching method. For example, teach with a mentor text, or by demonstration, but not both. Also, resist the temptation to show multiple examples of published or process mentor texts. Often, one good example will be enough!

Action 8.3: Teach Precisely with Mentor Texts

One of the most important teaching skills you can hone is your skill with describing craft techniques and conventions precisely when you teach with mentor texts in minilessons, small groups, and writing conferences (C. Anderson 2022b; Eickholdt and Vitale-Reilly 2022; Marchetti and O'Dell 2021). This skill makes your teaching accessible to children of all ages.

You may feel daunted by this. Perhaps your teachers didn't teach with mentor texts when you were in elementary and secondary school, and you didn't learn much about craft. And you may have been taught to use conventions by learning rules instead of studying how writers actually use them in texts.

To develop your ability to talk precisely about craft and conventions, you need to work on reading texts like a writer. This kind of reading has several steps that will help you analyze what the author of a mentor text is doing (Ray 1999, 2006; C. Anderson 2022b).

1. Reread the excerpt of the mentor text that contains the crafting technique.
2. Ask yourself, *What exactly do I notice the author is doing* as a writer?
3. Ask yourself, *Why do I think the writer used this technique?*
4. Ask yourself, *Where else have I seen writers use this technique?*

This action will help you improve your skill with reading like a writer so that you can talk more precisely about mentor texts.

Video 8.7 Teaching with a mentor text in an upper-grade minilesson

Watch Experienced Writing Teachers Teach Precisely About Mentor Texts

Begin by watching us teach with mentor texts, so you have a clear image of what it means to talk precisely about craft techniques and conventions.

As you watch the videos, use **Online Resource 8.7**: Studying How to Teach Precisely with a Mentor Text Form.

Watch Experienced Writing Teachers Analyze Mentor Texts

Watching experienced writing teachers read like writers is another way to help you envision how this kind of reading goes. Watch Videos 8.9 and 8.10 to see us go through the steps of reading like a writer to figure out how to describe a craft technique and a convention in a mentor text.

Video 8.8 Teaching with a mentor text in a primary conference

Practice This Yourself

Now it's time for you to hone your ability to talk precisely about craft techniques. The Analyzing a Craft Technique or Convention Form (**Online Resource 8.8**) will walk you through the steps of reading like a writer.

- Start by practicing analyzing several sample crafting techniques and conventions using the Tool for Analyzing Craft Techniques and Conventions (**Online Resource 8.9**). Afterward, compare what you've done with how we analyzed these same craft techniques in **Online Resource 8.10**: Matt and Carl's Analysis of Craft Techniques and Conventions.
- Once you've done this work, go through one of your mentor texts and select several craft techniques and conventions you'll be teaching your students, and use the guide to help you analyze them.

Video 8.9 Discussion about a craft technique

Try to do this work with colleagues who are also trying to get better at talking precisely about mentor texts. This will accelerate your learning, since together you'll notice more aspects of crafting techniques and conventions than you will yourself.

By doing this exercise several times, you'll internalize the process of reading like a writer, which will help you in any craft lesson.

Apply Your Skills to Your Lessons

Finally, apply what you've learned from these exercises in real-time lessons with students. You might start with a minilesson or small-group lesson, as you'll know what you're teaching ahead of time, but you'll ultimately want to practice during conferences, too.

Structure your teaching points in this way:

1. Name the craft technique or convention you're going to teach and why it's important to learn it.
2. Make the text visible to your student(s).
3. Read the craft technique or convention aloud.
4. Describe what the writer did in the technique or convention as precisely as you can.

Video 8.10 Discussion about a convention

To assess your teaching, record a lesson with a smartphone. Afterward, look to see which of these moves you made with success and which ones you could still work on. Of course, pay particular attention to how you describe the craft technique or convention. How clear and precise is your description?

Action 8.4: Help Students Read Like Writers in Inquiry Lessons

We have both had children who were learning to drive. After years of driving them everywhere, one day we each sat in the passenger seat (with a bit of reluctance—and nervousness) while our children took the wheel and began the process of becoming independent drivers.

When you teach about craft and conventions, it would be easy to always be the one who drives the conversation. After all, you're much more knowledgeable about craft and conventions than your students, and you've worked hard to be able to describe what writers do with precision and clarity.

However, it's important that you sometimes give students the wheel by giving them the chance to read like writers and notice what writers do. After all, just like parents can't drive their children everywhere forever, you're not going to be in students' lives forever, either. By giving them opportunities to read like writers, you give them much-needed practice with developing this important habit of mind that will serve them throughout their lives as writers (C. Anderson 2022b; Ray 1999, 2006).

How do you give students the wheel? By making one simple shift. Once you show a mentor text, ask them this question: "What do you notice the author did?"

This action will help you learn how to help students steer the conversation.

Video 8.11
Inquiry minilesson in primary

Watch Experienced Writing Teachers

Start by getting an image of what it looks and sounds like when experienced writing teachers invite students to read like writers by watching Videos 8.11–8.13.

As you watch the videos, fill out the Studying an Inquiry Lesson Form (**Online Resource 8.11**).

Video 8.12
Inquiry minilesson in upper grades

Decide What to Teach in Inquiry Lessons

How do you decide which craft techniques or conventions are good candidates for inquiry lessons? In general, students—especially ones who are new to craft study—will be more successful studying crafting techniques with obvious visual features. For example, primary students will notice interesting illustrations, such as the different kinds of text features in nonfiction books and articles. And students of all ages will be more able to talk about craft techniques that involve how text is written, such as the use of bold words and italics. Students will also be more successful studying craft techniques that are visually and aurally obvious, such as short and long sentences, ones that repeat a word or phrase, or lists of sentences. Since most writing conventions are visual, they lend themselves nicely to inquiry lessons.

Video 8.13
Inquiry conference in upper grades

With these criteria in mind, go through your stack of mentor texts for a unit, and identify which craft techniques and conventions are good candidates for inquiry lessons. When you find them, annotate them or use sticky notes to mark them so you can find them when you want to teach them in lessons.

Practice This Yourself

Now it's time to try this yourself. It may be less daunting to try an inquiry lesson in a minilesson or small-group lesson, where you know ahead of time what and how you're going to teach. However, since you've identified several craft techniques or conventions that lend themselves to inquiry lessons, if the opportunity to teach one of them comes up in a conference, you'll be prepared.

Wherever you've decided to try an inquiry lesson, structure your teaching in this way:

1. Name the craft technique or convention you're going to teach and why it's important to learn it.
2. Make the text visible to your student(s).
3. Read the craft technique or convention aloud.
4. Ask your students, "What do you notice about what the author did *as a writer* in this craft technique [or convention]?"
5. Support your students' attempts to talk about the craft technique or convention.

If inquiry lessons are new for students, then you can expect your first attempts to be a bit messy, and they'll need some support (see Figure 8–3).

To assess your inquiry lessons, record one or more with your smartphone and review it afterward. When you watch the lesson, assess how well your students talked about the text as well as how you supported their talk. Be on the lookout for places where you could have handled things differently, and imagine ways you could handle these situations better in the future.

How Students Respond to Questions About Craft Techniques or Conventions	Example Student Comments	Ways You Can Respond
Your students respond as readers.	"This is a really exciting part of the text." "I can see a picture in my head when I read this."	Redirect your student(s) by restating your initial question: "What do you notice the author did *as a writer* here?" Model how you would like your students to talk by discussing one aspect of the craft technique or convention.
Your students discuss the craft technique or convention in very general ways.	"This part is very detailed." "The author uses punctuation in this part."	Say to your student(s), "Say more about that." Say to your student(s), "What *exactly* do you see the author doing in this part?"

Figure 8–3

Action 8.5: Teach Precisely in Process Lessons

In process lessons, you teach students about how to navigate the stages of the writing process—how to find a topic, how to plan a piece, how to revise, how to edit, and so on (C. Anderson 2018; Eickholdt and Vitale-Reilly 2022).

When you teach process lessons, you don't use published texts as mentors. While the authors went through all the stages of the writing process while composing them, you won't usually know the strategies they used to plan their writing or to edit the text for spelling errors.

Instead, you'll use the writing of authors whose writing process you do know. Who are these writers? You, of course! And your students.

There are two types of process lessons. In one, you'll show the writing you or a student did at a stage of the writing process. For example, you can show your class the list of topics you brainstormed when you were trying to pick a topic. Or you can show them the revisions a student made to their draft.

The other type of process lesson is a demonstration, in which you write in front of students, showing them how you use a writing strategy. For example, you could show students how you plan a book by touching each page and saying what you're going to write on it and then jotting a word or two on a sticky note to help you remember. Or you might show students how you edit a draft by reading it aloud and listening for places where you might need to add punctuation. (See Figure 8-4 for more examples.)

Video 8.14 Process minilesson in primary

The key word in a process lesson is *how*. When you do a process lesson, it isn't enough just to show some writing you or a student did at a certain stage of the writing process or to write in front of your students. As you do these things, it's essential to explain *how* you or the student did the work or, if you're doing a demonstration, explain *how* you're doing it as you write.

In an effective process lesson, you'll explain how you're navigating a stage in the writing process with precision. This action will help you work on this skill.

Video 8.15 Process minilesson in upper grades

Watch Experienced Writing Teachers Teach

Watch us teach process lessons with primary and upper-grade students (Videos 8.14–8.17. These lessons will help you envision what a process lesson entails. Use the Studying a Process Lesson Form (**Online Resource 8.12**) as you watch the videos.

Stage of the Writing Process	Examples of Process Lessons
Rehearsal (or prewriting)	Brainstorming a list of possible topics Using writing territories to find topics Researching a topic Making a plan for a piece of writing
Drafting	How to start a draft by flash-drafting How to get restarted each day with a piece of writing How to study a mentor text to get craft ideas
Revision	How to reread a draft, looking for places to add on How to use revision tools—carets, arrows, footnotes, sticky notes, flaps, etc. How to reread a draft, looking for clutter to cut How to reread a draft and jot down revision plans in the margins
Editing	Self-editing by reading aloud Having a good peer editing conference
Getting ready to publish	How to decide upon a format for a piece you will publish/share

Figure 8–4

Video 8.16
Process conference in primary

Video 8.17
Process conference in upper grades

Video 8.18
Discussion of writing strategies

Watch Experienced Writing Teachers Talk About Their Process

Watching experienced writing teachers talk about their writing process will give you a sense of this kind of talk. This is especially helpful if you haven't yet thought much about how you move through the stages of the writing process yourself. In Video 8.18 you can watch us discuss writing strategies we use at various stages of the writing process and talk about how we use these strategies.

Practice This Yourself

Next, practice describing how you or a student used a strategy. Use the Describing a Stage of the Writing Process Guide (**Online Resource 8.13**) to help

Action 8.6

Improve Your Teaching Through Study and Reflection is in the Online Resources.

you think about what you could say about your own writing process or a student's writing process.

If you're using the guide to help you think about your process, select writing you did at the stage of the writing process that will be the focus of this exercise. You probably already have some writing like this—for example, you wrote process texts if you did Action 4.4.

If you're going to use student writing, then you probably learned about the student's process by talking with them in a writing conference, and you'll use what you learned from that conversation in this exercise.

Do this work with colleagues who are also trying to learn to talk precisely about process. When you share your thinking about your process or a student's process, you can get feedback about how clear you're being.

Of course, the ultimate point of doing this exercise is to help you describe process precisely when you do live lessons. Once you have the feel for how to talk about your own or a student's process, you'll find this will transfer into any process lesson you teach your students, whether you're teaching in minilessons, small groups, or writing conferences.

If you're teaching with a process text, structure your teaching in this way:

1. Name the strategy you're going to teach and why it's important to learn.
2. Make the process text visible to your student(s).
3. Describe what you or the student who used the strategy did and *how* you or the student did it.

If you're doing a demonstration:

1. Name the strategy you're going to teach and why it's important to learn it.
2. Start using the strategy in front of the student(s).
3. As you write, describe what you're doing and how you're doing it.

After you've tried these teaching moves in several lessons, record yourself. As you watch afterward, assess which moves you made successfully and which ones you could still improve. Pay special attention to the part(s) of the lesson where you tried to explain how you or the student used the strategy!

One of the qualities of a good writing teacher is a sort of planned obsolescence.

9

Support Student Independence

Why Is Supporting Student Independence So Important?

One of the qualities of a good writing teacher is a sort of planned obsolescence. That is, their goal is students will become able to compose pieces themselves, without assistance (Cruz 2004; Mermelstein 2013).

How do students develop this ability? They do so when you teach them about each stage of the writing process and the strategies writers use to navigate them. You'll also teach them strategies for handling the inevitable problems that will arise.

There are many benefits to teaching students to write independently:

- Students develop confidence in their ability to put pen to paper (or fingers to keyboard) and move through the writing process.
- Students develop a repertoire of writing strategies they'll use when you're no longer their teacher.
- While students are writing, you can focus on writing conferences and small-group lessons.
- Less of your time will be devoted to helping students who are stuck or unsure of how to proceed with their writing because they'll be able to work through these issues themselves.

Chapter 9

ACTIONS

9.1 Help *All* Students Write Independently

9.2 Teach Students to Navigate the Writing Process Independently

9.3 Envision How Students Can Help Each Other

9.4 Teach Students How to Work in Partnerships and Peer Conferences

9.5 Help Students Find and Use Their Own Mentor Texts (see Online Resources for this action)

The goal of this chapter is to help you envision the teaching necessary for students to learn how to navigate the writing process themselves.

What Can You Do to Support Student Independence?

Action	When to Take It
Action 9.1 Help *All* Students Write Independently	• If you spend a lot of time sitting with students who seem unable to do grade-level work without you. • If students are unable to write independently because the work you expect them to do is above their level.
9.2 Teach Students to Navigate the Writing Process Independently	• If you have students who are unsure of what writers do in some or most stages of the writing process and get stuck or skip stages entirely. • If your students need constant reminders about what to do when they get to each stage of the writing process.
9.3 Envision How Students Can Help Each Other	• If you would like students to make use of writing partnerships and peer conferences in every unit of study.
9.4 Teach Students How to Work in Partnerships and Peer Conferences	• If you want to know how to teach students about collaboration.
9.5 Help Students Find and Use Their Own Mentor Texts (in Online Resources)	• If students depend on you to help them figure out how to craft their writing or use conventions. • If students try only craft techniques and conventions you've taught them.

Figure 9–1

Action 9.1: Help *All* Students Write Independently

To write independently, students first need to be able to do the work we give them.

This isn't as simple as it sounds. In any classroom, there are students at a variety of levels as writers. In the best of all possible worlds, all of your children would be able do the grade-level work you teach them about in your minilessons, small-group lessons, and writing conferences.

However, you probably have some students who aren't yet ready to do grade-level work. It's often these children who have the most difficulty with working independently and whom you find yourself sitting with constantly to keep them writing. Of course, being with them constantly won't support their independence. How do you help these students write independently?

Identify Which Students Are Having Difficulty

First, make an honest appraisal of which students find it challenging to write on their own. For some students, this will be obvious. For example, students who stop writing when you don't sit with them and won't continue until you return are signaling there's a problem.

To determine which other children are having difficulty, ask yourself, *When I read student writing from a unit, are there students who would be unable to write something at a similar level if I asked them to write another piece completely on their own?* If the answer to this question is yes, then you probably gave them too much scaffolding. For example, perhaps a student's writing is well structured only because you gave them a graphic organizer and helped them fill it out, instead of giving them the opportunity to make their own plan. Or maybe you spent extra time when you conferred with them, making numerous suggestions about things they could improve on (and helping them carry out each suggestion), instead of teaching them about one aspect of writing. Or perhaps you did the writing for the child as they told you what their piece was about.

Figure Out What Students Can Do

Now that you've identified which students are having trouble with writing independently, the next—and most important—step is to figure out what they *can* do as writers.

This may be hard for you. The implication of this is that some students will be doing work at a level that's different from the rest of your class. For example, in the spring of kindergarten, when most students are making books that are a mixture of illustrations and text you can read, you may have some students making books with illustrations but text you can't read. Or you may have some sixth graders include fewer or shorter sections in their feature articles than you expect from most students.

Meeting students where they are is essential to their ability to work independently. Conversely, expecting them to meet you where they aren't yet makes independence highly unlikely, if not impossible, for them!

The first step in figuring out what students can do independently is to *step away from them as they write* so you can see what they do without your assistance. Be prepared for the probability that students will write at a significantly lower level on their own than when you give them support. This may be difficult for you, since it will reveal how much you've been overscaffolding them.

If students don't write much, or write nothing at all, this may be because they think they can't do the level of work you're expecting or they really can't do it at this point. If you think this is the case, try showing them a mentor text that is less sophisticated—for example, one with fewer sections or less elaboration. Students will be more likely to write when they think they can do the work.

Teach with Nudges

Once you've figured out what a child can do independently, the next step is to teach them with nudges, that is, teach them small step by small step.

To help you understand the concept of nudges, consider Matt's relationship with his smartphone. Like many adults, he sometimes needs help with using an app. When his four children are at home, he knows (without naming names) that Child A will show him how to use the app slowly, one step at a time, and won't be frustrated when he asks obvious questions. He also knows (without naming names) that Child B will tell him too many steps at once, get frustrated when he doesn't get it, and eventually take the phone from him and say, "Let me just do it for you!"

Child A, of course, is the one who teaches Matt with nudges! When you teach with nudges, you're not only helping students grow as writers over time but also helping them continue to write independently because what you're adding to their plate won't overwhelm them.

Teaching with nudges involves breaking down instruction into manageable steps. For example, suppose you have a student who includes character actions in their narratives, and you've decided to teach them to include dialogue, too.

You could show them a mentor text in which the writer has characters speak back and forth several times, but instead you show them one in which one character says one thing (like in *Owl Moon*). In a later conference, you might teach the student to have one character say something and another respond. And so on.

It can help to conceptualize nudges as the rungs of a ladder that you gradually help students ascend step-by-step, such as in the dialogue ladder in Figure 9–2.

How do you know which rung of a ladder to begin on with a student? Look at the writing the student did without assistance, and assess their strengths as a writer. (If you need help with this, read Action 2.5.)

When you start teaching at the appropriate rung, students will be able to take in what you teach, integrate it into what they can already do—and continue to work independently. It's when we start too high on the ladder or try to teach a child to climb too many rungs at once that we cause difficulty for children. If they can't do what we teach, it's likely they'll ignore what we teach them or shut down—or we'll take over their writing and do it for them.

Teaching with nudges requires you to accept and value student approximation. Until a student reaches the top

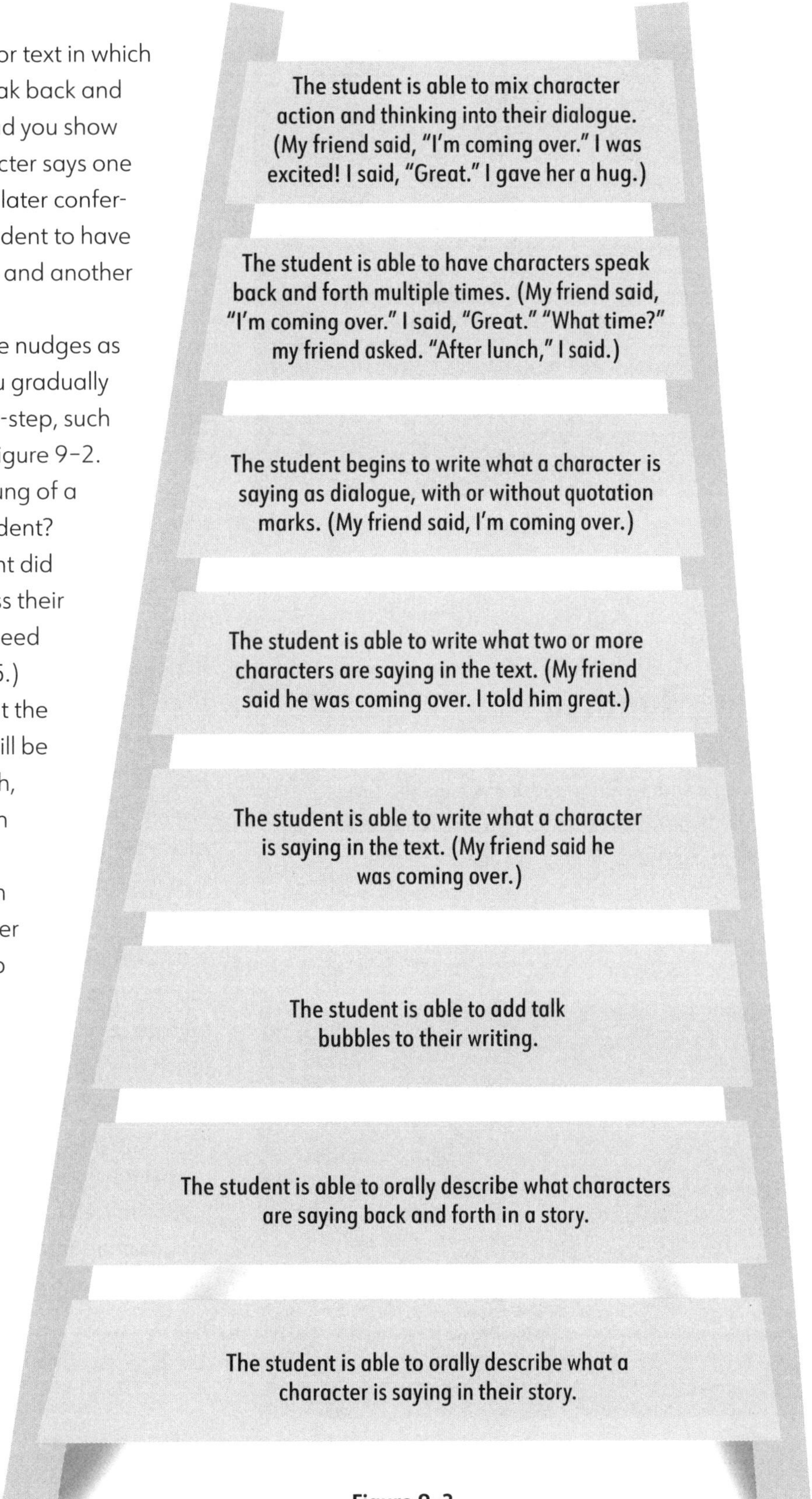

The student is able to mix character action and thinking into their dialogue. (My friend said, "I'm coming over." I was excited! I said, "Great." I gave her a hug.)

The student is able to have characters speak back and forth multiple times. (My friend said, "I'm coming over." I said, "Great." "What time?" my friend asked. "After lunch," I said.)

The student begins to write what a character is saying as dialogue, with or without quotation marks. (My friend said, I'm coming over.)

The student is able to write what two or more characters are saying in the text. (My friend said he was coming over. I told him great.)

The student is able to write what a character is saying in the text. (My friend said he was coming over.)

The student is able to add talk bubbles to their writing.

The student is able to orally describe what characters are saying back and forth in a story.

The student is able to orally describe what a character is saying in their story.

Figure 9–2

Do you have other ladders like these?

It's not possible for us to include ladders for the literally hundreds of different things we teach children K–8, from using periods to transitioning from part to part in a nonfiction piece!

Over time you'll envision your own ladders, which will be more effective than relying on someone else's. If you've taught on your grade level before, you probably already have a sense of students' typical strengths (the rungs of the ladders they're on), and you have also discovered which rungs you can move students up to through your teaching. The difficulty often lies when students are on rungs that are much lower than the ones your students are typically on. The key to discovering which rung you can move students up to is to ask yourself, *What logical small step can this student take next?*

Further Reading

For more information about working with students who struggle with writing, read Janet Angelillo's *The Struggling Writer: Strategies to Help Kids Focus, Build Stamina, and Develop Writing Confidence* (2010).

Should I acknowledge to my class that students are at different levels as writers?

Yes! It's not a secret to students they're at different levels at many kinds of activities and skills—however, sometimes students who are at a lower level than many of their classmates feel self-conscious, even stigmatized. By acknowledging that students are at different levels matter-of-factly, and by making it clear that you feel that all of your students have strengths as writers (which you can do when you use students as mentors—see Action 6.7), you'll create a workshop environment in which students will feel comfortable with whoever they are as writers at this point in time.

rung of the ladder—which may not happen during the year they're your student—they will have a partial understanding of the craft technique or strategy you're teaching them. Over time, as students move up the ladder step-by-step, their approximations will become more and more sophisticated. Of course, don't expect all students to be on the same rungs at the same time—no matter where a student is on the ladder. As long as (with your support) they're gradually moving up rung by rung at a pace appropriate for them as learners, you should be pleased with their progress as writers.

Confer with Some Students More Frequently

In general, you'll confer with most students about the same number of times across the school year. However, some students will need more support from you, and you'll confer with them more frequently. Fairness, after all, doesn't mean that all students get exactly the same thing. Instead, it means all students get what they need.

Conferring more frequently with some students will do two things. One, it'll help you feel more comfortable with giving them step-by-step nudges, as you'll have more opportunities to teach them and you won't be as tempted to overteach. Also, it can have the effect of accelerating learning for these students.

Another way to help students who need more individualized teaching is to teach them in small groups in addition to your individual conferences with them each week.

Action 9.2: Teach Students to Navigate the Writing Process Independently

One of the most important goals for students is that they learn to move through the stages of the writing process—rehearsal (or prewriting), drafting, revising, editing, and publishing—with independence. Learning how to do this is a key aspect of becoming independent writers.

As they learn to navigate the writing process with independence, students

- become aware of the stages of the writing process;
- learn about the moves writers make in each stage of the process and strategies they can use to make these moves; and
- make these moves with growing skill and independence.

Stage of the Writing Process	Moves at This Stage	Strategies Writers Use to Navigate These Moves
Rehearsal	Finding a topic	• Heart maps • Brainstorming lists of topics • Writing territories
	Developing a topic	• Drawing what you're writing about • Brainstorming details • Researching
	Figuring out what point to make about a topic	• Answering the question *What do I want to say about my topic in my draft?*
	Planning	• Touching each page of a book and thinking about what you'll write on it • Webs • Outlines • Flowcharts

continues

Stage of the Writing Process	Moves at This Stage	Strategies Writers Use to Navigate These Moves
Drafting	Getting started	• Talking about your topic with a partner before drafting • Reading over your notes and beginning • Flash-drafting
	Crafting your writing (illustrations and text)	• Referring to a mentor text for craft ideas
	Getting restarted with a draft	• Rereading what you've written so far • Referring to your plan
	Getting unstuck	• Freewriting until you get an idea for how to continue • Reading what you have so far to a fellow writer • Putting the draft aside until tomorrow

Revision	Coming up with revision ideas	• Rereading a draft and asking yourself:
		  • Do I want to add more to this part?
		  • Do I want to cut some details?
		  • Do I want to rework this part [a lead or ending]?
		  • Do I want to reorder the parts of the piece?
		• Comparing your writing with a mentor text
		• Using a revision checklist
		• Asking for feedback from your writing partner

	Making revision plans	• Rereading your draft and putting stars or comments on parts you want to revise
	Finding space for revisions	• On a written draft, using carets, arrows, sticky notes, flaps, etc. • On a draft written on a word processor, using functions like Cut and Paste
	Getting help with revision	• Asking your writing partner for help with a specific kind of revision • Looking at a mentor text to see how a more experienced writer does something

Stage of the Writing Process	Moves at This Stage	Strategies Writers Use to Navigate These Moves
Editing	Finding errors in punctuation, grammar, and spelling	• Reading your draft aloud to yourself • Reading your draft aloud to a peer • Using an editing checklist
Getting ready to publish	Deciding how to format your draft Deciding how to illustrate your draft	• Looking at mentor texts to see how they're formatted • Looking at mentor texts to see how similar texts are illustrated • In the upper grades, drawing illustrations yourself or using illustrations from the internet. In the younger grades when students are making books, illustrations will already be present.

Figure 9–3

Connect Your Lessons to the Corresponding Steps of the Writing Process

Build students' understanding of each stage of the writing process by naming which stage each one of your minilessons, small-group lessons, and conferences connects to. For example, say, "Today we're going to talk about how to find topics, which is something writers do during the first stage of the writing process, which writers call *rehearsal*," or "Today I want to talk to you about something writers do during the *revision* stage of the writing process, which is to reread their drafts and add some more details."

Make Process Connections Across Units

As you move from unit to unit, point out that the process moves you're teaching students about *are the same ones they've been making in previous units*. For example, say, "Today we're going to talk about how to come up with topics for feature articles. Of course, we've talked in previous units about how finding topics is something writers do in the rehearsal stage of the writing process," or "Today we're going to talk about how fiction writers sometimes add dialogue to the drafts of their short stories, just like we've talked in other units about how writers add details to their writing when they revise."

Also, have students try the same strategies for navigating a stage of the writing process in units across the year. For example, if you've taught students how to find topics by brainstorming lists of ideas in your first unit, revisit that same strategy in subsequent units. By using strategies over and over, students will get better and better at using them.

Include Units of Study on Aspects of Process in Your Curriculum

One of the advantages of a process study is it accelerates learning in the aspect of process that is the focus for the unit. For example, in a revision study, students make substantial growth in their ability to revise because they spend more time thinking about and practicing revision than they would in a genre study.

Include Units of Study in Which Students Can Choose Their Genres

In genre studies, you probably teach students some genre-specific strategies for navigating stages of the writing process. For example, you might teach students to plan out a fiction story by making a story mountain chart and then expect all of your students to use it.

However, when students are in a unit of study in which they can choose genres, they have to decide which strategies are the best ones to use for the genre they're writing. For example, to plan their writing, they'll ask themselves, *What are all the ways I know that writers plan their writing?* and *Which of these strategies is the best one for the genre I've chosen to write in?* (Note: This is an important minilesson to teach in these units.) To do this requires much-higher-level thinking.

Chart the Writing Process

Help students develop a clearer understanding of the writing process by charting each stage and listing the moves writers make and the strategies they use at that stage. You can refer to these charts in your whole-class and individualized lessons, and students can refer to the charts themselves. (See the examples in Figures 9-4 and 9-5.)

When writers revise, they:

- Reread their drafts, sometimes several times
- Put stars / notes next to parts they want to work on more
- As they reread, they may
  - add words, phrases and/or sentences to some parts
  - rewrite some parts
  - cut some parts
  - move some parts
- Use their revision tools to make changes: carets, arrows, footnotes, sticky notes
- Read their drafts to their writing partner to get feedback

Figure 9–4 Classroom Process Chart: Revision

When writers edit, they:

- Read their drafts aloud to themselves
  - Check spelling by tapping and looking at each word
  - Check punctuation by listening for when their voice pauses and stops
  - Check capitalization and punctuation by looking at sentences
  - Check grammar by listening to how sentences sound
- Read their draft to a partner
  - The writer sits next to the partner
  - The writer reads their draft aloud
  - The partner stops the writer when they think there should be an edit
  - The writer makes final decisions about edits

Figure 9–5 Classroom Process Chart: Editing

Let Students Move Through the Writing Process at Their Own Pace

An important part of becoming an independent writer is knowing when and how to move into the next stage of the writing process. However, in many writing workshops, students aren't allowed to make this decision. For example, in some classrooms, week one of a unit is devoted to gathering ideas, week two to drafting, week three to revision, and week four to editing and publishing. In other classrooms, students aren't able to revise or edit until all of their classmates are finished drafting or revising, respectively.

How do you help children learn to make decisions about moving from one stage to another? On one level, it's as simple as saying, "Go!" to your students. When you tell students it's up to them to decide when to move from one stage to the next—and you've explained to them what each stage is and what writers do in each—students are equipped to start making these decisions.

Of course, when students start moving through the writing process at their own pace, they'll be approximating the writing process of experienced writers. You should expect this and understand they'll have a lot to learn about navigating the process independently. For example, they may leave out a stage (such as revision), or they may not be that good at making one of the moves in a stage (such as editing for punctuation). As you confer, you'll figure out what students know so far about the stage they're in and then teach them how to navigate it better. And when you notice students have similar approximations of a stage, you'll address them in minilessons and small-group lessons, too. Over time, students' writing processes will become more sophisticated, and they'll become able to make the moves in each stage with growing skill and independence.

Create a "Where Am I in the Process?" Chart

Create a chart to help students be conscious of where they are in the writing process and think about the corresponding work they could be doing (see Figure 9–6). And when they're ready to go to another stage of the process, they can formalize their decision by moving a sticky note with their name on it to the next stage on the chart. When you introduce this chart to your class, teach a minilesson on how to use it, and afterward, give your students a chance to put their sticky note where it belongs before they start working on their writing. In that day's share session, ask students who thinks they'll be in the same stage of the process the next day and who is ready to move to the next stage. Students who are moving from one stage to another can move their sticky note before going back to their seat. Students will usually learn how to use the chart quickly but will need some occasional reminders to keep using it.

WHERE AM I IN THE WRITING PROCESS?

REHEARSING (prewriting)	DRAFTING	REVISING	EDITING	GETTING READY TO PUBLISH	PUBLISHING

Figure 9–6 "Where Am I in the Writing Process?" Chart

One caveat about this chart is that it oversimplifies the writing process. After all, the writing process isn't actually linear—a writer might be in the middle of drafting a feature article and realize they need to do some more research, which puts them back in the rehearsal stage for a bit before they continue drafting. Or a writer might be revising a draft but correcting the spelling of some words as they make revisions. It's important to explain this to your students, so they have a more nuanced understanding of the writing process. And it's for this reason that we suggest that teachers use this type of chart only with students in the upper-elementary or middle school grades.

The chart will also be a help to you, as it will give you a picture of where your students are in the writing process. You may wish to confer with some students when you see their sticky is in a particular stage because you know they need some help navigating it. Or you might want to give a minilesson to address a stage when you notice some students are getting to it.

The information on the chart can also be helpful for assessing your comfort level with students moving through the writing process at their own pace. If you notice your students are consistently at the same stage of the process at the same time, it may because you aren't allowing them to decide when it's time to move to the next stage themselves!

Further Reading

These books will give you information on teaching students about the rehearsal and revision stages of the writing process: Amy Buckner's *Notebook Know-How* (2005), Janet Angelillo's *Making Revision Matter* (2005), Chris Hall's *The Writer's Mindset* (2022), and Georgia Heard's *The Revision Toolbox* (2014).

Action 9.3: Envision How Students Can Help Each Other

Writing is not a solitary act. Throughout the writing process, writers talk about their work in progress with colleagues, fellow writers, and editors. Sometimes writers use these conversations to get validation that they're on the right track or to get feedback about a draft. And other times they need advice about how to navigate a tricky challenge they're encountering. For most writers, these kinds of conversations are essential to the success of their writing projects.

For students to become independent writers, they need to learn how to get help with their writing from other people besides you. The fact that you're not often available to an individual student—because you're conferring with their classmates or working with them in small groups—sets the stage for the conversations you'll have with them about how to have *partnerships* and *peer conferences*. A partnership consists of two students who establish a supportive writing relationship that continues for a period of several months or longer. A peer conference, on the other hand, is more ad hoc and involves students working together on a onetime basis, as needed.

When students have partnerships and peer conferences, they learn that

- talking about writing with someone else helps you think about it from someone else's perspective;
- when you're listening to someone else's writing and thinking about what to say, you're also informing your thinking about your own writing; and
- talking about your writing gives you the opportunity to receive a response from an audience, a crucial experience for a writer.

Most important, by teaching your students how to get help from their classmates, you'll help them have these conversations in the future.

TIP

It's important to be realistic about the quality of support students will give each other. After all, they don't have the same expertise you have about writing and won't be able to give each other the same kind of responsive feedback you give in writing conferences! The most important goal for partnership and peer conferring work is that students learn about the process of trying to help each other with their writing, something there is always more to learn about, no matter how experienced a writer is. After years of writing instruction and practice, students will gradually be able to give better feedback to each other. This is not to say that inexperienced writers can't give each other great feedback and advice—they sometimes do, but consider this a bonus when they're just starting to help each other.

Teach Students About Partnerships and Peer Conferences All Year

You won't successfully teach students how to have partnerships and peer conferences in just a minilesson or two at the beginning of the school year. To help students learn how to have these conversations, commit to teaching a series of lessons across the school year.

Have a goal for partnerships and peer conferences in *each* one of your units of study so that bit by bit and year by year, students learn how to talk about their writing with others. To meet each unit goal, teach a minilesson or two, and also look for opportunities to confer with students when they're working with each other. Over time, each lesson will build on what you've taught students before and will also give you the opportunity to respond to what you're seeing when you observe and confer with students who are working together.

There are different kinds of partnership and peer conference goals:

- how to sit and talk with a writing partner
- how to select a writing partner who is a good fit for you

- what to talk about
- how to give feedback
- how to make use of feedback

Decide on How You'll Form Partnerships

You have two choices when you form partnerships. You can decide which students to put together, or you can give students a chance to have some input into who their partners will be, so they can learn how to choose a good partner.

If you decide to form partnerships, you'll weigh all you've learned about your students as you pair them together. Making these decisions yourself also prevents students who aren't socially sought-after partners from feeling anxious and left out. When creating partnerships, we pair students who are able to support each other in having meaningful conversations. We don't put our two most talkative students together, or two students who talk much less. And regardless of their writing levels, students can give each other feedback and advice.

If you're going to give your students input into forming partnerships, we suggest that in the beginning of the school year, you give students an opportunity to work with several different classmates to try out potential writing partners and help them identify whom they might want to work with for the next several months. Then, after several weeks, you can ask them to tell you who they think would make a good partner for them. (Since you'll be observing and conferring with students as they talk with each other, you'll be getting some information about how well students work with each other, too.) While ultimately you'll make the final decisions, giving students some input helps them feel a sense of ownership of the process as well as provides them with the experience of sizing up potential partners.

Decide How Long Partnerships Will Last

It's important to keep partnerships going for several months, upwards of half a year. Since partner work is built upon trust and a good working relationship and takes time to develop, it makes sense to keep successful partnerships together for a while. (Of course, you may need to disband some partnerships if students aren't a good match.)

By the midyear mark, put students in different partnerships so they can learn how to apply the relationship skills they've developed with another classmate.

Decide When Partnerships Will Meet

Schedule set times for partnerships to meet. Otherwise, it's likely some students will choose not to meet, and they won't gain experience with this important collaboration. Here are three options for when partnerships can meet:

- ***At a regular point in time:*** For example, partnerships might meet every Monday during the beginning of independent writing to discuss where each student is with their current piece.
- ***At a point in the writing process:*** Partnerships could meet when one or both of the members are ready to start a new piece or when they're ready to revise or edit. This will mean some students will be meeting with their partners in designated areas of the classroom while others are working on their writing. (You could support this by asking students at the end of a minilesson if some of them are at a point in the writing process where they could meet with their partners.) At other times, such as when the whole class may be editing before getting ready to publish their writing, many or even all partnerships may be meeting to help each other.
- ***As needed:*** There will be times when students need some feedback or help and will want to meet with their partners.

Plan for Missing Partners

Students won't always be able to rely on their writing partners. There will be times when one partner is absent. In these situations, students need the option of having a peer conference with another classmate.

And as the year progresses, some students will develop reputations as being particularly good at helping their partner with an aspect of writing, such as finding topics or editing. Other students may want to seek them out when they have need of their special expertise. (You can celebrate students' unique areas of expertise by making a chart for the class to refer to—see Action 6.7.)

To help students have peer conferences, explain to students when and how they can approach each other for help and where they should meet while other students are working. And, since all students have various strengths, make sure that all students are seen as experts in some area.

Action 9.4: Teach Students How to Work in Partnerships and Peer Conferences

There are three ways to teach students about writing partnerships and peer conferences:

- In each unit of study, teach a minilesson to address your partnership or peer conferring goal for that unit. This way, students get better at talking about their writing incrementally across the year.
- Confer with students when they're talking with each other about their writing.
- Include a unit of study about partnerships and peer conferences in your writing curriculum.

In this action, we'll discuss the first two ways. (You can read about a unit on peer conferring in Matt's book *Craft and Process Studies* [2019].)

Envision *What* You Can Teach

While you'll teach your class about only one aspect of partnership or peer conferring work in a minilesson, in your conferences, you'll teach students about a wider range of things, depending on what you learn about how their conversations are going when you confer with them (see Figure 9-7).

Decide *How* You'll Teach Students

There are several methods for teaching students about partnerships and peer conferences. The first two—demonstration and fishbowl—work best in minilessons. You can use the other one—showing video—in both minilessons and conferences.

DEMONSTRATION

You can demonstrate a partnership or peer conference with another teacher (your coteacher or a colleague who is free during your minilesson) or a student.

Partnership or Peer Conference Unit Goal	Possible Teaching Points
Learn how to sit with a partner	• Sit next to your partner. • Take one piece of writing out at a time; both partners should be able to see it. • Use positive body language.
Learn what to talk about	• Writers talk about where they are in the writing process and any feedback or help they may want. • Writers talk about how they're crafting their writing and any feedback or help they may want. • Writers talk about problems they're having with process or craft.
Learn how to set an agenda for the conversation	• (In a partnership) Decide who will talk about their writing first. • (In a peer conference) The partner who initiates the conference starts by talking about their reason for seeking out the conversation (getting affirmation, seeking help with a specific issue, getting feedback about their draft, seeking help with editing). • Decide who will read the writing and how (the writer out loud or the partner silently). • Tell your partner about what your piece is about (without reading the whole draft aloud) before telling what kind of feedback you want.
Learn how to be an active listener	• Use positive body language. • Reflect back what a partner is saying about their writing ("What I'm hearing you say is . . ."). • Ask good questions about your partner's writing.
Learn how to give feedback	• Give positive feedback. • Give specific feedback. • Give feedback about a specific part of a partner's writing.
Learn how to give advice	• Use an anchor chart to help you get ideas for giving your partner advice. • Talk about what you do as a writer. • Look at a mentor text together.
Learn how to use your partner's advice or feedback	• Decide whether to take your partner's advice or not. • Try out your partner's advice to see if you like it—you can always change it back!

Figure 9–7

Before you do the demonstration, explain what goal you're addressing in the lesson and the specific aspect of partnership or peer conference work you want students to watch for.

Video 9.1
Minilesson: How to have a good partnership conversation

FISHBOWL

You can also teach by having two students do a fishbowl partnership or peer conference in front of the class. Just as you do in a demonstration, start by explaining what goal the lesson addresses and the specific aspect of partnership or peer conference work you want students to watch for in the fishbowl. As the students talk, point out what they do well that's connected to the focus of the lesson. And as the students talk, coach as needed, stopping first to explain to the students and the rest of your class what you're noticing and what you want them to do differently. All the students will benefit from watching you coach!

SHOW A VIDEO

Finally, just like you show mentor texts to teach students about the craft of writing, you can show students a mentor video of a partnership or peer conference that illustrates what you want to teach them. You could record a demonstration partnership or peer conference outside of writing workshop or record students as they talk with each other during writing workshop. You can show the video as part of a minilesson or a conference (using your cell phone in the latter), pointing out what the writing partners are doing in the video that you would like students to learn to do.

Video 9.2
Mentor peer conference conversation

Confer into Students' Needs

When you confer with partnerships or peer conferences, you'll learn some students need help with your partnership or peer conferring goal for the current unit of study while others have different collaboration needs. To make sure you're addressing students' actual needs, incorporate these moves when you confer into partnerships and peer conferences:

- Begin conferences by observing the partnership or peer conference and listening to how the conversation is going.
- Ask students one of these questions:
  - How is your conversation going?
  - What are you trying to get better at in your conversations with each other?
  - What's been going well in your conversations recently?

Action 9.5

Help Students Find and Use Their Own Mentor Texts is in the Online Resources.

Video 9.3 Conferring into a partnership

Video 9.4 Conferring into a peer conference

  - » What are some of the challenges of having these conversations?
  - » How have your conversations been influencing your writing?

- Look for and listen for student collaborative strengths, however emergent, and then point them out and build on them in your teaching point. For example, if you hear one student say to the other, "Your lead is great!" point out you're hearing they're trying to give feedback—an important part of a writer-to-writer conversation—and that their next step is to learn how to give each other more specific feedback, which you'll then teach them how to do (by referring to a video).

WORKS CITED

Abraham, Anita, and Amy Matthusen. 2021. *Speaking Up: Manageable, Meaningful, and Student-Driven Conferences.* New York: Rowman and Littlefield.

Ahmed, Sara K. 2018. *Being the Change: Lessons and Strategies to Teach Social Comprehension.* Portsmouth, NH: Heinemann.

Alexander, Kwame. 2019. *The Write Thing: Kwame Alexander Engages Students in Writing Workshop (and You Can Too!).* Huntington Beach, CA: Shell Education.

Anderson, Carl. 2000. *How's It Going? A Practical Guide to Conferring with Student Writers.* Portsmouth, NH: Heinemann.

——. 2005. *Assessing Writers.* Portsmouth, NH: Heinemann.

——. 2008. *Strategic Writing Conferences: Smart Conversations That Move Young Writers Forward.* Portsmouth, NH: Heinemann.

——. 2018. *A Teacher's Guide to Writing Conferences, K–8.* Portsmouth, NH: Heinemann.

——. 2022a. "Teach Students to Read Like Writers During Whole-Class Text Study." *Heinemann Blog*, December 8. https://blog.heinemann.com/teach-students-to-read-like-writers-during-whole-class-text-study.

——. 2022b. *A Teacher's Guide to Mentor Texts, K–5.* Portsmouth, NH: Heinemann.

——. 2024. *Magical Writing: Teaching Fantasy Writing in Grades K–6.* Thousand Oaks, CA: Corwin.

Anderson, Jeff, with Travis Leech and Melinda Clark. 2021. *Patterns of Power: Inviting Adolescent Writers into the Conventions of Language, Grades 6–8.* Portland, ME: Stenhouse.

Anderson, Jeff, and Whitney La Rocca. 2017. *Patterns of Power: Inviting Young Writers into the Conventions of Language, Grades 1–5.* Portland, ME: Stenhouse.

——. 2021. *Patterns of Wonder: Inviting Emergent Writers to Play with the Conventions of Language, Pre-K–1.* Portland, ME: Stenhouse.

Anderson, Mike. 2016. *Learning to Choose, Choosing to Learn: The Key to Student Motivation and Achievement.* Alexandria, VA: ASCD.

Angelillo, Janet. 2005. *Making Revision Matter: Strategies for Guiding Students to Focus, Organize, and Strengthen Their Writing Independently.* New York: Scholastic.

——. 2008. *Whole-Class Teaching: Minilessons and More.* Portsmouth, NH: Heinemann.

——. 2010. *The Struggling Writer: Strategies to Help Kids Focus, Build Stamina, and Develop Writing Confidence.* New York: Scholastic.

Ask staff. 2022. "Short and Curly, Long and Swirly?" *Ask* 21 (9): 14–17.

Atwell, Nancie. 1987. *In the Middle: Writing, Reading, and Learning with Adolescents.* 1st ed. Portsmouth, NH: Heinemann.

——. 2014. *In the Middle: A Lifetime of Learning About Writing, Reading, and Adolescents.* 3rd ed. Portsmouth, NH: Heinemann.

Ayres, Ruth. 2013. *Celebrating Writers: From Possibilities Through Publication.* Portland, ME: Stenhouse.

Bishop, Rudine Sims. 1990. "Mirrors, Windows, and Sliding Glass Doors." *Perspectives* 1 (3): ix–xi.

Bomer, Katherine. 2005. *Writing a Life: Teaching Memoir to Sharpen Insight, Shape Meaning—and Triumph over Tests.* Portsmouth, NH: Heinemann.

——. 2010. *Hidden Gems: Naming and Teaching from the Brilliance in Every Student's Writing.* Portsmouth, NH: Heinemann.

——. 2011. *Starting with What Students Do Best: How to Improve Writing by Responding to Students' Strengths.* DVD. Portsmouth, NH: Heinemann.

——. 2016. *The Journey Is Everything: Teaching Essays That Students Want to Write for People Who Want to Read Them.* Portsmouth, NH: Heinemann.

Bomer, Katherine, and Corinne Arens. 2020. *A Teacher's Guide to Writing Workshop Essentials: Time, Choice, Response*. Portsmouth, NH: Heinemann.

Bomer, Randy. 2011. *Building Adolescent Literacy in Today's English Classrooms.* Portsmouth, NH: Heinemann.

Bomer, Randy, and Katherine Bomer. 2001. *For a Better World: Reading and Writing for Social Action.* Portsmouth, NH: Heinemann.

Boswell, Kelly. 2021. *Every Kid a Writer: Strategies That Get Everyone Writing.* Portsmouth, NH: Heinemann.

Brunn, Peter. 2010. *The Lesson Planning Handbook: Essential Strategies That Inspire Student Thinking and Learning.* New York: Scholastic.

Buckner, Aimee. 2005. *Notebook Know-How: Strategies for the Writer's Notebook.* Portland, ME: Stenhouse.

Caine, Karen. 2008. *Writing to Persuade: Minilessons to Help Students Plan, Draft, and Revise, Grades 3–8.* Portsmouth, NH: Heinemann.

Calkins, Lucy. 1986. *The Art of Teaching Writing.* Portsmouth, NH: Heinemann.

Cambourne, Brian. 1988. *The Whole Story: Natural Learning and the Acquisition of Literacy in the Classroom.* Auckland, NZ: Ashton Scholastic.

Chavez, Felicia Rose. 2021. *The Anti-Racist Writing Workshop: How to Decolonize the Creative Classroom.* Chicago: Haymarket Books.

Cherry-Paul, Sonja. 2021. "We Need Books That Center Black Joy." Chalkbeat. February 5. https://www.chalkbeat.org/2021/2/5/22267415/black-joy-books.

Cornwall, Gaia. 2017. *Jabari Jumps.* Somerville, MA: Candlewick.

Costa, Arthur L., and Bena Kallick, editors. 2008. *Learning and Leading with Habits of Mind: 16 Essential Characteristics for Success.* Alexandria, VA: ASCD.

Crews, Donald. 1996. *Shortcut.* New York: Greenwillow Books.

Crouch, Debra, and Brian Cambourne. 2020. *Made for Learning: How the Conditions of Learning Guide Teaching Decisions.* Katonah, NH: Richard C. Owen.

Cruz, M. Colleen. 2004. *Independent Writing: One Teacher—Thirty-Two Needs, Topics, and Plans.* Portsmouth, NH: Heinemann.

——. 2015. *The Unstoppable Writing Teacher: Real Strategies for the Real Classroom.* Portsmouth, NH: Heinemann.

——. 2018. *Writers Read Better: Nonfiction.* Thousand Oaks, CA: Corwin.

——. 2019. *Writers Read Better: Narrative.* Thousand Oaks, CA: Corwin.

Culham, Ruth. 2003. *6 + 1 Traits of Writing: The Complete Guide, Grades 3 and Up.* New York: Scholastic.

——. 2005. *6 + 1 Traits of Writing: The Complete Guide for the Primary Grades.* New York: Scholastic.

——. 2014. *The Writing Thief: Using Mentor Texts to Teach the Craft of Writing*. Portland, ME: Stenhouse.

Daniels, Harvey "Smokey." 2017. *The Curious Classroom: 10 Structures for Teaching with Student-Directed Inquiry*. Portsmouth, NH: Heinemann.

Davies, Nicola. 2003. *Surprising Sharks*. Somerville, MA: Candlewick.

Ebarvia, Tricia. 2017. "Tricia Ebarvia: How Inclusive Is Your Literacy Classroom Really?" *Heinemann Blog*, December 12. https://blog.heinemann.com/heinemann-fellow-tricia-ebavaria-inclusive-literacy-classroom-really.

Ehrenworth, Mary, Pablo Wolfe, and Marc Todd. 2020. *The Civically Engaged Classroom: Reading, Writing, and Speaking for Change*. Portsmouth, NH: Heinemann.

Eickholdt, Lisa. 2015. *Learning from Classmates: Using Students' Writing as Mentor Texts*. Portsmouth, NH: Heinemann.

Eickholdt, Lisa, and Patricia Vitale-Reilly. 2022. *A Teacher's Guide to Writing Workshop Minilessons, Grades K–8*. Portsmouth, NH: Heinemann.

Feigelson, Dan. 2008. *Practical Punctuation: Lessons on Rule Making and Rule Breaking in Elementary Writing*. Portsmouth, NH: Heinemann.

——. 2014. *Reading Projects Reimagined: Student-Driven Conferences to Deepen Critical Thinking*. Portsmouth, NH: Heinemann.

——. 2022. *Radical Listening: Reading and Writing Conferences to Reach All Students*. New York: Scholastic.

Fletcher, Ralph. 2006. *Boy Writers: Reclaiming Their Voices*. Portland, ME: Stenhouse.

——. 2010. *Pyrotechnics on the Page: Playful Craft That Sparks Writing*. Portland, ME: Stenhouse.

——. 2013. *What a Writer Needs*. 2nd ed. Portsmouth, NH: Heinemann.

——. 2015. *Making Nonfiction from Scratch*. Portland, ME: Stenhouse.

——. 2017. *Joy Write: Cultivating High-Impact, Low-Stakes Writing*. Portsmouth, NH: Heinemann.

——. 2019. *Focus Lessons: How Photography Enhances the Teaching of Writing*. Portsmouth, NH: Heinemann.

Fletcher, Ralph, Peter Johnston, and Katie Wood Ray. 2007. "Where Has All the Real Choice Gone? Revisiting an Essential Element of Writing Instruction." Lecture presented at NCTE Annual Convention, New York City, November 17.

Fletcher, Ralph, and JoAnn Portalupi. 2001a. *Nonfiction Craft Lessons: Teaching Information Writing, K–8*. Portland, ME: Stenhouse.

——. 2001b. *Writing Workshop: The Essential Guide*. Portsmouth, NH: Heinemann.

——. 2007. *Craft Lessons: Teaching Writing, K–8*. 2nd ed. Portland, ME: Stenhouse.

Gibbons, Gail. 1979. *Clocks and How They Go*. New York: Crowell.

——. 1993. *Frogs*. New York: Holiday House.

Glover, Matt. 2009. *Engaging Young Writers, Preschool–Grade 1*. Portsmouth, NH: Heinemann.

——. 2019. *Craft and Process Studies: Units That Provide Writers with Choice of Genre*. Portsmouth, NH: Heinemann.

Glover, Matt, and Mary Alice Berry. 2012. *Projecting Possibilities for Writers: The How, What, and Why of Designing Units of Study, K–5*. Portsmouth, NH: Heinemann.

Graves, Donald H. 1983. *Writing: Teachers and Children at Work*. Portsmouth, NH: Heinemann.

———. 1994. *A Fresh Look at Writing*. Portsmouth, NH: Heinemann.

———. 2006. *A Sea of Faces: The Importance of Knowing Your Students*. Portsmouth, NH: Heinemann.

Hall, Chris. 2022. *The Writer's Mindset: 6 Stances That Promote Authentic Revision.* Portsmouth, NH: Heinemann.

Harris, Towanda. 2019. *The Right Tools: A Guide to Selecting, Evaluating, and Implementing Classroom Resources and Practices.* Portsmouth, NH: Heinemann.

Hattie, John. 2009. *Visible Learning: A Synthesis of over 800 Meta-analyses Relating to Achievement*. New York: Routledge.

Heard, Georgia. 1989. *For the Good of the Earth and Sun: Teaching Poetry.* Portsmouth, NH: Heinemann.

———. 1999. *Awakening the Heart: Exploring Poetry in Elementary and Middle School.* Portsmouth, NH: Heinemann.

———. 2013. *Finding the Heart of Nonfiction: Teaching 7 Essential Craft Tools with Mentor Texts.* Portsmouth, NH: Heinemann.

———. 2014. *The Revision Toolbox: Teaching Techniques That Work*. 2nd ed. Portsmouth, NH: Heinemann.

———. 2016. *Heart Maps: Helping Students Create and Craft Authentic Writing*. Portsmouth, NH: Heinemann.

Hertz, Christine, and Kristine Mraz. 2018. *Kids 1st from Day 1: A Teacher's Guide to Today's Classroom.* Portsmouth, NH: Heinemann.

Horn, Martha, and Mary Ellen Giacobbe. 2006. *Talking, Drawing, Writing: Lessons for Our Youngest Writers*. Portland, ME: Stenhouse.

Jackson, Peter, dir. 2021. *The Beatles: Get Back.* Burbank, CA: Walt Disney Studios, Apple Corps, and WingNut Films.

Johnston, Peter H. 1997. *Knowing Literacy: Constructive Literacy Assessment.* Portland, ME: Stenhouse.

———. 2004. *Choice Words: How Our Language Affects Children's Learning*. Portland, ME: Stenhouse.

Kaufman, Douglas. 2000. *Conferences and Conversations: Listening to the Literate Classroom.* Portsmouth, NH: Heinemann.

Keene, Ellin Oliver. 2018. *Engaging Children: Igniting a Drive for Deeper Learning, K–8.* Portsmouth, NH: Heinemann.

———. 2022. *The Literacy Studio: Redesigning the Workshop for Readers and Writers.* Portsmouth, NH: Heinemann.

Kittle, Penny. 2022. *Micro Mentor Texts: Using Short Passages from Great Books to Teach Writer's Craft.* New York: Scholastic.

Kittle, Penny, and Kelly Gallagher. 2021. *4 Essential Studies: Beliefs and Practices to Reclaim Student Agency.* Portsmouth, NH: Heinemann.

Kleinrock, Liz. 2021. *Start Here, Start Now: A Guide to Antibias and Antiracist Work in Your School Community.* Portsmouth, NH: Heinemann.

Laman, Tasha Tropp. 2013. *From Ideas to Words: Writing Strategies for English Language Learners*. Portsmouth, NH: Heinemann.

Laminack, Lester L. 2007. *Cracking Open the Author's Craft: Teaching the Art of Writing.* New York: Scholastic.

Lane, Barry. 2016. *After the End: Teaching and Learning Creative Revision*. 2nd ed. Portsmouth, NH: Heinemann.

Larsen, Mylisa. 2016. *How to Put Your Parents to Bed.* New York: HarperCollins.

Lehman, Christopher. 2012. *Energize Research Reading and Writing: Fresh Strategies to Spark Interest, Develop Independence, and Meet Key Common Core Standards, Grades 4–8.* Portsmouth, NH: Heinemann.

Linder, Rozlyn. 2016. *The Big Book of Details: 46 Moves for Teaching Writers to Elaborate.* Portsmouth, NH: Heinemann.

Marchetti, Allison, and Rebekah O'Dell. 2015. *Writing with Mentors: How to Reach Every Writer in the Room Using Current, Engaging Mentor Texts.* Portsmouth, NH: Heinemann.

——. 2021. *A Teacher's Guide to Mentor Texts, 6–12.* Portsmouth, NH: Heinemann.

McCardie, Amanda. 2019. *Our Very Own Dog: Taking Care of Your First Pet.* Somerville, MA: Candlewick.

McGee, Patty. 2017. *Feedback That Moves Writers Forward: How to Escape Correcting Mode to Transform Student Writing.* Thousand Oaks, CA: Corwin.

Medina, Meg. 2020. *Evelyn Del Rey Is Moving Away*. Somerville, MA: Candlewick.

Meehan, Melanie. 2022. *Answers to Your Biggest Questions About Teaching Elementary Writing.* Thousand Oaks, CA: Corwin.

Meehan, Melanie, and Kelsey Sorum. 2021. *The Responsive Writing Teacher: A Hands-on Guide to Child-Centered Equitable Instruction*. Thousand Oaks, CA: Corwin.

Mermelstein, Leah. 2013. *Self-Directed Writers: The Third Essential Element in the Writing Workshop*. Portsmouth, NH: Heinemann.

Minor, Cornelius. 2019. *We Got This.: Equity, Access, and the Quest to Be Who Our Students Need Us to Be.* Portsmouth, NH: Heinemann.

Mraz, Kristine, and Christine Hertz. 2015. *A Mindset for Learning: Teaching the Traits of Joyful, Independent Growth.* Portsmouth, NH: Heinemann.

Muhammad, Gholdy. 2020. *Cultivating Genius: An Equity Framework for Culturally and Historically Responsive Literacy*. New York: Scholastic.

Murray, Donald M. 1999. *Write to Learn.* 6th ed. New York: Harcourt Brace.

Owocki, Gretchen, and Yetta Goodman. 2002. *Kidwatching: Documenting Children's Literacy Development*. Portsmouth, NH: Heinemann.

Painter, Kristen. 2006. *Living and Teaching the Writing Workshop.* Portsmouth, NH: Heinemann.

Parr, Todd. 2010. *The Earth Book.* Boston: Little Brown.

Parsons, Stephanie. 2005. *First Grade Writers: Units of Study to Help Children Plan, Organize, and Structure Their Ideas.* Portsmouth, NH: Heinemann.

——. 2007. *Second Grade Writers: Units of Study to Help Children Focus on Audience and Purpose.* Portsmouth, NH: Heinemann.

Ray, Katie Wood. 1999. *Wondrous Words: Writers and Writing in the Elementary Classroom*. Urbana, IL: NCTE.

——. 2002. *What You Know by Heart: How to Develop Curriculum for Your Writing Workshop.* Portsmouth, NH: Heinemann.

——. 2006. *Study Driven: A Framework for Planning Units of Study in the Writing Workshop.* Portsmouth, NH: Heinemann.

——. 2010. *In Pictures and In Words: Teaching the Qualities of Good Writing Through Illustration Study*. Portsmouth, NH: Heinemann.

Ray, Katie Wood, and Lisa B. Cleaveland. 2004. *About the Authors: Writing Workshop with Our Youngest Writers*. Portsmouth, NH: Heinemann.

——. 2018. *A Teacher's Guide to Getting Started with Beginning Writers*. Portsmouth, NH: Heinemann.

Ray, Katie Wood, and Matt Glover. 2008. *Already Ready: Nurturing Writers in Preschool and Kindergarten*. Portsmouth, NH: Heinemann.

Rief, Linda. 2018. *The Quickwrite Handbook: 100 Mentor Texts to Jumpstart Your Students' Thinking and Writing*. Portsmouth, NH: Heinemann.

Roberts, Kate, and Maggie Beattie Roberts. 2016. *DIY Literacy: Teaching Tools for Differentiation, Rigor, and Independence*. Portsmouth, NH: Heinemann.

Robb, Laura. 2010. *Teaching Middle School Writers: What Every English Teacher Needs to Know*. Portsmouth, NH: Heinemann.

Salesses, Matthew. 2021. *Craft in the Real World: Rethinking Fiction Writing and Workshopping*. New York: Catapult.

Sanchez, Anita. 2019. *Rotten!: Vultures, Beetles, Slime, and Nature's Other Decomposers*. New York: Clarion Books.

Scieszka, Jon. 2008. *Knucklehead: Tall Tales and Almost True Stories of Growing Up*. New York: Viking.

Serravallo, Jennifer. 2014a. *The Literacy Teacher's Playbook, Grades K–2: Four Steps for Turning Assessment Data into Goal-Directed Instruction*. Portsmouth, NH: Heinemann.

——. 2014b. *The Literacy Teacher's Playbook, Grades 3–6: Four Steps for Turning Assessment Data into Goal-Directed Instruction*. Portsmouth, NH: Heinemann.

——. 2017. *The Writing Strategies Book: Your Everything Guide to Developing Skilled Writers*. Portsmouth, NH: Heinemann.

——. 2021. *Teaching Writing in Small Groups*. Portsmouth, NH: Heinemann.

Shubitz, Stacey. 2016. *Craft Moves: Lesson Sets for Teaching Writing with Mentor Texts*. Portland, ME: Stenhouse.

Shubitz, Stacey, and Lynne R. Dorfman. 2019. *Welcome to Writing Workshop: Engaging Today's Students with a Model That Works*. Portland, ME: Stenhouse.

Slaughter, Holly. 2009. *Small-Group Writing Conferences, K–5: How to Use Your Instructional Time More Efficiently*. Portsmouth, NH: Heinemann.

Smee, Nicola. 2006. *Clip-Clop!* London: Boxer Books.

Smith, Frank. 1983. "Reading Like a Writer." *Language Arts* 60 (5): 558–567.

Spandel, Vicki. 2012. *Creating Writers: 6 Traits, Process, Workshop, and Literature*. 6th ed. New York: Pearson.

Swift, Keilly. 2020. *How to Make a Better World: For Every Kid Who Wants to Make a Difference*. London: DK Children.

Tomlinson, Carol Ann. 2014. *The Differentiated Classroom: Responding to the Needs of All Learners*. 2nd ed. Alexandria, VA: ASCD.

VanDerwater, Amy Ludwig. 2018. *Poems Are Teachers: How Studying Poetry Strengthens Writing in All Genres*. Portsmouth, NH: Heinemann.

Vygotsky, Lev. 1986. *Thought and Language*. Edited by Alex Kozulin. Cambridge, MA: MIT Press.

Weaver, Constance. 1996. *Teaching Grammar in Context*. Portsmouth, NH: Heinemann.

Woodson, Jacqueline. 2016. *Brown Girl Dreaming*. New York: Puffin Books.

Yolen, Jane. 1987. *Owl Moon*. New York: Philomel Books.